THE SEVERE STYLE IN GREEK SCULPTURE

THE
SEVERE STYLE
IN GREEK SCULPTURE

By Brunilde Sismondo Ridgway

PRINCETON UNIVERSITY PRESS
PRINCETON, NEW JERSEY

This book is set in Linotype Caledonia

Printed in the United States of America by Princeton University Press

Illustrations printed by The Meriden Gravure Company, Meriden, Connecticut

Preface

During the Academic Year 1966-1967 at Bryn Mawr College, I held a Seminar on the Severe style: this book is the direct result. Primarily, it is intended as a help to students who, like mine, have found themselves confronted with a wealth of specific articles and a few limited handbooks, and who have emerged from their readings with rather uncertain notions about Severe sculpture.

In intention at least, this book is a cross between a handbook and a monograph on sculpture in Severe style, yet it is by no means as comprehensive as Lippold's *Handbuch* nor as knowledgeable as Poulsen's *Der strenge Stil*. Far from being exhaustive, the treatment of Severe sculpture has here been limited to a few sample cases, moving from undoubted Severe originals to copies and finally to controversial pieces. Though I have personal convictions on many of them, I have tried not to solve problems as much as to point them out, at times attempting to reopen questions that have long been considered closed. Undoubtedly the specialist will find much cause for impatience with this approach, but I hope the student will find sufficient information and enough bibliography to proceed further on his own. Descriptions have been limited to a few salient points, leaving mostly to illustrations the task of bringing out differences and similarities; this is especially the case with the difficult "classicistic" works of Roman times, whose stylistic discrepancies and cultural inheritances often defy analysis and even recognition. In such cases it is hoped that photographic juxtaposition with truly Severe works will prove more effective than the accompanying text.

The book has been planned so that the reader need not interrupt his perusal of the main text. Only footnotes with relevance for the discussion in progress have been introduced and need be read in conjunction with the text; all supporting documentation and bibliographical information will be found in the Bibliography sections at the end of each chapter. Furthermore, since not all pertinent works could be discussed in detail, additional items have been selected for inclusion in Appendices to each chapter, to give students a more rounded idea of the monuments which belong to the Severe style. Both Bibliographies and Appendices are intended to provide separate reading material for research in greater depth, but not to interfere with the continuous reading of the basic text.

Bibliography has been limited to the most recent sources, partly because they usually summarize all previous important scholarship, and partly because they supplement Lippold's *Handbuch*, which was published in 1950. Invaluable, in this connection, have been the two volumes of Helbig, *Führer durch die öffentlichen Sammlungen klassischer Altertümer in Rom*, fourth edition, which appeared in 1963 and 1966 respectively. In some cases early publications have also been cited because of their relevance or lasting value, but Lippold's *Handbuch* is quoted only seldom since its indispensability is taken for granted. Ancient passages have mostly been taken from J. J. Pollitt, *The Art of Greece, 1400-31 B.C.* (Sources and Documents in the History of Art Series, New York 1965), because his comments are up to date, his quotations in English, and the book, being a paperback, is easily accessible to students.

One source from which I have heavily drawn without always being able to acknowledge it is Professor Rhys Carpenter's vast understanding of Greek Sculpture. I was privileged to study under him, and I have absorbed his theories and methods so thoroughly that I can no longer distinguish his inspiration from my own ideas. Though in no way responsible for my mistakes, Professor Carpenter is undoubtedly responsible for my desire to look at old monuments with fresh eyes, and I hope that he will be pleased, if not with my suggestions, at least with my approach. My indebtedness to him is more than I can express.

I have also greatly profited from spending one sabbatical semester as a member of the Institute for Advanced Study in Princeton, New Jersey, where the bulk of my book has been written. Besides the exceptional material facilities it provides and the quiet isolation of its accommodations, the Institute gives as its greatest gift the opportunity for communication with outstanding scholars, who willingly share their knowledge and indulgently discuss wild theories. I was particularly fortunate in having as fellow members during my term Professors Jale Inan and Werner Fuchs, both recognized experts in my field, and Dr. Klaus Vierneisel of the Munich Glyptothek. All three were constantly subjected to my questions and arguments. Mrs. Dorothy Burr Thompson has greatly helped me with advice and bibliography. To her and to Professor Homer A. Thompson, as well as to Drs. Inan, Fuchs, and Vierneisel, I wish to express here all my gratitude.

There are many other persons who should rightly be mentioned in these acknowledgments, but I find it impossible to list them all. I specifically wish to name the students in my Seminar, who with their discussion and interest encouraged me to write this book: Mrs. Carol W. Carpenter, Miss Diane Grossman (now Mrs. Paul Sheldon), Mr. F. Tyko Kihlstedt, Miss Sara A. MacVane, Miss Fernande Scheid (now Mrs. Tonio Hölscher), Miss Phoebe Sherman (now Mrs. Roger Sheftel), Miss Mary Sturgeon, and Mrs. Helen R. Young. I also sincerely thank the readers of my manuscript, particularly Professor Martin Robertson, for helpful criticism and encouragement; completely beyond the possibility of thanks was the task of Harriet Anderson, Fine Arts Editor of Princeton University Press.

One of the major undertakings of the book was the gathering of illustrations. I am most grateful to Miss Alison Frantz for allowing me the use of so many of her photographs; I am also particularly indebted to Professor F. Brommer for Fig. 15, to Dr. H. Biesantz for Figs. 76-77, 131-132, to Dr. G. Dontas for Figs. 100-102, to Professor E. Berger for Fig. 150. All the various Museum Curators were also most helpful in supplying photographs of pieces in their collections; of the many I wish to name specifically J. D. Cooney, of the Cleveland Museum of Art, who allowed me to publish in the Cleveland Museum Bulletin the head of Figs. 88-91, a purchase from the J. H. Wade Fund.

Finally I gratefully acknowledge the contribution of the Madge Miller Research Fund of Bryn Mawr College toward the expenses of typing and illustrating my text.

But without the help and understanding of the father of my four sons this book would not have been possible.

BRUNILDE SISMONDO RIDGWAY

Bryn Mawr College, Bryn Mawr, Pa.
Institute for Advanced Study, Princeton, N.J.
22 August, 1968

POSTSCRIPT: During the summer of 1969 I was able to visit several museums and sites in North Africa and Turkey, and therefore to examine personally several of the pieces mentioned in my text. I wish to thank the National Endowment for the Humanities for their Summer Stipend, and the American Philosophical Society for their Grant from the Johnson Fund, which financed my trip.

Contents

List of Illustrations and Photographic Sources

For sculptures owned by museums, it is to be understood that the proprietor supplied the photograph unless another source is acknowledged.

xiii

List of Abbreviations

The system of abbreviation followed throughout the text is based on "Notes for Contributors and Abbreviations," *American Journal of Archaeology* 69 (1965) 199-206. Works most frequently cited have been abbreviated according to the list below. Other titles, which may appear abbreviated in the footnotes, will be found quoted in full in the bibliography related to the pertinent chapter.

For German books of large scope, the English edition is used, where available, to accommodate the students with limited libraries at their disposal.

AntK: Antike Kunst

Arias and Hirmer: P. E. Arias and M. Hirmer, *A History of a Thousand Years of Greek Vase Painting,* revised by B. Shefton; New York 1961.

ArteAntMod: Arte Antica e Moderna

Beyen and Vollgraff: H. Beyen and W. Vollgraff, *Argos et Sicyone, Etudes relatives à la sculpture de style sévère,* The Hague 1947.

BerlWinckPr: Berliner Winckelmannsprogramm

Boardman/Dörig/Fuchs/Hirmer: J. Boardman, J. Dörig, W. Fuchs, and M. Hirmer, *The Art and Architecture of Ancient Greece,* London 1967.

Buschor and Hamann: E. Buschor and R. Hamann, *Die Skulpturen des Zeustempels zu Olympia,* Marburg 1924.

Carpenter, *Greek Sculpture*: R. Carpenter, *Greek Sculpture,* Chicago 1960.

Critd'Ar: Critica d'Arte

Dedications: A. Raubitschek, *Dedications from the Athenian Acropolis, A Catalogue of the Inscriptions of the sixth and fifth centuries B.C.,* Cambridge, Mass. 1949.

EncArAn: Enciclopedia dell'Arte Antica, Classica e Orientale, Rome 1958-1966.

FdD: Fouilles de Delphes, École Française d'Athènes.

FdX: Fouilles de Xanthos, Institut Français d'Archéologie d'Istanbul.

Fuchs, *Vorbilder*: W. Fuchs, *Die Vorbilder der neuattischen Reliefs* (*Jahrbuch des deutschen archäologischen Instituts, Ergänzungsheft* 20) Berlin 1959.

Harrison, *Agora 11*: *The Athenian Agora,* Vol. 11, E. Harrison, *Archaic and Archaistic Sculpture,* American School of Classical Studies at Athens, Princeton 1965.

Helbig[4]: W. Helbig, *Führer durch die öffentlichen Sammlungen klassischer Altertümer in Rom,* 4th edition supervised by H. Speier, Tubingen Vol. 1: 1963; Vol. 2: 1966. (Vol. 1 ends at no. 1160; Vol. 2 at no. 2116.)

JdI HE: Jahrbuch des deutschen archäologischen Instituts, Ergänzungshefte.

Jeffery, *Local Scripts*: L. Jeffery, *The Local Scripts of Archaic Greece,* Oxford 1961.

Korai: G. M. A. Richter, *Korai, Archaic Greek Maidens,* London 1968.

Langlotz, *FrühBild*: E. Langlotz, *Frühgriechische Bildhauerschulen*, Nuremberg 1927.

————, *Magna Graecia*: E. Langlotz and M. Hirmer, *The Art of Magna Graecia*, London 1965.

Lippold, *Handbuch*: W. Otto, *Handbuch der Archäologie im Rahmen des Handbuchs der Altertumswissenschaft*, Vol. 6:3,1, G. Lippold, *Die griechische Plastik*, Munich 1950.

Lullies and Hirmer: R. Lullies and M. Hirmer, *Greek Sculpture*, 2nd ed., New York 1960.

MarbWinckPr: *Marburger Winckelmann-Programm*

Paribeni, *Catalogo*: E. Paribeni, *Catalogo delle Sculture di Cirene*, Rome 1959.

————, *Sculture V Sec.*: E. Paribeni, *Museo Nazionale Romano, Sculture greche del V secolo, originali e repliche*, Rome 1953.

Poulsen, SS: V. H. Poulsen, *Der strenge Stil, Studien zur Geschichte der griechischen Plastik 480-450 v. Chr.* (ActaA 8, 1937)

Schefold, *Meisterwerke*: K. Schefold, *Meisterwerke griechische Kunst*, Basel 1960.

Schrader: H. Schrader, E. Langlotz, and W.-H. Schuchhardt, *Die archaischen Marmorbildwerke der Akropolis*, Frankfurt am Main, 1939.

Sculpture and Sculptors: G. M. A. Richter, *The Sculpture and Sculptors of the Greeks*, New Haven 1950.

Studies Robinson: *Studies presented to David M. Robinson*, ed. by G. Mylonas, 2 v., St. Louis 1951-1953.

TEL iii: *Encyclopédie photographique de l'art*, Paris Editions "Tel," Vol. iii, *Le Musée du Louvre, Grèce, Rome*, 1938.

THE SEVERE STYLE IN GREEK SCULPTURE

CHAPTER 1

What Is the Severe Style? Methods of Approach

Acccording to a recent definition, the term Severe style refers to the "style of that generation of artists active in Greece between 480-450 B.C." (L. Vlad Borrelli, *EncArAn*, s.v. Severo, Stile). The adjective is a translation of the German *streng*, which as a stylistic label was first used by Gustav Kramer in 1837 to refer to the early Red Figure vases (*Über den Styl und die Herkunft der bemahlten griechischen Thongefässe*, Berlin 1837, p. 101). The "starkness of design" recognized by the German scholar in these early Fifth century vessels is also apparent in the sculpture of the same period, but though Winckelmann had already called pre-Pheidian works "severe," the term did not acquire a specific and chronological meaning until recently, when it was extended to include all artistic manifestations of the post-Persian years. In particular, the definition "Severe style" became especially connected with sculpture as a result of Vagn Poulsen's important monograph, *Der strenge Stil*.

The history of Greek Art is generally divided into periods, whose terminal dates are more or less firmly connected with important political events, but the determining factor behind the subdivision remains the style typical of each chronological bracket. Only a change in style justifies the beginning of a new period; historical factors *per se* are of no consideration if their occurrence does not affect stylistic continuity. The so-called Transitional or Severe period is therefore that chronological span in Greek art during which the Severe style predominated in sculpture. When a new sculptural manner developed through the influence of Pheidias and the building of the Parthenon, the previous artistic phase gave way to the High Classical, at least in scholars' definitions. It is in fact fully understood that such divisions serve only a practical purpose, and that none of them can be considered a watertight compartment to be studied in isolation.

Yet it is not equally understood that this method of approach to Greek art and its terminology are open to dangers. If by Severe style is meant the sculptural manner developed between 480-450 B.C., these thirty years can be rightly called the Severe period. But to assume that Severe style and Severe period are synonymous is wrong since we would thus tend to attribute to the early Fifth century all works which display Severe characteristics. We would fail to distinguish between works that *are* Severe in style, because they were indeed created during those crucial thirty years, and works that *appear* Severe but actually represent an adaptation or a revival at a later time of the conventions of the early Fifth century. By grouping all such works within the Severe period we obviously run the risk of clouding and distorting our understanding of the Severe style; we also tend to underestimate the impact that the art of the 460's exercised over later phases of Greek and even Roman sculpture—a misestimate partly abetted by ancient literary sources which stress the value of individual Severe artists but still define their works as "hard," "stiff," and "dry." Many classicistic creations or pastiches are still taken to be bona fide though perhaps misguided copies of true Severe originals, and the Severe period, as a result, is inflated with works which contribute nothing to our appreciation of that phase and actually endanger it.

This difficulty partly stems from the fact that the Severe period has not been properly investigated. Individual monuments have received thorough and competent attention, but Severe art as a whole has been the subject of few studies and, in recent years, only of Poulsen's monograph. The Severe phase is mostly known through short chapters in handbooks or general treatises on Greek art, books which by their very nature can cast only a superficial glance at such a short span of Greek sculpture.

Basically, the subject has hitherto been approached in two ways: *chronologically*, by trying to arrange extant monuments in a relative sequence based on stylistic development; and *geographically*, by trying to distinguish different regional schools or by sketching the careers of prominent artists and their pupils. The first method leads to excess, too many monuments usually being included within the Severe period; the second method, though also open to that danger, is at the same time threatened with penury since our information on individual artists is at best slanted and limited, and our knowledge of regional schools conditioned by chance finds. A combination of the two approaches gives approximately the same results, and so does the *typological* method, which tries to group monuments by categories in an attempt to discover the inner development within each class. The conception of the period also varies: to some scholars it represents the logical development of the archaic phase, and the natural forerunner of classical art; to others it appears as a sharply differentiated link in the chain of sculptural evolution, quite distinct from what precedes and what follows.

The most authoritative handbook, G. Lippold's *Griechische Plastik*, vol. 6:3:1 in W. Otto's *Handbuch der Archäologie*, remains the fundamental source of information on the Severe monuments and their bibliography up to 1950. It treats the subject geographically, trying to outline the production of famous masters whenever possible; it therefore incurs the difficulties pointed out above, but especially that of considering sculptures produced at a later time as true copies of Severe works. The same basic approach appears in Ch. Picard's *Manuel d'Archéologie Grecque, La Sculpture* 2:1, published in 1939. The text of E. Buschor and R. Hamann, *Die Skulpturen des Zeustempels zu Olympia* (Marburg 1924) is mainly concerned with one specific monument, but it includes a useful geographical listing of Severe originals and copies, though with cautionary comments on the method (p. 39). G. M. A. Richter's *Sculpture and Sculptors of the Greeks*, in its 1950 edition, follows more closely the chronological system within the framework of individual sculptors' careers; the 1959 *Handbook of Greek Art* by the same author concentrates on typology, with the added difficulty of trying to categorize by types a period which is by far freer and more inventive than the archaic, and which does not cater to the same demands. L. Alscher's *Griechische Plastik* 2:1 (1961) includes an interesting historical excursus, but still relies on regional schools and focuses on few important monuments, mostly Greek originals of the early Severe phase.[1] The same holds true, on a necessarily more restricted scale, for works of larger scope, often lavishly illustrated, which consider other fields of Greek art besides sculpture or even related cultures, such as Etruscan, Iberian, etc. Of these, particularly important are J. D. Beazley and B. Ashmole, *Greek Sculpture and Painting* (1932, republished in 1966); G. Becatti, *The Art of Ancient Greece and Rome* (1965, English ed. 1967); J. Boardman, J. Dörig, W. Fuchs, and M. Hirmer, *The Art and Architecture of Ancient Greece* (1966, English ed.

[1] His book, 2:2, which presumably would deal with the more advanced Severe style, has not yet appeared; see, however, his *Götter vor Gericht*, 1963, supplement to Vol. 2:2, and "Nachwort," p. 138.

1967); P. E. Arias, *L'Arte della Grecia* (Storia Universale dell'Arte 2:1, 1967); K. Schefold, *Die Griechen und ihre Nachbarn* (Propyläen Kunstgeschichte 1, 1967). Separate mention should here be made of the comprehensive book by F. Schachermeyr, *Die frühe Klassik der Griechen* (1966), which investigates the period from historical, literary, and artistic points of view; specifically, chapter 11 is devoted to sculpture and painting and contains many illuminating and penetrating observations; but the major emphasis, and therefore the greater value, of the work lies in the recreation of the general background for the entire phase 500-450 B.C. R. Carpenter, in his *Greek Sculpture* (1960), concentrates on only a few monuments, but his main interest is in making specific points; the reader acquires considerable stylistic insight in the few spotlighted works, the development of the style and the aims of the period as a whole, but he is then expected to proceed on his own in gathering and applying those criteria to the various sculptures that may be called Severe.

As for the evaluation of the stylistic period as a whole, Carpenter considers the Severe style an abrupt but inevitable and predictable change from the artificiality of the late archaic phase (p. 86). A similar point of view is upheld by Schuchhardt, *Epochen der griechischen Plastik* (1959), who selects the Persian war as the major turning point in Greek art until the appearance of Alexander the Great. Richter, in *Three Critical Periods* (1951), chooses to stress the difference not with the preceding but with the following style. She sees the Severe phase as representative of a realistic trend in art which was abruptly shifted and held back by Pheidias and his idealizing approach to sculpture. Without the powerful personality of this master and the influence he exercised over later generations, she claims, Greek sculpture would have probably continued to pursue a realistic course, with emphasis on motion, emotion, and portraiture—a course which was actually resumed at the end of the Fourth century B.C. and reached extreme expressions during the Hellenistic period. B. Ashmole (*Some Nameless Sculptors of the Fifth Century B.C.*, 1962) considers the Severe period the logical link between archaic and high classical.

The single recent study in depth of the Severe period is the 1937 book by V. H. Poulsen, *Der strenge Stil*. Following in the footsteps of Langlotz's *Frühgriechische Bildhauerschulen* (1927), Poulsen divides his material by regional schools. His approach varies from the traditional, in that he fully realizes the problem presented by the "major" art of monumental sculpture, with its exceptional demands and its traveling artists. He therefore concentrates on the minor arts, terracotta figurines first, then small bronzes, on the assumption that these lesser works would be more representative of local traits and schools, and less likely to be exported for their value. The point is valid and the study useful, but the subsequent step from the minor arts to monumental sculpture is at least somewhat arbitrary, as there is no guarantee that the two productions developed along parallel lines or influenced each other since they responded to different needs. It is perhaps useful to repeat here some of the main criticisms expressed by Ch. Picard in his review of Poulsen's book, *Gnomon* 15 (1939) 411-17, since they seem eminently reasonable and pertinent: that terracottas are particularly apt to suffer great deformations, based on individual modification of standard moulds; that the choice of types would be largely based on their suitability for moulds (that is, the ease with which they could be cast into moulds and then removed from them); that they are meant to appeal to the general public and are therefore bound to be most "canonical"; and finally, that the centers considered the seats of the most important schools may simply be those which produced and exported the greatest quantities of terracottas, without necessarily having a corresponding output of monumental sculpture in bronze and stone. The products of the minor arts travel easily and far and can be imitated here and there; indeed terracottas from Olynthos resemble those from Boeotia, there are contacts and similarities from East to West, from Rhodes to Sicily, and by and large the illustrations of Poulsen's book appear standard and monotonous, hardly testifying to the importance of the period as a whole.[2]

A further objection to the regional approach lies in fact in the nature of the period itself. At that time political and historical conditions favored the diffusion of artistic trends and prototypes, as well as the traveling of individual artists. The break with the past came perhaps as a natural consequence of the tension created by the Persian war.[3] Under the threat of invasion the minds of the Greeks were, perhaps for the first time though still for different reasons, focused toward one major problem, and there was little time left for great public enterprises or for more than a few private dedications. While in 490 the Athenians and the Euboeans alone had felt the hardship of the war (and the Athenians not even in Athens, but only at Marathon), in 480 the invading Persian army occupied Greek soil for a considerable length of time, and even cities not directly touched by the invader were hastily building up defenses or sending men into battle. Athens and its monuments were destroyed. It was a marvelous opportunity, once the danger had passed, to make a clean sweep and start on a new direction, which had already been sighted in the preceding years. The Acropolis buildings may have lain in ruins, but private dedications started springing up all over the citadel shortly after 480/479, as the various inscribed bases from the Acropolis attest. Without the obvious confrontation with earlier works, now all piously buried with the rest of the Persian debris, the new statues had free field for assertion and might have come to symbolize the true rebirth of the state.

These *tabula rasa* conditions, of course, apply only to Athens. Yet the same artistic manifestations occur throughout the Greek world. How can we account for the phenomenon? A contributing factor to the spreading of the Severe style to the East and to the Aegean islands must have been the great political power developed by Athens during the years of the Delian confederacy. The Kimonian campaigns spread Athenian influence not only to Greek Asia Minor, but also to non-Greek areas such as Lycia and Caria. The Great Panathenaic games were resumed, and perhaps from the early days of the confederacy Athens expected her allies to attend and participate. Indeed the Panathenaic procession, like a Roman triumph, became such an outward manifestation of Athenian power and influence that by 447 B.C. it was considered an appropriate subject for the

---

[2] A more recent, general, discussion of terracottas points out further dangers. R. A. Higgins (*Greek Terracottas*, Methuen's Handbooks of Archaeology series, London 1967, 57-58) affirms that the stylistic transition from late archaic to early classical was more gradual and less important in terracotta than in major sculpture, and that only by the middle of the Fifth century had Severe simplicity truly replaced archaic elaboration. The British scholar also reverses Poulsen's chronological order for the two major Attic types (Higgins, pl. 30 E, ca. 450 B.C. = Poulsen p. 73 fig. 43, dated hardly before the middle of the Fifth century; Higgins, pl. 30 F, about 440 B.C. = Poulsen, p. 53 fig. 30, 460-450).

[3] For a more specific discussion of chronology, see infra, Ch. 2.

adornment of the Parthenon, the most ambitious building of the Periklean program and a true "Treasury of Athens" in the archaic sense.

But more important than the Panathenaic were the Olympic games. In the Severe period Olympia became the focus of the Greek world and a center of great artistic activity, with the erection of the magnificent Temple of Zeus, the first ever to be built in the sacred Altis for its main divinity. The agonistic spirit of the events, the glory attached to a victory in the games, provided the strongest moral stimulus to participate, while access to the contest was facilitated by the famous Olympic truce, which allowed free transit to heralds and athletes alike. Though the games had been held since 776, if we believe the traditional dating, never before had they attained the importance and emphasis bestowed on them after the Persian war. The victory against the enemy had been won by the physical fitness and training of Greek men, as well as by their courage, and the games promoted, glorified, and displayed this excellence. Historical circumstances also contributed to this climate of internationalism. Olympia had always been somewhat westward-oriented in its affiliations, as the many archaic treasuries dedicated by western cities amply attest. Now the colonial ties with the mainland were strengthened by the victory of the Sicilian tyrants over the Carthaginians, which was hailed as a true triumph of Greeks against barbarians. Its contemporaneity with the victory over the Persians, true though perhaps overemphasized, made for a freer and more united Greek world than had ever been possible before, and from South Italy, Sicily, and North Africa competitors flocked to the great contests of Olympia and Delphi with a filial spirit not felt since the first colonial waves had left the motherland. It was the time of the great Deinomenids and the other Sicilian princes immortalized by Pindar in his odes. It was the time when the best poets were recruited to glorify the victors and the best masters enlisted to cast their monuments in bronze. The statues are now mostly lost, or known to us only through copies, but the verses of the poets have survived and attest to the glory of the era.

This briefly sketched picture may suffice to list the basic traits which characterize the thirty years between 480 and 450 B.C. It is a period of internationalism, when people travel in relative security; the booty taken from Persians and Carthaginians, as well as the tribute exacted from allies, have created a certain economic prosperity; the victory over the barbarian has aroused a certain ethnic pride. Thus the renewed interest in the Panhellenic competitions promotes a new kind of nationalism as well as a specific form of artistic production, centering on athletic statuary in bronze. As Greek competitors come to the agonistic centers from all over the Greek world, so do Greek artists travel from everywhere to satisfy the athletes' demands. It is usually said that in the archaic period stylistic motifs and technical innovations spread with the rapidity and excitement promoted by the novelty of experimentation, so that "new discoveries were welcomed and shared" and "regional distinctions became merged in a common progression" (Richter, *Kouroi²*, p. 5). Yet local schools are more readily discernible in archaic than in Severe sculpture, and it is the Severe period which should be truly termed international, or perhaps national, in the Greek sense of the term.

If these premises are accepted, it is easy to see why a study of Severe sculpture along regional traits is fraught with difficulties. Local characteristics can perhaps prevail in cheap terracotta votives, but the great monuments must be steeped in the main stream of the art of the time. Study of Severe sculpture through the study of artists is not much safer. It has been claimed that only great personalities could have diverted the trends of the archaic period so radically.[4] Yet none of these masters is for us more substantial than a shadow, or is at best safely known through more than one of his works. Literary sources have preserved for us many names which remain unidentified despite repeated attempts at attributions, while the extant inscriptions on statue bases attest that many more masters were active than one would suspect from the lists compiled by Roman authors. In the wake of German philological scholarship in the last century, some recent efforts have been made to define the artistic personalities of masters like Kalamis, Pythagoras, or Myron; but not even the added archaeological evidence from recent excavations or the more scientific method of approach have yielded reliable results.

It seems best therefore to attempt a study of the Severe style on stylistic criteria alone, bringing to bear whatever archaeological information or external evidence are available on any point.[5] To distinguish between the Severe style of the Severe period proper and that of later times, we shall begin by analyzing a few Greek monuments of undoubted Severe date, in the attempt to define some basic elements of the original style. To this purpose a few general statements can be anticipated, not as dogmatic pronouncements *ante factum*, but to serve as guide lines during the analysis of single works. Most treatises on Greek sculpture seem to agree on these points, and they should be weighed against the evidence, to be tested, and then either accepted or rejected.

BASIC TRAITS OF THE SEVERE STYLE

1. *A certain simplicity or "severity" of forms*, visible both in facial features and in the treatment of drapery; a heaviness of traits in open contrast to the lighter features of archaic sculpture; a feeling for the tectonics of the human body which conceives each figure as composed of certain basic structural sections, as contrasted with the lack of articulation and the emphasis on outlines in archaic statuary. More especially, in the human face the eyelids acquire volume, often appearing as thick rims around the eyes, and chins become particularly heavy; in drapery, cloth also is made to look heavier and "doughy."

The Severe period owes its present name to this most evident of all its traits. Contrary to the decorative approach of archaic sculptors, who multiplied details and fractioned into a variety of patterns the basic unity of single garments,[6] Severe artists proceeded as if by a process of elimination, thereby focusing emphasis on the few elements retained. From this point of view, the term Severe describes the style more accurately than the terms transitional or early classical, which stress continuity rather than difference.

2. *A change in drapery*, readily apparent in two forms: (a) a shift from Ionic to Doric fashions; (b) a change in the treatment of the folds.

[4] Richter, *Sculpture and Sculptors*, p. 199: "such an epoch produced and was probably largely conditioned by great leaders."

[5] Occasional reference to painting and the minor arts will be included but limited to a minimum because of its relative validity. Vase painting, for instance, which toward the end of the Sixth century had forged ahead of sculpture, after 480 B.C. seems to lag behind or at least to move in different directions. Painting and minor arts, moreover, perhaps because of their media or their more secular nature, appear concerned with themes which do not necessarily occur also in monumental sculpture.

[6] Cf., e.g. the many different borders used for the same mantle on the Acropolis korai: Schrader, *passim*; *Korai*, pp. 69-82.

(a) A desire for greater simplicity must have prompted the adoption in art of a different costume which more readily lent itself to the sober rendering in favor at the time. Conversely, the actual appearance of the peplos must have encouraged sculptors in their "severe" approach. Yet contemporary fashions cannot be made entirely responsible for the change in style since the more conservative and decorative vase painters continue to give their figures the plissé richness of chiton and himation. Contemporary female statues wear the heavy Doric peplos, either alone or over a thin chiton, which becomes all but hidden by the heavier upper garment. When a mantle is worn, it is longer than the archaic himation and draped in a different way. The peplos can be of two varieties, the Argive, closed along the side by two pins, or the Lakonian, left open. It basically consists of a rectangle of heavy material, presumably wool, folded over for about a third of its length to create an overfold or *apoptygma*. The garment thus prepared is draped around the body below the armpits, with enough looseness to allow the wearer to gather it and fasten it over both shoulders by means of long pins or brooches. The vertical opening usually falls on the right side. The peplos (or Doric chiton as it is sometimes misleadingly called), can be worn either loose, with just the basic horizontal accent created by the edge of the apoptygma, or belted. Athena usually prefers to tie her belt over the overfold, but another arrangement is possible, with the belt below it, so that a second horizontal line is formed under the apoptygma. When the material is shown loosely gathered *above* the belt, so that it bulges slightly, the effect is called a *kolpos*. Within the Severe period, the kolpos changes chronologically from a straight line into an arc, as the gathered material is shown increasingly voluminous and drooping down at the hips on either side of the roundness of the stomach. Similarly, the free leg is progressively moved sideways, breaking the vertical outline of the skirt. Both these deviations from the compact rectangular forms of the early period herald the classical style.

(b) In any costume, whether masculine or feminine, the folds are treated differently. They no longer cover the entire surface of the garment, but endeavor to betray the stance or the contour of the underlying human body by their irregular grouping. More important, while archaic folds were basically grooves sunk into the depth of the marble, and the wide ridges of the pleats stood closely packed side by side, the Severe folds are more widely spaced, and in some instances, equal emphasis is given to the ridges and valleys which separate them, so that the final effect resembles corrugated iron. Since now the pattern relies for its effect on the voids as well as the masses, fewer folds become imperative.

3. *A change in subject matter.* One aspect of this phenomenon is the increase in *characterization*. The basic Kouros type now becomes sharply differentiated into either Apollo or a human being, and the difference no longer rests on the attributes held by the statue. Apollo is recognizable not only through a certain grandeur or *ethos* (one of those intangible elements in Greek art which are so difficult to pinpoint but with which one has inevitably to reckon), but mostly because he now wears his hair long while the common athlete has his short. This hairstyle must have reflected contemporary fashions, since a wrestler offers less of a grip to his opponent if his hair is closely cropped. In the Fifth century the Greeks did not specialize in specific sports, but were all-around athletes; each one was therefore a potential wrestler and was portrayed as such; likewise, all athletes were represented with the swollen ears of the boxer. By leaving Apollo's curls long, the

9

artist emphasized the otherworldliness of the apparition, the conservatism typical of all religions. On the other hand, no longer depending on bow and arrow to characterize his subject, the artist had freed the hands of his god for a variety of actions: hence potential *narrative*. Similarly, the athlete can be characterized not only by his physical aspect but by a portrayal of some specific athletic feat or the addition of some item of athletic equipment. Once a break with traditional typology has been made, partly determined by the specific demand for agonistic monuments, the forms of representation multiply, for male as well as for female or even animal statuary, so that one should no longer speak of *types*, but more correctly, of subjects.

4. *Interest in emotion.* The increase in characterization, with its potential for narrative, is obviously accompanied by an interest in the mechanics of expression. The range goes from quiet brooding to worried forethought to physical distress, and ends with the uncontrollable muscular distortions of death. Naturally, these indications remain fairly superficial and linear, more like the wrinkles on a mask than the true structural alterations of a human face under stress or pain; but the interest in emotions cannot be mistaken. Side by side with these "expressionistic" renderings appear the "idealized" countenances: faces which at best seem serious and at worst merely vacant. The technical changes in the rendering of the mouth contribute to a certain wistfulness. While the archaic artist emphasized depth by shaping the lips into a shallow arc with upturned corners, the Severe artist makes the upper lip slightly longer than the lower, with the result that the mouth seems to dip down at the corners and thus to "pout."

5. *Interest in motion.* Emotions or physical distress are usually dependent upon strain or action. Characterization has led to narrative. Thus traits 3 and 4 combine to produce a series of "statues in motion." This feature is not wholly dependent upon the demand for athletic sculpture, nor can it be considered a total innovation of the Severe period since figures in action had already appeared during the archaic phase. What is of special interest is the kind of motion portrayed: either a violent physical action which still relies on an eloquent silhouette, or a moment of rest immediately preceding or following a physical action of any sort, be it even the quiet action of walking. Groups seem to be glorified metopes in the round, and this change from the purely paratactic archaic arrangement may be dependent on architectural and hence, ultimately, on pictorial sources. But a major factor must be the greater freedom permitted the artist by what now becomes his favorite medium:

6. *The predominant use of bronze.* The Acropolis bases attest that the use of marble was virtually discontinued after 480 B.C. Since a bronze statue has a different static balance from a marble one, the advantages of using bronze for athletic statuary, or for any narrative sculpture in general, are immediately obvious. They were not so readily apparent to the late archaic sculptor, who at first conceived his bronze figures along the same restrained lines of his stone work. But by the Severe period the potential of the medium had been realized.

Another aspect of metal statuary (which is usually inadequately emphasized) is the *decorative value* of cold work. From this point of view, Severe figures are as highly, though less garishly, decorative as archaic statues, and not so much "severe" as "naturalistic." The intricacies in the hair rendering permitted by chasing and engraving, or even by the moulding, solid casting, and separate additions of curls and strands, allow the adoption of coiffures which would look heavy and improbable in stone.

The change in medium, with the consequent demand of clay prototypes for casting purposes, allowed a freedom of experimentation impossible in stone, where every tool mark was irrevocable and often beyond correction. The handling of the softer material might have prompted comparable effects in marble statuary, thus lending drapery the doughy appearance mentioned above.

One final trait, usually mentioned by the handbooks, is the new conception of Man, that tragic or epic spirit which seems to imbue Severe sculpture and finds eloquent expression in contemporary literature. Without denying the validity of such parallels and comments, it seems best to limit our list to material features, or at least features which find a material and more or less tangible expression. Ethos and grandeur, though obviously perceptible, are difficult to describe and are not localized in specific features. They are therefore best left to the individual reader's subjective reaction.[7]

[7] Among the "tangible traits" should perhaps be listed a change in proportions; it is here omitted because the great fluctuation from monument to monument does not allow general definition. Some works, e.g. the Omphalos Apollo, seem to have rather small heads and elongated bodies; others, e.g. the New York stele of the Girl with Doves, show exactly the opposite.

CHAPTER 2

Greek Originals and Their Chronology:
Architectural Sculpture

WE ARE fortunate in having so many original works of the Severe period preserved for our inspection; yet few of them can be definitely dated on external evidence, and many differ so greatly in type and appearance as to prove difficult to correlate in terms of relative chronology. The differences between the very ornate late archaic and the striking simplicity of the early Severe monuments seem so pronounced as almost to imply a definite turning point, as indeed advocated by some scholars on the basis of historical events. Nonetheless, incipient signs of the Severe style are amply attested as far back as 500 B.C.,[1] and in marginal cases it is difficult to decide exactly whether a certain work falls just before or just after the fateful date of 480 B.C. It is simpler, in many instances, to determine whether the style of a certain piece is still archaic or already Severe, and it might be safer to leave the upper chronological limit of the Severe period somewhat fluid. German scholarship has sometimes bracketed the transitional phase as 490-450 or even 500-450 while other students of Greek sculpture have stressed the harbingers of the new formulas in the early Fifth century and have tried to lower traditional archaic chronology. Since, however, no absolute date can be found for the beginnings of the Severe period, the divisions remain a matter of terminology, and it seems expedient to retain the one historical date—the destruction of Athens in 480 B.C.— which can at least stake a reasonable claim for a turn of events and a need for replacement and change. The chronology followed in this book will therefore retain the traditional thirty years span 480-450, with the full understanding that a margin of at least five years could be allowed on either side of these limits. But in ultimate analysis, as G. M. A. Richter writes (*Kouroi²*, p. 5), "it is the style, not the individual that counts," and the Severe style finds its full expression and coherent formulation only in the second quarter of the Fifth century. The official date of the Tyrannicide group by Kritios and Nesiotes, 477 B.C., can therefore be considered the legal birthday of the Severe style.

A tentative list of the best known Severe originals, with some basic information for each piece, will be found in the Appendices. Here only representative monuments will be discussed, not for descriptive purposes but with the aim of pointing out those stylistic characteristics which can be considered truly Severe. In order to emphasize their "early classical" traits, these monuments will be compared and contrasted, as far as is feasible, with earlier and later pieces without consideration of regional schools, not to deny that regional differences exist, but to acknowledge the difficulty of correctly assessing them and to stress instead the wide diffusion of the style. This procedure obviously has faults and is open to legitimate criticism, but on the basis of the factors outlined in Chapter 1 it may not be wholly irrational at the present state of our knowledge. It is further assumed that masterpieces, as such, rise above local peculiarities and are typical only of their time.

---

[1] Notice for instance the heavy jaws and the plastic treatment of the drapery in the Theseus/Antiope group from the pediment of the Temple at Eretria (Lullies & Hirmer, pls. 66-68); the himation over the back of Kore Akr. 684 (Schrader, no. 55, pl. 79; *Korai*, figs. 578-82); the peplos of the Fleeing girl from Eleusis (on which see infra, ch. 2, App. 1), and other similar cases.

All extant Greek originals can be divided into three basic categories:

(a) architectural sculpture

(b) sculpture in the round

(c) reliefs (votive and funerary)

It seems best to begin with architectural sculpture, since in many cases the details of the architecture provide some chronological clues; moreover, though artists can travel and influences reach from distant regions, the actual carving of the sculptures usually takes place locally and—except in cases of later depredation and shipment—the works remain firmly bound to their edifices. The Severe period provides a good range of architectural decoration, varied also in its geographical distribution: the pediments of the Temple of Aphaia on the Island of Aegina, the pediments and metopes of the Temple of Zeus at Olympia, the metopes of Temple E at Selinus in Sicily, and the architectural reliefs from Xanthos in Lycia. Attica, at this time, is conspicuously absent, though better represented in the two other categories, and the explanation lies probably in the fact that no extensive building program was to be carried out until the time of Perikles (though see infra, Ch. 7, on the "Kimonian" Parthenon metopes).

The Temple of Aphaia at Aegina provides the ideal parallel and contrast between late archaic and early classical style; it is almost the answer to a scholar's dream for exemplification of the changes between the two periods. Its date is based exclusively on stylistic criteria, both in terms of the architecture and of the sculpture. The most recent discussion of the temple plan places the inception of the construction at ca. 500 B.C., on the strength of the experimentation with proportions evident in the 6 x 12 peristyle. W. B. Dinsmoor would even favor a date after the turn of the century, though presumably before 490. The slenderness of the columns, combined with the ramp of access and the double-tiered inner colonnade, seem to indicate a mixture of Ionic influence and Doric elements, as befits a structure located at a central point between Attica and the Peloponnese.

A comparable date would seem to be suggested by the sculpture, but here the picture is complicated by the fact that three, not two, pedimental compositions are preserved, and even three great central akroteria. Various hypotheses have been formulated, without carrying complete conviction, the least likely of which postulates the same date for all three sets: the extra one would be the rejected product of a sculptural competition between two artists, the loser having decided to dedicate his work on the ground east of the temple. Most scholars, however, recognize the difference in style between the East and West pedimental compositions, while the "rejected" set seems contemporary with the earlier, West sculptures. The sequence of events would, therefore, provide for the simultaneous manufacture of two pedimental sets shortly after work on the temple had begun; for some unknown reason the Eastern set (East I) was later discarded and another set (East II) carved, approximately fifteen years after the completion of the Western. Since the remains of East I were found in the proximity of the temple, one must assume that they stood there in antiquity, again for unfathomable reasons. It has been suggested that East I was damaged, either by human or atmospheric agents, and therefore had to be totally replaced. But if the damage had been slight, proper patchwork, such as that carried out at Olympia, should have proved adequate, while massive damage should have extended also to the architecture, which on the contrary appears well preserved. Furthermore, heavily damaged sculpture could hardly have been appropriate for setting within the sanctuary. The nature of the evidence is also peculiar since East I consists mostly of helmeted heads, hands, and feet;[2] granted that the sculptures were long exposed to the predatory habits of the local peasants, it is unlikely that such peasants would be so selective in their choice of parts since ancient marbles were usually taken as building material or to be burned into lime. Could some special significance be read into this fact, and could one postulate that the missing bodies were in a different medium?

Aegina was known during the late archaic and early classical periods as a famous bronze-casting center. Given the chosen subject of Trojan battles to fill the gables, the artists might have thought it natural to make only the naked parts of the warriors in stone, and to cover bodies in cheaper material with bronze armor and shields.[3] Figures entirely of bronze would have been too expensive, and the color contrast between marble and metal might have been counted a quality rather than a fault. The procedure is certainly complicated, and it was perhaps deemed expedient not to follow it for the less conspicuous West pediment. When, however, the Western figures were set in place they probably looked vastly superior to their hybrid Eastern counterparts, and equally colorful with added metal ornaments and painted details: the Aphaia temple is indeed notable for its polychromy, both sculptural and architectural. After a number of years it must have been decided to make the Eastern pediment conform, and East II was carved, while the original set was displayed nearby. The perishable nature of the bodies, possibly of wood, and the value of their metal coverings and additions, might have caused their complete disappearance and the puzzling survival of only the parts in stone. Unfortunately, no traces of dowel holes or attachment surfaces are preserved in the extant fragments, and therefore this "akrolithic" theory has no objective support.

Be this as it may, no hypothesis can be firmly anchored to an absolute date and the ultimate answer rests on stylistic criteria. Until recently, the reading of the sculptures was somewhat confused by the modifications and additions made by Thorvaldsen in the last century, but preparations for a new display in 1962/63 prompted the removal of all restorations (which were fortunately only glued onto the ancient parts), and a complete restudy of the compositions, based also on extant pedimental markings. It is perhaps presumptuous to discuss "the Aeginetans" before their complete publication by the Munich Museum, but some comments may be ventured, based on those pieces which suffered least from restoration. Also a preliminary report has been made by D. Ohly, who, on stylistic criteria, dates the inception of the temple around 510 B.C., the carving of East I and West around 500 and the replacement with East II by 490 B.C., and certainly not more than fifteen years after the completion of the West pediment. Though the German

---

[2] As also pointed out by Invernizzi, *I Frontoni*, p. 247, who however comments on the weathering of the surfaces, implying even partial exposure to the elements and therefore definite use. It should nevertheless be admitted that it is at times difficult to determine whether a fragment belongs to East I or to the "official" pediments. The difference lies mostly in sculptural scale, that of East I being presumably smaller than that of East II. However, see *infra*, p. 17, and reference in bibliography for a case of a head originally attributed to East I and now

convincingly assigned to East II. Other such changes in attribution have also occurred. But the number of preserved heads and the definite differences in style and scale apparently make it impossible to distribute all available fragments between two pediments only.

[3] The central Athena, being a totally draped figure, might have been carved almost entirely of marble; this possibility might explain the survival of the large fragment with her skirt and feet.

scholar clearly perceives the formal and material differences between East II and West, his chronology would make the second East pediment still fall within the archaic period. Yet, as Ohly himself stresses, West is late archaic, while something new can be detected in East II: that something new could be called the Severe style. It is not only manifest in individual sporadic details, but appears as a coherent program, both in the composition—much more tridimensional than the West gable—and in the rendering of all the figures. This new conception is too clearly formulated to be purely experimental. Since no external evidence is available and stylistic analysis is bound to be somewhat subjective, the chronology here accepted will be ca. 490 for the West pediment, and 480-470 for East II.

The stylistic argument in defense of such dating may also be stated as follows. The figures of the West pediment already show a "tired" brand of archaism. This is not so obvious in the male anatomy, which in the early Fifth century represents the vital element of experimentation, but is more apparent in the garment of the central Athena (Fig. 1), which looks definitely artificial because of its excessive elaboration. The so-called swallow-tail patterns, adopted at first as symbolic of the ins and outs of voluminous garments, have now been meaninglessly multiplied for the sake of sheer decoration. The double curves in the zigzag hanging from the right arm, again an initial attempt at suggesting fullness and free movement of cloth, are so flat as to be purely linear. The excessive thickness of the chiton's central pleat (the *paryphe*), obvious in the various convolutions of the lower end, disappears into unreal flatness over the stomach, though thin vertical lines on either side still suggest the gathering of the material as in an Indian sari. Furthermore, the himation is incongruous: if it can hang so low over the right side, it must obviously be worn diagonally;[4] yet the strictly horizontal central portion, with only a minimum dip over the left hip, is incompatible with this arrangement. Contrast the Athena in the metope with Theseus from the Athenian Treasury at Delphi (Fig. 2): the paryphe is narrower and the more feminine drapery hangs low between her feet; the zigzag patterns are fairly inconspicuous and the mantle is more coherent. It is true that we lack the shorter tip of the himation over the left leg, but this was carved separately and attached by means of the large square socket at present visible on the figure. The French have usually interpreted this hole as the point of insertion for a belt ornament; but traditionally Athena wears no such belt, and moreover the rendering of the himation would be unprecedented, without a counterpart to its right mass. The position of the tenon hole, somewhat displaced toward the proper left, indicates that the tip of the

[4] As indicated also by the small section of the upper border visible below the left armpit. Yet the lower edge of the mantle is so horizontal as to recall the apoptygma of a peplos, and one wonders whether the artist might have been influenced by his knowledge of this Doric garment. For a comparable rendering in numismatics, of proven later date, cf. the nymph Himera on Sicilian coins, C. M. Kraay and M. Hirmer, *Greek Coins*, 1966, pl. 21, 68 R, ca. 440-430 B.C.

Along these lines one may also note the manneristic way in which the akroterial figures hold their skirts well in front of their bodies. Sixth century korai tend to pull their garment aside, while Fifth century maidens pull it forward. The Aeginetan girls, in this respect, are comparable to Euthydikos' kore, which dates from the very end of the archaic period; this mannerism is also found in bronze peplophoroi supporting mirrors, which, because of their costume, definitely belong to the Severe period (e.g. Mitten and Doeringer, *Master Bronzes*, no. 88, p. 93, Baltimore; ca. 460 B.C.) and in works of manneristic vase painters (e.g. the Killing of Tityos by the Penthesilea Painter, Arias and Hirmer, fig. 170, dated ca. 455 B.C.).

mantle was similarly slanted, or at least that over that area lay the greatest weight, in contrast with the straight accent of the Aeginetan Athena. It has recently been claimed that this Aeginetan emphasis on horizontals and verticals is to be interpreted as Peloponnesian tectonics. I see it as the last step after the Athenian Treasury, the epitome of that "linear definition" which caused the collapse of archaic formulas and led to the simplicity of the Severe style. The Athenian Treasury has recently been convincingly dated to the 490's. Aegina West should be slightly later, for its "archaizing" rather than truly archaic flavor. Since it is generally admitted that approximately fifteen years intervene between West and East II, this chonology would place East II around 475.

Comparison between the two pediments is obviously conditioned by the chances of preservation. Of the two central Athenas only the heads allow confrontation, and the most striking change lies in the different proportions. Athena West is built horizontally (Fig. 3), Athena East vertically (Fig. 4). This impression is not caused by the lack of hair (added separately) in the latter, since measurements taken from the edge of the helmet to the tip of the chin in both figures confirm that, regardless of the hairline, the features of Athena West occupy slightly more than the lower half of the face, while those of Athena East expand over more than two-thirds. In the earlier Athena the area of the cheekbones coincides with the greatest width of the face; a hypothetical line joining temples and chin in an elliptical curve would leave part of the cheek out. A similar experiment tried on the Eastern Athena shows that the facial oval is more regular and the cheeks approximate the flat rendering typical of early Severe works. Finally, notice the shape of the mouth: the longer upper lip dominates the lower, thus preventing the smiling formula of Athena West; since the part between the lips is not completely straight but faintly curved upward, the result still suggests a concealed smile.

The same comments apply to the two archers facing left: that from the Western gable wears an Oriental costume (Fig. 5), while the Eastern is identifiable as Herakles because of his lion-headed helmet (Fig. 6). Besides the changes in composition,[5] the differences in outlines are significant. The earlier figure is still a silhouette pattern of an archer, whose arms clear the face so that the whole human body is visible. Herakles' left arm is level with his shoulder, but the head bends slightly forward, so that the chin is blocked from sight; when the torso is in profile, the head is in three-quarter view; his right knee does not touch the ground, so his weight must rest on the ball of his right foot; in consequence, his back is straighter as contrasted with the forward lean of the Oriental archer. A more striking comparison is offered by the cuirassed archer from the West pediment (Fig. 7), shooting to the right. His chitoniskos, appearing under the leather flaps of the thorax, is neatly arranged in symmetrical swallowtails, all drawn perpendicular according to the law of gravity. Herakles' drapery shows only incipient zigzags, promptly merging into the first true rippling folds of Greek sculpture, with wider valleys than ridges.

These comparisons and contrasts could be expanded, but with relative value. More general comments are perhaps in order. The variety and freedom of the poses have often been stressed and sometimes attributed to the influence of bronze technique. Yet con-

[5] The Western Archer shoots into the corner, at close quarters; Herakles shoots across the gable, through the center; see *AA* 1966, p. 521 figs. 5 and 6.

temporary bronzes, or the impressions they left on statue bases, appear more sedate. Presumably the relative safety of a temple gable, and the necessity to narrate a story, prompted the lively actions. Forerunners of the Aeginetans are indeed to be found in the few preserved figures from the Peisistratid Temple in Athens. Once the idea of a fight as subject matter had been accepted, pictorial tradition provided an ample repertoire of poses for the stonecutter also. It is presumably from similar pedimental—and metopal —compositions that later more lively and narrative bronze groups were derived, though unfortunately we know them mostly from literary descriptions. As for the Aeginetans, it is interesting to note that such daring renderings as combatants falling backwards[6] (Fig. 8) do not find pertinent parallels in later extant sculpture until the Attalid dedications (Fig. 9). Similarly the rendering of death in Warrior L from East II (Fig. 10), with one eye narrower than the other in uncontrollable spasm, find its best comparison in the Hellenistic head of a Dead Persian in the Terme museum (Fig. 11). This affinity between the Severe and the Hellenistic periods is confirmed time and again, and shows that similarity of content and goals is stronger than morphological and stylistic difference.

One final point: if the second East pediment is to be dated in the Severe period, why do coiffures imitate so closely the archaic styles of the West warriors? Partly because the replacement figures were indeed meant as counterparts for the rear gable, partly also because they represented "heroes" who, as such, did not belong to the contemporary generation of men. The conservative touch of the snail-curls, though typical of late archaic kouroi, would be sufficiently old-fashioned in the 470's to identify the wearer as "ancient." Perhaps snail-curls were indeed considered typical of heroes, as shown by the coiffure of Theseus in the Athenian Treasury metopes and the pediment of the Temple of Apollo at Eretria. Signs of the new fashion are also apparent: the "Companion" I from the right wing of the East gable wears a braid, one of the most popular arrangements for long hair in the early Severe period (Fig. 12).[7] A helmeted head, formerly considered part of East I but recently attributed to East II, has its beard rendered only as volume and mass, without inner details, quite similar to the beard of Atlas in the famous Olympia metope, or, even closer, to that of Herakles in the metope with the Amazon (Fig. 30).

The Temple of Zeus at Olympia is firmly dated within a fifteen years' span by Pausanias' statement (5.10.2) that it was built from the spoils of the war between Elis and Pisa (470 B.C.) and that a shield from the battle of Tanagra (457 B.C.) was dedicated at the apex of the Eastern gable. Hence the temple had its raking cornice in position by that date or shortly afterwards. The temple and its sculpture have been so recently discussed and superbly illustrated by B. Ashmole, N. Yalouris, and A. Frantz (*Olympia, The Sculptures of the Temple of Zeus*, London 1967) that the reader is referred to their publication for all pertinent information. An interesting discussion of the drapery and its use for modeling purposes can be found in Carpenter, *Greek Sculpture*, pp. 128-34.

---

[6] *Not* forward; see the newly positioned torso from the East pediment, AA 1966, p. 518 figs. 3 and 4, for a contrast between the old and the new restoration.

[7] It looks as if the figure wore only *one* braid, instead of the customary two, but since the plait tapers at both ends behind the ears, it should be visualized as originating at the center of the nape; for a good photographic detail and a classical parallel, see G. Hafner, *Theoria*, Festschrift Schuchhardt, p. 83 fig. 4 and comments.

Here only specific comments will be made, again as clarification of the Severe style rather than as explanation or description of the Olympia sculptures. Hence problems of composition, arrangement of figures, and identification will not be discussed.

It may be useful, however, to repeat in this context the well-known fact that the corner figures of the West gable are replacements for the originals, damaged at some time in antiquity. Though Ashmole does not mention it, the suggestion has been made that the name of Alkamenes in antiquity became connected with the rear pediment, not because he had made the entire set of sculptures but because he had replaced the corner figures. Since the earliest damage to the temple occurred in the early Fourth century B.C., Alkamenes might still have been active, and his fame as pupil of Pheidias may have prompted the commission to repair what was by then one of the most famous buildings of antiquity. The use of Pentelic marble for the repairs may also point in the direction of Athens. However, only figure A (ills. 62-63) dates from the Fourth century; B and U are additions of a later date, presumably the first century B.C. This replacement is important in demonstrating later interest in the Severe style, and the partial understanding of it which could create statues so close to the original types as to have looked convincing from the ground level.

Two misunderstandings of the later sculptor should, however, be noted because incompatible with the Severe style: the engraved hair in the eyebrows of figure U (ill. 68), a rendering which is not found earlier than at least the Fourth century B.C.;[8] and the curls in the center of figure B's forehead with their stilted ivy-leaf pattern (Fig. 13). In the late archaic korai frilly strands were usually carried directly across the forehead, with complete disregard for the laws of nature; the proper understanding, or at least the proper rendering of the behavior of hair began at the time of Euthydikos' Kore, which displays a normal central part. The consequent triangular shape of the forehead, with the hair receding to a peak on the vertical axis of the face, is to be found in several Olympia heads, but either in conjunction with a complete part or with the part disappearing under a scarf or indicated in paint. On the other hand, this central motif appears at times on both archaic and Severe male heads, and is eventually transformed into the horizontal "parenthesis" of Polykleitos' Doryphoros (Fig. 42). The closest parallel to figure B's locks occurs in the mid Sixth century Nike from Delos (Fig. 55), and in the Archaic period the diminution in the size of the curls toward the center and the inver-

[8] In the bronze Boxer head from Olympia: Lullies and Hirmer, pls. 238-39; however Carpenter, *MAAR* 18 (1941) 39, would date this work in the Roman Republican period, not only because of the eyebrows pattern but also for the technique employed in inserting the eyes. Perhaps one should also differentiate between eyebrows engraved on marble and on bronze statues, since the latter seem more common (see, e.g. the head of an African from Cyrene, Lullies and Hirmer, pl. 210, though its date is also controversial and oscillates between the early Fourth and the Third century B.C.). An early example may even date from the Severe period: see the Mt. Holyoke Ephebe and the detail photograph in *AJA* 33 (1929) 46 fig. 2. In marble the practice may have started considerably later; the earliest example I know is the child on the Ilissos stele, but Adam considers this feature a substitute for a wrinkled brow (see S. Adam, *The Technique of Greek Sculpture*, p. 122 and detailed photograph, p. 68a). Engraved as well as plastic eyebrows are common in the Pergamon Altar, but usually introduced as an emotional and expressionistic device. Roman copies of Fourth century portraits are not safe evidence, since they could be copying original bronzes, and the original marble portrait head in Delphi (M. Bieber, *Sculpture of the Hellenistic Age*[2], figs. 692-93) has been variously dated from the Second century B.C. to the First A.D. It seems, however, reasonable to assume that the practice became fashionable in marbles by the Second century B.C.

sion of the movement at the axis seem usually reserved for Nikai, sphinxes, or similar semi-human beings.[9] The First century artist who made the Olympia corner statue either confused his periods or did not distinguish between male and female renderings.

These corner figures are particularly appropriate for establishing a further point of contact between Severe and Hellenistic sculptors: their interest in age range. As pointed out by Ashmole (p. 11) all phases of human life are represented in these pediments: from youth through maturity to old age. The inclusion of some aged figures, such as the seer, can be justified perhaps in terms of the story, but the old women in the Western gable are the intelligent contribution of the individual master.[10] They satisfy the same requirements as a Greek chorus: they must be present, yet unable to interfere with the main course of action. Their age makes them less desirable to the excited centaurs and also prevents them from taking active part in the struggle. They can, therefore, conveniently and plausibly recline to fill the corners, the eternal problem areas of all pedimental compositions.

The most striking feature of the Olympia sculptures is the drapery, not because of its ability, or occasional lack of it, to model the bodies, but because of its physical appearance. It clings to the figures, or it bulges out, with a plasticity and a heaviness completely different from archaic renderings. It is best described as "doughy," since it falls and waves with that wet consistency typical of a sheet of dough, and it is not difficult to assume that the artist experimented, if not with actual flour paste, with slabs of soft clay. As others have already pointed out, clay must have been an important factor in the making of the Olympia sculpture, but not the sharply tooled clay meant to appear like carved stone—the clay that we see for instance in the Zeus and Ganymede group, also in Olympia and from approximately the same period. The temple sculptors might have used what we could term "experimental clay," trying out different effects of drapery over their armatures and clay models. The process has been reversed, and instead of treating clay like stone, in imitation of marble statuary, now stone is cut like clay, in an intentional, and perhaps even somewhat mechanical, duplication of the models. Archaic marble sculpture was not similarly treated possibly because the sculptors made no use of preliminary models but sketched the outlines of their compositions directly on the quarry block, as seems suggested also by the residual block-like squareness of archaic statuary. This change in sculptural technique, from four-sided carving of outlines to transference of specific points from model to block, is perhaps the factor of greatest consequence in the change from the archaic to the Severe style.[11] It may be that the need

---

[9] This statement does not imply that korai with triangular foreheads did not exist (see for instance the Lyons kore, Schrader, pl. 36; *Korai*, figs. 275-79) or that no examples of parts appear before Euthydikos' kore (see, e.g. Akr. 683, Schrader, pl. 19; *Korai*, figs. 381-84), or Akr. 671 (Schrader, pl. 26; *Korai*, figs. 341-44), but they are the exception, not the rule.

[10] Although B and U are later additions, they were presumably patterned after a Severe model. It is therefore assumed that the now headless figure v was elderly and served as inspiration to the First century master; see Ashmole, p. 22.

[11] Cf. A. J. B. Wace, *An Approach to Greek Sculpture*, p. 50: "It is this pointing off into marble from a clay or wax model which gives the later Greek sculpture in marble a quality different from that of the Archaic sculpture. The latter was conceived as stone or marble and executed directly in that material." For possible archaic experiments along the same lines see supra, n. 1 (Eretria sculpture and Akr. 684). H. J. Etienne (*The Chisel in Greek Sculpture*, Leiden 1968, p. XIII and passim) advocates that the difference between sculpture carved before and after 500 B.C. is caused by the use of different tools (steel as against the earlier bronze)

for clay models was made necessary by the experimentations with balance and the new breaking of the law of frontality; perhaps the greater scale and complexity of pedimental compositions urged preliminary planning; and possibly also the idea of making clay models could not have originated until increased production in bronze had proved the advantages of such procedure. It has been objected that "the glyptic and unplastic character of the surviving monumental bronzes makes it clear that they are not cast replicas of clay models" (Carpenter, *Greek Sculpture*, p. 75; see also pp. 71 and 77); yet in those cases it is easy to assume that the bronze-caster was intentionally imitating the more familiar and popular stone production, just as did the *clay* sculptor of the Zeus and Ganymede. If the Peiraeus kouros is, however, to be considered truly archaic, it provides ample evidence of the use of clay in the making of bronzes with the "doughy" appearance of its locks and its rounded forms.

A revealing comparison can be made between the back of the kneeling girl O from the East pediment of Olympia (Fig. 14), and the back of Selene from the East pediment of the Parthenon (Fig. 15). As the belts indent the drapery at the waist, small furrows are formed both above and below, which often terminate with slightly rounded ends, as if a stick had been drawn through a soft medium and brought to a sudden stop. The classical rendering differs from the Severe in that each furrow either continues into a valley or terminates within an equally narrow ridge. In the Olympia figure, these ridges are wide and flat, as if formed by several pleats merged together, and they do not stand out with the relief of the high classical folds.

A comparison between Oinomaos (Fig. 16) and an archaic statue, the so-called Ilissos Kouros (Fig. 17), is equally illuminating. In the latter the symmetrically arranged mantle narrowly enframes the emphatic abdominal partitions, thus lending great value to the decorative effect of the anatomy and creating a play of horizontals and verticals; the folds are flat, the ridges sharp, the zigzags prominent and regular. In the Oinomaos the mantle is bent double, then swung over the left arm, but below the right, before being thrown over the right shoulder and back. While the folds on the left side hang downward, those on the right curve under the armpit and then swing upward. There is only residual reminiscence of zigzags over the right thigh, and the decorative effect has almost vanished. The folds are irregular and thus destroy the impression of pattern. Since the mantle lies partly on the left arm, most of the torso is bare, therefore the anatomy asserts itself on its own and not because of an established focus. Notice the difference between Oinomaos' curved *linea alba* and the straight line of the kouros.

It is difficult to compare the central Zeus (Fig. 18) with an archaic counterpart since the entire conception of the representation has changed. Formerly Zeus was shown participating in the action, either sitting at the Introduction of Herakles into Olympus, or actively interfering between Herakles and Apollo struggling for the tripod (Fig. 19). Here Zeus is an apparition.[12] But, more important, while the archaic Zeus was heavily dressed, and with the same costumes used by female figures, the partial nudity of gods and heroes has here been introduced in what shall remain the canonical rendering of

which allowed a different technique; but the point is not convincing and the pitted marble surfaces mentioned as evidence seem to occur (from his own photographs) both before and after the turn into the Fifth century.

[12] In this respect, he is comparable to the Athena of Aegina West: another argument in support of her late date?

20

later periods. Exact parallels do not occur even later, since the Dresden Zeus (Fig. 20), or the "Zeus-Hero" from Pergamon (Fig. 21), also drape part of the mantle over their shoulders. Compared with these later renderings, the Olympia Zeus' drapery reveals all its tentative formulation: against the lively sharpness of the classical folds, it is again the Olympia flatness which stands out, and the collapsing, more than the overlapping, of the folds. Everything remains more or less at the same level, and the artist seems reluctant to cut deeply into his block.

Even more block-like are the two main female personages, Sterope (Fig. 22) and Hippodameia (Fig. 23). They both wear the peplos, but in two different fashions that could almost, as it has been claimed, exemplify two different regional schools or two different masters. It is, of course, more likely that they exemplify the repertoire of the main master and should be further proof of the relative value to be attached to such differences, since the conception of both pediments is too unified to justify divisions among more than just the various workers. In comparison with earlier or later figures, the two peplophoroi stress certain Severe style traits. The famous Acropolis 679 (Fig. 24), the so-called Peplos Kore (now dated by Harrison as late as 530-525 B.C., and therefore almost a precursor of new forms rather than conservative), though wearing the same garment displays a minimum of folds, and only a slight depression along the vertical axis of her body suggests the division of the legs. At Olympia the artist is interested in balance. What male figures have achieved relatively simply, with shifts in musculature quite obvious in a naked body, the female figure must suggest through a thick covering. The master of the Peplos Kore disregarded a problem which could not yet face him; the artists who made the latest Acropolis korai gave them thin transparent chitons pulled tight across their legs, virtually eliminating the drapery in favor of the body (Fig. 25.)[13] The Severe artist has the courage of virtually eliminating the body in favor of the drapery; or rather, of sacrificing one part of the body in order to suggest the other. To put it in other words, the archaic master reveals the body by means of outlines, emphasizing the contours of his figure. Conversely, within the blocklike mass of his figures the Severe master reveals the presence of the body by its position, which determines the gathering of steep folds over the weight leg and the stretching of the cloth over the slightly protruding, slightly bent free leg. One leg is thus hidden (or "sacrificed") in order to display the other and to suggest that shift in balance which male figures conveyed through the slanting of their hips. This Severe formula will survive until Hellenistic times, with changes only in the number and material appearance of the folds. Only the late Fifth century could find a different formula which, by massing the drapery *between* the legs, could manage to reveal both,

[13] See, e.g. Akr. 682 (Schrader, pl. 53; *Korai*, figs. 362-67) or Akr. 680 (Schrader, pl. 68; *Korai*, figs. 389-93). Toward the end of the archaic period artists even experiment with poses which do not involve the pulling aside of the chiton, so that the skirt can more plausibly cling to the legs; cf., e.g. Akr. 685 (Schrader, pl. 70; *Korai*, figs. 573-77) or Akr. 615 (Schrader, pl. 82; *Korai*, figs. 401-4). Euthydikos' kore, probably the latest of extant Acropolis korai, retains the skirt-holding pose, but the dichotomy between upper and lower body is made even more apparent and disturbing than in earlier statuary because of the almost Severe massiveness of the torso (Schrader, text, fig. 42 on p. 78, gives four views of the lower fragment with its base; see also *Korai*, figs. 565-72). The discrepancy would probably be even more noticeable if the statue were entirely preserved: the left arm seems excessively outstretched, even considering the unusual stance with the left foot well forward, almost like a kouros', as against the almost even alignment of feet in earlier korai.

but in so doing sacrificed the volume of the drapery just as the archaic artist had done.[14]

The Olympia peplophoroi are also a good example of the tectonic approach of Severe sculptors. The one major horizontal accent of the figures, the edge of the overfold, is echoed in a minor key by the two other articulations of the body: the bend of the knee and the protrusion of the breasts, in Hippodameia (figure F; our Fig. 23) underlined by the crossed arms to compensate for the weaker accent at the waist. A similar conception of the figure in sections can be seen in the Apollo of the West pediment, where the horizontal accents are more numerous: pectoral, waist,[15] groin, and hips, and, at a great distance, knees. The vertical patterns are all but lost in this emphatic "building up" of the figure as if in separate sections.

Finally consider the lunging Lapith, West pediment C (Fig. 26). The original composition has been changed with the elimination of the drapery, which has left only residual waves on the plinth under the left foot. The outline of the naked body is thus all the more forceful and quite unparalleled. The giants at the corners of the Peisistratid Temple cannot compete in effort, nor can the poros giant (Fig. 27) from the West pediment of the Delphic temple. If such daring statuary in the round existed, presumably in bronze, it has not survived. The nearest chronological parallel, incredibly, remains the Borghese Warrior (ca. 120 B.C.) (Fig. 28), where the effort has again been expressed by means of a continuous line from leg to arm. The flayed musculature of the Hellenistic body points up the extreme simplicity of the Severe sculpture, but in the latter the basic articulations are given, and the head bent toward the chest clears the arms and reveals the strain.[16]

A few comments on stylistic traits may be in order. The faces are heavy, with rounded chins and flat cheeks. The eyes bulge between rim-like lids, which end in a peculiarly stunted outer corner.[17] The mouths are often open to express distress, even in Oinomaos, who seems otherwise composed. Additional signs of emotion are linear: a pronounced nostril, a groove across the forehead, crow's-feet at the eyes (Fig. 29). In the centaurs these lines are multiplied and deepened to make the rendering grotesque. These emotions result from deep foreboding and fatigue, as well as from great physical violence: the brutality of the Olympia fight is evident even with so few combatants to represent it, and finds close correspondence in the Selinus metopes to be discussed below. Lines in the faces correspond to lines on the bodies: the centaurs wrinkle at their joints, and long veins cross their equine bellies. The rendering of veins is one of the features of the Severe

[14] The typical example is the Frejus Aphrodite type: Lippold, *Handbuch*, pl. 60:4.

[15] This marking of the waist is surprising and not quite true to nature. Notice also the rather pointed epigastric arch, which approximates that of the *older* Tyrannicide (Fig. 115).

[16] Obviously in pedimental sculpture one has to take into account the differences and distortions caused by a view from below. The high setting and the oblique sighting line may also explain the great length of Apollo's legs. On optical corrections in the Olympia sculptures see S. Stucchi, "La decorazione figurata del Tempio di Zeus ad Olimpia,"

ASAtene 30-32, N.S. 14-16 (1952-54) 75-129.

[17] This rendering is peculiarly Severe and may stem from the fact that the artist, perhaps under the influence of bronze techniques, presumably conceived the lids mainly as the edges of a cavity to be filled by the eye. He therefore rendered these edges as a continuous rim. Increased accuracy toward the end of the Severe phase led to the mannerism of making the upper lid overlap the lower at the outer corner, so that the separation of the two would be obvious. This new rendering predominated during the Fifth century and was again revived in the Second century B.C.

style which lost popularity with the passing of time,[18] to re-appear in the Hellenistic period. The theme of the tired Herakles, as he appears in the Metope with the Nemean Lion, will also be revived only at the end of the Fourth century, in the so-called Farnese type.

The most distinctive characteristic of the Olympia heads is the treatment of the hair. It varies from a solid mass to be detailed in paint (Fig. 30), to a series of engraved strands which recall metal work (Fig. 73), to a close-fitting cap of tight curls pierced by drill holes (Fig. 29). This use of the drill is spectacular; it is contemporary with a variant of the snail-curl which appears as a protruding tight spiral[19] and which might be an imitation of the blobs of glaze used in contemporary vases to indicate curly hair. But to drill the center of curls is unusual and creates a tonal contrast not to be exploited again until Flavian times, or, significantly enough, reappearing only in neo-Attic and archaistic creations of the First century B.C.–First century A.D. With long hair, or in beards, the drill is used with more moderation (Fig. 31), perhaps simply as a matter of coherence, since longer hair creates fewer curls. That the Severe artist could be capable of such different conceptions for hair as the "impressionistic" mass and the drilled contrast of light and shadow suggests his complete break with the limiting conventions of Archaic times.[20]

Let us turn to the Selinus metopes. Metopal narrative is fully at home in Magna Graecian temples, where it has been employed since the early Sixth century, in contrast to their pediments which were left plain or filled simply with a gorgon mask as an apotropaic device. Contacts with the mainland of Greece, so dramatically renewed after the victory against the Carthaginians, brought in the first tentative pedimental sculpture, while the metopes, once proudly displayed across the fronts, in Temple E are demoted to the porches, perhaps under influence from Olympia. Thus cross-strains are adapted locally to suit particular tendencies.

Temple E has the most "canonical" plan of all temples in Selinus and the most "Greek." It was probably dedicated to Hera and was started when the victory of Himera had brought a revival of prosperity to the Sicilian towns. This fact makes it definitely later than 480 B.C., but the exact date is still in dispute. Some scholars think it precedes the Temple of Zeus at Olympia; others (and among them some architects) think that Olympia influence is already evident in both plan and sculpture and favor a date of 465-450 B.C. Attic influence has also been advocated, perhaps through vase painting or even because the master of the Selinus metopes had been to Athens. The most frequently cited parallels are the resemblance between Harmodios and the Herakles of the Amazonomachy metope (Fig. 32), and between the head of the Artemision bronze (Fig. 99) and that of

---

[18] Veins are still found in the Parthenon frieze, where however they are used to characterize old age. Cf., for instance, the smooth hand of Apollo on the East frieze with the strongly veined hand of his neighbor Poseidon (Fig. 142).

[19] Cf. for instance the head of Harmodios (in its various replicas) or the Herakles of the metope from temple E at Selinus (Fig. 32).

[20] S. Adam (*The Technique of Greek Sculpture*, p. 50) comments that "the archaic habit of drilling single holes to emphasize the centres of the curls of hair and beards is seen for almost the last time at Olympia." Indeed the rendering at Olympia differs from that on archaic statuary, where it had a purely decorative function and was therefore adopted only sporadically. By contrast, the *tonal* effect of the Olympia drilling can be considered a Severe innovation, typical only of the Severe period. I therefore see it as the beginning, rather than the end of a sculptural practice.

the seated Zeus of the Hieros Gamos metope (Fig. 33). The most recent stylistic analysis is by E. Langlotz, *Die Kunst der Westgriechen* (1963) 80-83 in the notes to pls. 100-13 (= *Magna Graecia*, pp. 280-83).

Stylistically the metopes are at the same time progressive and conservative, perhaps as reflection of the approach of different masters. Costumes retain archaic fashions and patterns, even in the rather fussy rendering of the peplos which looks as if it were made of thin material and shows swallowtails! Yet these latter hang from the protruding breasts, with a correct understanding of modeling drapery; and the wearer, Artemis, stands in the new position, with one knee straight and one bent. But if the draperies look tormented and over-elaborate, the heads are in pure Severe style. A surprising innovation, partly dictated by the poor quality of the local stone, consists in the insertion in marble of all exposed areas of the female figures: heads, hands, and feet. The result is a pseudo-akrolithic technique, a typical experimentation of the Severe period in textural contrast which at the same time suggests the delicacy of women as contrasted with the ruddy vigor of the men, mostly naked and carved entirely in limestone. There is no question that the additions in marble were also carved *in situ,* to be fitted to the limestone panels; notice for instance how Herakles' left foot curls over the marble foot of the Amazon. Therefore the advanced style of the heads should determine the date for the entire sculptural program, despite the "Lingering Archaic" of the costumes. Particularly significant, in many of the faces, is the rendering of the eyelids, thick but with sharp edges, the lower lid often forming a ledge slightly sloping downward. Obviously all the heads in the metopes betray many different influences: besides the resemblances already cited, one could mention the peculiar "tongue" in the center of Zeus' beard, to be found also in the Poseidon from Kreusis and the bronze head of a warrior in the National Museum in Athens; the typical hairstyle of Aktaion, so close not only to mainland renderings but also to the Agrigento kouros and the bronze Selinus/Castelvetrano Youth; and finally the same *range* as Olympia in the rendering of the hair, from simply blocked-out masses, as in the Artemis, to the finely detailed strands of the Zeus, to the blobs of Herakles. Whether this variety should indicate different artists or simply different influences and prototypes, it is difficult to say. The use of local stone, and the considerable skill required in erecting a temple, speak in favor of a local workshop; and even the imported marble does not necessarily imply an imported master. Where the lack of a strong personality is indeed apparent, as contrasted with the unified program of Olympia, is in the different quality of the single compositions, some being well planned and successful, others with such strong oblique accents as to look out of balance. Yet even such judgment is arbitrary since architectural sculpture should not be examined away from its structural setting, where one oblique composition might have been counterbalanced by another.

The myths chosen are unusual and disjointed; I cannot help feeling that the Western Greeks had a greater flair for narrative—an interest in the story as such rather than true interest in decoration. It is the mainland Greeks who combine decorative and narrative purposes into a "program," unified by an underlying theme, with typical sense for order, clarity, and coherence.

The reliefs from Xanthos have only recently been attributed to definite architectural contexts, though some of the evidence is uncertain. The buildings, erected ca. 470 B.C.

in imitation of wooden structures, have a typically local character and were presumably heroa, therefore dedicated to strictly local beliefs and cults. Yet the carvings are unquestionably Greek in style, though the subject matter may be Lycian (Figs. 33-34). The slabs with the procession presumably decorated the outside and inside walls of Building G; the sphinx pediment surmounted Building H (Fig. 38).

While the emphasis on smooth surfaces may be characteristic of Asia Minor, and perhaps even of Persian, influence, and the drapery still seems archaic, the types of faces, with the heavy chins and smooth, linear hair, are in pure Severe style. The diffusion of Greek art to non-Greek territory cannot be ascribed exclusively to Kimon's campaigns, since Xanthians traditionally employed Greek workmanship for their sculpture. However, these Severe reliefs are particularly important, in that corresponding monuments from Ionia are lacking, and the Xanthos sculptures have to stand as proof that the Severe style had spread also to the opposite shores of the Aegean Sea. It is, of course, not impossible that Greek artists had been summoned from Greece proper, but it is more logical to assume, especially in view of the Ionic quality of the carving, that they came from Asia Minor, thus attesting to a flourishing tradition in sculpture in that area despite the scantiness of our present evidence.

In chronological terms, the conclusions to be derived from the monuments just discussed are as follows. The most reliably dated structure remains the Temple of Zeus at Olympia, which conveniently falls within a span of time median to the whole period and in itself limited enough to be useful. All the traits of the Severe style mentioned in the first chapter find full and complete expression in the pedimental and metopal sculptures, with, nonetheless, a specific application which seems peculiarly "Olympic" and cannot be exactly paralleled in other sculpture. This peculiarity may perhaps be attributed to the master mind who planned the entire "program" and who cannot be identified by name; the imprint of his style is completely independent of the idiosyncrasies of the various carving hands. It is all the more remarkable that the *style* in general can assert itself so strongly over the *manner* of the individual master, and that this is the case is proved not only by what is contemporary, and of course by what follows, but especially by what precedes the Olympia sculptures, namely the second East pediment in the Temple of Aegina. There again all traits of the Severe style are present, but in what obviously appears as a coherently earlier phase.

Conversely, the metopes at Selinus and the reliefs from Xanthos show a certain retention of archaic traits discrepant with the appearance of fully developed Severe style features. It could be argued that this mixture is the hallmark of provincial art in peripheral areas, yet the important conclusion should be not this slightly derogatory judgment of "colonial" sculpture but rather the acknowledgment of the wide diffusion of an unmistakable style. A distinction should also be made between the local workshops necessarily employed for temple sculpture, and the itinerant artists of sculpture in the round. Where a major sculptor was not responsible for the entire program, as was probably true at Selinus, or when he was under specific commission from a non-Greek client, the "retarding" elements had more room for assertion.

1. *Fleeing maiden from Eleusis* (Figs. 36-37). The statuette, 0.645 m. high, was found in 1924 near the area of the so-called Sacred House, and has been generally attributed to the pediment of that structure. The building, though going back to earlier years, seems to have been remodeled or re-erected in Peisistratean times, as shown by some of the wall blocks and marble roof tiles still extant. It was destroyed by the Persians in 480/479 B.C. The Fleeing Maiden, because of her advanced style, is dated between 490-480. (For the latest account on this subject see G. Mylonas, *Eleusis and the Eleusinian Mysteries*, Princeton 1961, 102-3; paperback ed. 1969.)

It seems unlikely that the pedimental decoration of a structure approximately the size of the Athenian Treasury at Delphi should have required several decades, especially when the roof tiles conform to the standard of ca. 525. Should the Fleeing Maiden therefore be dissociated from the building? A post-Persian date for the statue has been maintained by E. Buschor (*Die Antike* 2 [1926] 175-76) and Lippold (*Handbuch*, p. 197). But recent studies have tried to support a date just before 480, and to assign other figures to the same pedimental composition and to the same workshop: see F. Willemsen, "Zu dem laufenden Mädchen aus Eleusis," *AthMitt* 69/70 (1954-55) 33-40 Beil. 19-21, pls. 1-2; N. Himmelmann-Wildschütz, "Eine eleusinische Bildhauerwerkstatt des frühen fünften Jahrunderts," *MarbWinckPr* (1957) 9-10.

Within this grouping, the most interesting figure is the Nike assigned by Willemsen to a pedimental composition for reasons not entirely clear to me. The distinctive treatment of the drapery, with serrated flat ribbon-like folds, recalls the pedimental figures from Selinus (Item 2 infra) and especially the torso from Paros illustrated by B. Ashmole, "Greek Sculpture in Sicily and South Italy," *ProcBritAc* 20 (1934) pl. 19 fig. 82.

For the Fleeing Maiden's hairstyle see infra, p. 117 (Fig. 156).

2. *Pedimental Figures from Selinus*: E. Gabrici, "Il Santuario della Malophoros a Selinunte," *MonAnt* 32 (1927) 165-66, pls. 25-26. B. Ashmole, "Greek Sculpture in Sicily and South Italy," *ProcBritAc* 20 (1934) 117, pl. 19 figs. 80-81. E. Paribeni, "Un torso di peplophoros da Piazza Barberini," *ASAtene* N.S. 8-10 (1946-1948) 106 fig. 3. Two female figures, one seated and one reclining, were found in the Sanctuary of Demeter, Gaggera (Selinus) in 1926. They are cm. 19 and 23 respectively (though headless) and therefore must come from a very small structure. Gabrici has suggested that they adorned the pediment of one of the votive naiskoi common in the area. The figures can, therefore, hardly qualify as true architectural sculpture, but the resemblance between the reclining Selinus woman and the corner statues of the Olympia pediments is interesting and significant of the influence exercised by the Mainland over the Italian colonies at this time. Ashmole, however, advocates a local school, perhaps with Cycladic connections because of the affinities with a torso from Paros (see supra). A further connection, with a peplophoros torso in Rome, has been suggested by Paribeni (see infra, Ch. 9, App. 5).

3. *So-called Prytaneion Reliefs, Thasos*: see Ch. 7, App. 1.

4. *Apollo the Archer (Apollo Sosianus)*: see Ch. 7, App. 3.

FOR PAGE 12

Dating of the Severe period: 490-450 B.C. = Lippold, *Handbuch*, 94-135; 500-450 B.C. = Dörig, in Boardman/Dörig/Fuchs/Hirmer, 263-94.

For a general lowering of archaic chronology, see Harrison, *Agora* 11, p. 10 n. 61 and chronological table on pp. 12-13.

FOR PAGE 13

Temple of Aphaia: the main publication remains A. Furtwängler, *Aegina, das Heiligtum der Aphaia*, Munich 1906. A recent architectural discussion in G. Gruben, *Die Tempel der Griechen* (Munich 1966) 112-15. See also W. B. Dinsmoor, *The Architecture of Ancient Greece* (London 1950) 105, 107.

A discussion of the various chronological phases of the entire sanctuary, with some support for a low chronology, can be found also in G. Gruben's article, "Die Sphinx-Säule von Aigina," *AthMitt* 80 (1965) 170-208, especially pp. 196 (III:A) and 205.

For a summary of theories up to 1965: A. Invernizzi, *I Frontoni del Tempio di Aphaia ad Egina* (Turin 1965) Ch. 9.

FOR PAGE 14

On Aegina as a bronze-casting center, see e.g. the comments by Carpenter, *Greek Sculpture*, pp. 115-16. Yet a school of marble carving must also have existed, witness the (still unpublished) archaic sculptures from the Temple of Apollo and the Severe stelai and sphinx from the island. Preliminary report by D. Ohly: *AA* (1966) 515-28, with a brief history of the vicissitudes of the statues and related scholarship.

FOR PAGE 15

The chronology here followed is also accepted, e.g. by E. Buschor and R. Hamann, p. 33; Lippold, *Handbuch*, p. 99; Carpenter, *Greek Sculpture*, p. 114, though presumably because these authors accept the theory of "damage to East I" in connection with a possible Persian raid after Salamis.

Athena/Theseus Metope in Delphi: *FdD* IV:4 pls. 15-18. On the interpretation of the socket, *ibid.* pp. 21, 51, 52 n. 2.

FOR PAGE 16

For the rendering of the Aegina Athena seen as Peloponnesian tectonics, cf. Invernizzi, *I Frontoni* pp. 132-41 and especially p. 139.

On the collapse of archaic formulas and the change into the Severe style see Carpenter, *Greek Sculpture* p. 87.

On the new dating of the Athenian Treasury: Harrison, *Agora* 11, pp. 9-11.

For a contrast of the two pediments along similar lines see e.g. M. Wegner, "Das griechische Menschenbild im Wandel von der archaischen zur klassischen Kunst," *Gymnasium* 65 (1958) 107-21, especially pp. 115-16.

FOR PAGE 17

Dead Persian in Terme Museum: Bieber, *Sculpture of the Hellenistic Age*[2], fig. 425, p. 108.

Helmeted Head, formerly East I, now reattributed to East II: Furtwängler, *Aegina* no. 121 pls. 71-72 and figs. 221-22, in conjunction with fragment no. 121a = Glyptothek 114. Cf. G. Treu, *Olympia* III pl. 41. This comparison had already been made by Furtwängler, p. 262.

The fundamental publication on the Temple of Zeus at Olympia is by E. Curtius and F. Adler, *Olympia. Die Ergebnisse der v.d. D.R. veranstalteten Ausgrabung* (Berlin, 1890-1897) and especially Vol. 3, by G. Treu, on the sculptures. The book by B. Ashmole, N. Yalouris, and A. Frantz will, however, be quoted in this text for all references to illustrations. See also my review, *Archaeology* 22 (1969) 72-75.

FOR PAGE 18

On the connection with Alkamenes see, e.g., *EncArAn* s.v. Alkamenes.

The date of the earliest damage is given by the architectural fragments from the temple incorporated into the foundations of the Leonidaion; see Yalouris, *Olympia*, p. 179, figs. A, B, and U.

FOR PAGE 19

For the use of clay models in connection with the Olympia sculptures, see, e.g. Ashmole, p. 10, who postulates models of wax or clay, and p. 20, for traces of *puntelli*. These were first detected by C. Blümel, *Griechische Bildhauerarbeit*, *JdI EH* 11 (1927) 29-30, pls. 14-15. A. Rumpf ("Tettix," *Symbola Coloniensia*, Festschrift J. Kroll, Cologne 1949, 85-99) revived Treu's theory that the markings are for the addition of metal tongues, which he believed to be the "tettiges" mentioned in ancient texts; but the supposition seems unlikely.

P. Bianchi Bandinelli, *EncArAn*, s.v., Greca,

Arte: Età dello Stile Severo e Classico, asserts that the Olympia sculptor must have been familiar with bronze and clay. A. J. B. Wace, *An Approach to Greek Sculpture* (Cambridge 1935) 36, calls the Olympia pedimental figures "definitely plastic," and quotes Blümel, *loc.cit.*, for the evidence of the pointing system.
Terracotta group of Zeus and Ganymede: see infra, Ch. 3, App. 12.

FOR PAGE 20
Ilissos Kouros: *BrBr* 781-82 (text by H. Riemann, 1939).

FOR PAGE 21
Zeus-Hero from Pergamon: Carpenter, *Greek Sculpture*, pl. 38.
On the stylistic differences between Sterope and Hippodameia see, e.g. Poulsen, SS, pp. 40-42 and figs. 22-23 on p. 43. For a discussion of the identification, based on physical characteristics, see Ch. Kardara, "Sterope kai Hippodameia," *ArchEph* 1965, pp. 168-73.

FOR PAGE 23
On Temple E being influenced by Olympia on architectural grounds see e.g. H. Berve and G. Gruben, *Greek Temples, Theatres and Shrines* (N.Y. 1962) 431-32.

On Attic influence, see, for most comprehensive treatment, W. Fuchs, "Zu den Metopen des Heraion von Selinus," *RömMitt* 63 (1956) 102-21, where he insists, on good grounds, on a date after 466 B.C.

FOR PAGE 24
For a good detail of eyelids, see, e.g. Richter, *Sculpture and Sculptors*, fig. 187, Zeus on the Hieros Gamos metope. A characteristic form of elongated eye has been considered by Langlotz typically Sicilian provincial; cf. also Fuchs, *op.cit.*, p. 104 and n. 10 with further references. Bronze head of a Warrior in Athens, Nat. Mus.: Boardman/Dörig/Fuchs/Hirmer, pl. 168.
Agrigento and Castelvetrano youths: Langlotz, *Magna Graecia*, pls. 54-55 and 81 respectively.
Reliefs from Xanthos: H. Metzger and P. Coupel, *FdX* 2 (1963); processional reliefs from Building G, Brit. Mus. B 311-B 314 and probably B 309-B 310, figs. 14 and 16 and pls. 38-39; sphinx pediment from Building H, Brit. Mus. B 290-B 291, figs. 22-23, pl. 47. Newly found relief from Building G: *AJA* 73 (1969) 216, pl. 59 fig. 14.

FOR PAGE 25
On the relationship between Kimon's campaigns and the history of Xanthos, see *FdX* 2, pp. 81-82.

CHAPTER 3

Greek Originals: Sculpture in the Round

W<small>HILE</small> virtually all original monuments of extant architectural sculpture could be discussed in the previous chapter, it would be impossible to include here all extant Severe sculpture in the round. The discussion will therefore be limited to significant pieces, as already stated, and the reader is referred to the Appendix for succinct information on additional pieces.

Like the Aegina pediment, some pieces of Attic sculpture have long been debated in chronological terms, some authors favoring a date before 480 and others claiming post-Persian manufacture. In terms of sheer originality, as herald of the Severe style, the most important of these works is perhaps Angelitos' Athena, Acropolis 140 (Fig. 39).

It is only a statuette, at present 77 cm. high, certainly well under life-size even when a tall-crested helmet increased its total height; yet it has the stamp of monumentality characteristic of all major works. The statue was connected by Raubitschek with a column and an inscribed capital stating that the monument was dedicated by Angelitos to Athena and that Euenor had made it. This association provides a nickname for the piece but very scanty information otherwise, though Raubitschek has advanced the intriguing theory that the Athena might have been carved not by Euenor himself but by a pupil in his workshop, perhaps the young Pheidias. It is among the earliest representations of the goddess in the Doric peplos, with the belted apoptygma which also becomes a constant feature seemingly reserved for her alone.[1] The left hand, which in traditional

---

[1] The fashion seems so constant in Attic Athenas that the particular arrangement is sometimes called the Attic Peplos. Yet the emphasis should be on Athena, not on Attic. The belted apoptygma may actually have been used to characterize the goddess, thus serving almost the function of an attribute. This theory could explain why some Severe Athenas may even dispense with the formerly all-important aegis: the typical "girded peplos" combined with a helmeted head and a spear, as in the Mourning Athena or the Frankfurt Athena, may have provided ample identification.

During the course of the Fifth century, the fashion may also have been adopted by other personages: see e.g. the Artemis on the name-krater by the Niobid Painter (Boardman/Dörig/Fuchs/Hirmer, pl. 159), or the Selene of the Parthenon East pediment, where however the belt appears in conjunction with the crossed straps of the charioteer. It would seem that the arrangement is confined to figures in action, though Harrison (*Agora* 11, p. 52) suggests rather that it is appropriate for maiden divinities. If, however, either or both surmises are correct, this interpretation of the fashion would disqualify the so-called Agorakritos' statue in Eleusis (Lippold, *Handbuch*, pl. 70:1) as a representation of Demeter. It is not unlikely that the Eleusis peplophoros repre-

sents Athena, since stylistic affinities and subject matter can be easily explained through the close ties existing between Athens and Eleusis.

The action-connotation of the belted peplos seems to disappear, or at least to diminish ca. 400 B.C. (cf. e.g. the stele of Krito and Timarista, Lullies and Hirmer, pl. 185), and the fashion is adopted also for archaistic renderings (cf. Harrison, *Agora* 11, pp. 52-54). Conversely, even in the Severe period Athena may occasionally wear her peplos belted *under* the apoptygma, as for instance in the Olympia metopes. The aesthetic effect is however entirely different: the unbelted overfold creates an over-all rectangular effect in which the flat upper panel is only a horizontal subdivision of the entire figure; the belted apoptygma stresses the articulation of the body at the waist and breaks the straight vertical contour above the hips. This "hourglass" effect is progressively emphasized as the inner folds, at first arranged vertically, gradually become slanted and finally form a V-pattern. Also the flat expanse of the unbelted overfold is relieved by occasional folds, but their course is more erratic, and tends to resemble a U rather than a V. See, e.g. the so-called Candia type (Lippold, *Handbuch*, pl. 47:2) (Fig. 168), the Hestia Giustiniani (Fig. 103), and other monuments discussed below. This difference between

---

29

korai held the chiton aside, has lost its task in Peplophoroi and become cumbersome, as empty hands always are for inexperienced actors. The sculptor needs to anchor it firmly against breakage, and can therefore place it only on the hip. This "housewifely" pose is later slightly modified by making the hand rest with its back, not with its palm, against the hip, in a more elegant fashion, but the mannerism continues until Hellenistic times. Comparably, the Zeus from the East pediment at Olympia fingers the edge of his mantle.

In Angelitos' Athena the right arm is held high and Langlotz suggests it might have held a spear, not as support but in a swinging position. This reconstruction, though possible, is not strictly required by the extant portion of the arm, and it seems unlikely, since the "attacking" gesture is usually combined with a striding pose, as common in small bronzes. In marble, the sculptor seems to have chosen a quieter moment: the goddess bends her right knee, thus supporting her weight on the left leg and perhaps partly on the spear; her shoulders slant, her feet are at a slight angle, and her head must have been turned to her left, as suggested by the tip of the crest lying on her hair somewhat to one side; the hair mass itself is not centered on her wide back. In many subtle ways, therefore, the master has broken the archaic "law of frontality," which requires that an imaginary line drawn vertically through the center of a figure divide it into two equal halves.[2] Yet the artist has virtually drawn such a line himself, by building the lower part of his statue out of two *different* halves. This procedure was not so obvious in the Olympia figures because the long vertical folds of the skirt were somewhat irregularly grouped and more closely spaced; moreover, the garment over the bent leg was less smooth and a vertical fold hung from the protruding knee. In the Athena the dress clings so closely to the right leg as to reveal it entirely, while the vertical folds over the weight leg are widely spaced and tubular, more closely related to the flutings of a column than to human forms. This is obviously an early stage of the Severe style, comparable to that of the Herakles Archer at Aegina (cf. Fig. 6) where the valleys in the drapery do not merely emphasize the projection of the ridges but are an integral part of the composition.

Surprisingly, the rear of the skirt appears as a reversal of the front. It is now the left leg which is modeled by the clinging drapery, whereas the right side is marked by the same heavy pleats as those of the front. This interpretation of folds is eminently logical: if the right leg, by being bent, pushes the material forward and makes it adhere to its front, obviously the same effect could not prevail in the back, where the folds, undeviated by the body, should follow the natural law of gravity; the weight leg, by being straight, touches the skirt at the rear, and therefore flattens it into quasi-transparency. Logical though this rendering may be, it is not aesthetically valid, and in more advanced classical times the back will be uniformly fluted by steep vertical folds, or the free leg will

---

the two types continues beyond the Severe period (contrast e.g. the Erechtheion Karyatids and the stele of Krito and Timarista already mentioned), and should, therefore, be considered typological and not chronological.

[2] The breaking of the "law of frontality" in the Severe period seems almost a new law in itself. Notice how consistently the purely static Severe statues thrust one foot to the side or turn and incline their head. Modern scholarship has invested this last trait with a psychological and introspective meaning which was probably entirely subordinate to the physical appearance in the ancient sculptor's intent.

not only bend forward but move sideways, therefore making the drapery cling smoothly both front and back. During most of the Severe period, however, the block-like regularity of the outer contour will be preferred over the irregularity of a motion pose.

One final comment on the treatment of cloth: while the skirt is so rigid as to suggest only wood or marble carving, the small grooves in the overfold above the belt look as if a stick had been drawn through a soft medium, making it bulge at the sides and at the rounded end. Could this be an early indication of modeling in clay? Another rendering of the new style is the coiffure: while previous representations of Athena showed her with long strands flowing over the chest in the typical kore fashion, now hair appears only over her shoulders, a prelude to the more practical, rolled-up fashion of the Olympia metopes and later depictions.

The Athena was found in building the foundations of the Acropolis Museum, together with the Moschophoros, the Kritian Boy (Fig. 41), and the head of the Athena from the Peisistratid temple. Of these sculptures two are undoubtedly archaic, but Angelitos' Athena and the Kouros could be later, and a chronological discussion may be here attempted for both monuments. Because of the inscription, and because of the possibility that Pheidias might have carved the statue and that some Red Figure vases of ca. 460 B.C. might reproduce it, Raubitschek dates Akr. 140 after the Persian invasion. Langlotz places it around 480, questioning whether some tool marks over the aegis may be traces of repair after damage by the enemy. Both speculations are open to question, mostly because they do not rest on firm enough grounds. The surfaces of both the Kritian Boy and the Athena are remarkably well preserved, a fact which seems to argue for limited exposure to the weather and thus for a pre-480 date. On the other hand, the surface of the Moschophoros, considerably earlier than the two other pieces, is also well preserved, yet burial before the Persian attack is hardly likely. As additional evidence one may mention that Kore Akr. 688, also dated ca. 480 and often termed Severe, was found incorporated into the foundations of the Propylaia. Therefore one must assume that the Periklean building program was removing early classical dedications which were in the way or that statues destroyed by the Persians were still lying around in 438 B.C. In consideration of the careful manner in which archaic monuments were disposed of, both at the time of the Tyrants and after the sack of the Acropolis (the so-called *Tyrannenschutt* and *Perserschutt*), the second supposition is unlikely and the first acquires credibility. The mixed fill of the finding spot for both the Kritian Boy and Angelitos' Athena, if not valid as positive evidence for a post-Persian date, is at least valid as negative evidence, in being mixed and therefore not closely datable. Once again, the main criterion for chronology seems to be the style of the statues. Angelitos' Athena, in its new awareness of the reality of cloth, its Doric costume, its deviations from the law of frontality, its tectonic articulation, its experimentation with balance, has every right to stand at the origin of the classical Athena type.

The balance of the Athena is more obvious in the naked Kritian Boy (Fig. 41), who however turns his head on the side of his free leg. The bend of his right knee is so slight that both feet, though presumably at an angle, must have been flat on the ground, yet it is sufficient to make the hips slant, causing different compressions and distensions in the musculature. This pose, with all its corresponding innovations in the anatomical rendering, has been used both for and against a pre-Persian date. Slight shifts in the alignment of the hips are apparent in other torsos, which however are themselves such marginal cases as to be equally disputable in chronological terms. Comparable positions of feet are also known, not only from actual fragmentary statues but also from traces of attachments for bronze figures on inscribed statue bases, which on epigraphical grounds can be dated before 480 B.C. Yet it is unsafe to assume that the diverging position of the feet necessarily corresponded to a differentiation between weight and free leg, or even to a shift of the pelvis, since the Athena from Aegina West also has her feet at an angle, yet appears rigidly symmetrical and static. Conversely, this position of the feet continues unchanged in the Olympia sculpture, where the proper balancing of the body is carefully worked out. It is therefore impossible to judge the stance of a statue from the feet alone or from their imprints since in the late archaic period considerable experimentation was carried out, and kouroi were represented contemporaneously with both legs straight or both bent. The great innovation of the Kritian Boy lies not in the position of his feet but in the awareness that such a position results in a shift in balance, and that movement in musculature is compatible with a balance of repose, as contrasted with earlier representations experimenting with actual or at least potential movement.

In order to evaluate fully the stylistic position of the Kritian Boy, contrast it with Aristodikos (ca. 490 B.C.) on the one hand (Fig. 40), and the Doryphoros (ca. 440 B.C.) on the other (Fig. 42). The Severe youth is closer in spirit to the high classical than to the archaic, though a shorter span of time separates him from the earlier work. But while Aristodikos can be considered the true predecessor of the Acropolis Boy in the rendering of the facial features, the "potential motion" implicit in his stance will probably lead to athletic statuary in action, not to the quiet pose of the youth. The Doryphoros, on the other hand, has inherited and developed all the basic traits: the rendering of the features, the experimentation with static balance, the consequent changes in musculature. Aristodikos' face, with its "dimples" and prominent cheek bones, appears strongly articulated. The Kritian Boy, by contrast, looks vacant and smooth, through that process of elimination or lack of emphasis which the Severe sculptors seem to have adopted to unify their figures (Figs. 43-44). As a result, the one prominent detail looks incongruous and the youth's face seems absurdly divorced from the rest of the head by the encircling roll of hair so strongly contrasting with the thinly engraved dome. This dichotomy is eliminated in the Doryphoros, whose short locks tightly cover the skull and fuse smoothly with the rest of the head. The dome of the head has also been flattened and shaped, in contrast with the more abstract regularity of the Kritian Boy. Within the face, the Doryphoros' mouth is larger and slightly parted, the nose longer and heavier, the eyebrows at right angles to the nasal bridge. In the Kritian Boy the full cheeks and massive jaws have been simplified into a more obvious contour culminating in the rounded chin, with an emphasis on oval shapes almost comparable to the abstraction of the Dipylon Head; under the roll, the outline of the face continues into the skull without obvious widening or tapering, while in the Doryphoros his cranial structure, not his hair, bulges. This almost archaic return to pattern in early Severe heads is distinctive and significant. Pronounced at the beginning, this patternization disappears toward the end of the phase, absorbed and superseded by the classical renderings. Carpenter writes of "measured heads" and symmetry, with the restricted meaning of measurable concordance, and wants to date the Kritian Boy a full decade after the Persian invasion.[3]

Both the Kritian Boy and Angelitos' Athena are under life-size. This type of figure, not quite three quarter but more than half natural height, seems popular for private dedications toward the end of the archaic and the beginning of the Severe period. But heroic, over life-size, renderings are also possible, both for public and private monuments, and by the same masters. Indeed the Kritian Boy owes its nickname to its alleged similarity to the Harmodios of the second Tyrannicide group made by Kritios and Nesiotes. (Since this latter work is known only through copies, it is reserved for discussion in a later chapter.) Recently, however, another comparison has been suggested in terms of common origin: the Delphi Charioteer (Figs. 47-48). The resemblance is undeniable, stressed by the fact that the Kritian Boy seems to have been conceived as a work in bronze rather than in marble. The engraved hair, the roll so awkward in marble but which could be so plausible in metal, the fine curls so closely adhering to the nape, the once inserted eyes with the consequent need for hollowing out the orbital cavities (a difficult process in stone), even the minute struts at the wrists, are all criteria which in a later work could be construed as proof that the marble statue copies a lost bronze. The find spot makes this supposition unlikely, and the only alternative is that the stone-cutter intentionally imitated bronze work,[4] or was himself a bronze-caster. Yet to ascribe the Delphi Charioteer to the same hand, or even the same workshop, would be a purely hypothetical assumption. What creates the similarity between the two works is common style rather than common authorship.

If the Kritian Boy emphasizes balance in a naked body, the Charioteer provides the rare example of a draped male figure. By the Severe period, gods were shown in partial nudity and athletes continued the tradition of the naked kouroi. Few draped men have survived from the archaic period itself, mostly from Ionia or Magna Graecia, where the type seems to have been more frequent than on the Greek mainland. There is, however, an example from the Athenian Acropolis, instructive because closer in date to the Charioteer, Akr. 633 (Figs. 49-50).

Obviously the marble youth is not intentionally imitating bronze. The various items of clothing are only a wrapping for the body, which asserts itself powerfully through them. Color once differentiated the garments more effectively than the width or number of the folds, yet a certain progression is followed, from narrower to wider pleats whose spacing also varies within the single garment according to logical principles. The pose

[3] Raubitschek has tentatively connected the Kritian Boy with an inscribed capital and column (*Dedications*, no. 21, pp. 24-26, with previous bibliography; for a recent comment on the capital see H. Möbius, *Studia Varia* [1967], Nachtrag on p. 97 and pl. 18:3-4); however, even the architectural and epigraphical evidence is inconclusive since the connection between statue and capital/column is not assured. Raubitschek elsewhere (*Hesperia* 8 [1939] 156) also is uncertain whether to date the related victory soon after or soon before 480 B.C. He has, moreover, stated that even monuments found in the Persian debris may date after 480 B.C. (e.g. *Dedications*, nos. 39, 217, 294, and, on his own assumption, Angelitos' Athena), and that "some dedications which were set up after 480 B.C. were buried before the middle of the Vth century" (*ibid.*, p. 462).

[4] Interestingly enough, this imitation of techniques typical of a different medium occurs again in the Hellenistic Period when, however, bronze statuary imitates marble. See B. S. Ridgway, "Stone and Metal in Greek Sculpture," *Archaeology* 19 (1966) 31-42 and especially p. 42.

is frontal and quiet, the wide-shouldered torso distinctly tapers toward the well-indented waist and the whole composition gradually narrows down to the feet.

The Delphi Charioteer is in striking contrast. The composition is basically columnar, with an abrupt break at the hem of the skirt and a stem-like effect at the ankles. The body seems to serve mainly as support for the garment, and the high girdle marks not the waist line but a convenient point below the breasts. The difference in folds, achieved in the Acropolis statue through three different garments, is here obtained through three different treatments of the same costume, as conditioned by the crossing of the straps and the seams along the upper arms. The folds are intentionally irregular, so that they appear natural rather than logical, but each "frequency" of waves is disturbed only slightly, so that the basic pattern still predominates. There is no concern for balance: the lower body of the Charioteer is so successfully hidden under the cloth that no hint is given to visualize its articulation; the existing divisions are tectonic accents of the composition, not of the human figure. Obviously the master was interested in composure, since even a slight bending forward of the body would have created an impression of eagerness and tension such as that portrayed in Syracusan coins. This choice of moment, *after* not during the competition, is distinctive of the Severe style, which usually chooses to portray anticipation or aftermath, rather than the action itself, as evident in many of the Olympia sculptures.

Was the simplicity of the figure stressed not to overburden a complex composition? It is difficult today to remember that the Charioteer stood on a bronze quadriga, whose large horses must have competed for aesthetic interest with the driver himself. Literary sources mention artists who were particularly famous for their statues of animals, and artists who supplied human figures for chariots made by other masters. This type of dedication seems to have been favored by powerful rulers, understandably enough since such bronze groups must have been extremely costly, and the very participation in chariot racing involved the expenses of a well-equipped stable. It was also the only athletic event in which the prize could be received without personal physical effort, since the winner was not the charioteer but the owner of the horses. The Delphi Charioteer was dedicated by the Sicilian prince Polyzalos, son of Deinomenes, for a victory won presumably in 478 or 474. Though the problems of the twice-inscribed base have not been solved to everybody's satisfaction, there is general agreement that on historical grounds the statue should be dated not later than 470 B.C., and possibly around 474. The heavy, stolid features all compressed into a relatively small area within the large face, the high-set mouth which emphasizes the already considerable chin, the cubic structure of the head with the uniformly rounded skull and the closely adhering locks, make the Charioteer look almost earlier than the Kritian Boy. Once again, contrast with the archaic face of the draped Acropolis youth no. 633: the basic structure of the heads is similar, and the facial oval equally pronounced; but the earlier work is characterized by the ins and outs of the cheeks, with the consequent horizontal accents of light and shadow; in the Charioteer the accents are vertical, as the light catches the edges of the flat cheeks turning into the frontal view.

The same differences may be noticed between archaic and Severe female faces. The best comparison is perhaps not with the much publicized Euthydikos' Kore, but between the late archaic Acropolis 684 (Fig. 45) and the early classical Propylaia Kore 688

(Fig. 46). In the earlier figure notice the hair running horizontally across the forehead, the linear definition of the zygomatic bones, the protruding chin which in profile seems almost hinged to the rest of the face. This last impression is heightened in the Propylaia Kore, but the demarcation of the cheekbones has disappeared, thus making the face more unified, and, in consequence more massive. The eyes, with their pronounced rims, dominate the face. The hair parts in the center and flows in waves on either side, thus forming a pointed frame for the forehead; the long strands bulge and bend as they are caught by the mantle around the nape. It is significant that, though wearing her hair loose, this kore hides her long tresses under the himation, with the consequent effect of looking short-haired. Severe ladies with their change of costume seem to have also changed coiffures, and tend to wear their hair pushed back over the shoulders, either loose or gathered in a knot, but more frequently rolled up in a chignon above the nape. The wavy strands over the breasts, so typical of archaic korai, disappear in female figures, to reappear only exceptionally in the early Fourth century, for instance in the Eirene with Ploutos by Kephisodotos (Fig. 177), while they are retained for male figures only, specifically Apollo, as an archaizing trait of religious conservatism. The Severe artist takes particular delight in the intricacies of hair, which he often renders quite linearly and loops over and under fillets in unprecedented fashions: see for instance the head, Athens Nat. Mus. 1949, or the already mentioned sphinxes from Xanthos (Fig. 38), which imitate in the new style the archaic "roundels" still present in the Propylaia Kore.

This new approach to hair, combined with a general "humanizing" trend, is further pursued in another head, not strictly belonging to a human being: that of the Aegina sphinx (Figs. 51-52). We shall return to this monument later, in discussing its affiliations to regional workshops or masters (p. 64); for the moment let us concentrate on its importance as a Severe rendering of a monster especially popular in the archaic period. During the Sixth century, sphinxes were mostly used in Attica as the crowning ornament of funerary monuments, and therefore as guardians of graves. The purely dedicatory sphinx, however, is also known from examples in Delphi (the colossal Naxian Sphinx), in Delos, and also on the Athenian Acropolis. Nothing distinguishes a votive from a funerary sphinx, except perhaps the position of the head, which in a sphinx associated with a one-sided stele requires a turn of the neck so that the monster can face the beholder, while her body remains in its most extensive view, the profile. A votive sphinx, freely set on a column, can be seen from any point since the support itself is fairly neutral and presents no principal face; the head is therefore often in line with the body, facing straight ahead. But even this distinction is not absolute, since sphinx 632 from the Athenian Acropolis (Fig. 53), hence votive, turns her head at an angle.

Schuchhardt saw a special significance in this position. Since an earlier Acropolis sphinx faces forward, he considered this a pose of aloofness relegating the monster to the realm of myth and mythological beings; Akr. 632, by turning her head, would establish a link with the realm of men in a humanizing process taking place around the middle of the Sixth century. There is no denying that a "humanizing" process occurred in the rendering of all monsters; but the date proposed by Schuchhardt seems too early for its beginning, and the reason for the specific position is perhaps purely technical: the sphinx turns her head not to establish contact, but either because of a special setting (of which the sculptor was notified in advance), or, more probably, under the influence of contemporary funerary art. Other votive sphinxes, later than 550, continue to be made facing forward, as for instance the one recently found in Cyrene.

The Aegina sphinx holds her head in a position of compromise, not at the 90 degree angle of funerary renderings, but equally not in the straightforward pose of the Naxian sphinx. She is perhaps the last successful sphinx of the Fifth century, and indeed after the Severe period the monster appears seldom, and mostly in reliefs representing burial plots. The reason for the disappearance of the type lies perhaps in the strident contrast produced by the humanizing process already noted. A partly human, partly beastly creature was possible as long as the details were not worked out in great elaboration and naturalism. Even a centaur is at its most plausible when his face resembles a mask, yet the partly equine creature, with a fully human torso, does not present as great a problem as the combination of a purely human head and a completely animal body. The Egyptian, who created the sphinx as an abstract symbol of Pharaonic might, was not disturbed by the incongruity, yet the Middle Kingdom sphinxes of Sesostris III and Amenhemet III, with their touch of humanity in the careworn faces, are as startling and incongruous as the humanized Greek sphinx. An archaic sphinx head, though fully patterned after contemporary korai, retained a sufficient degree of abstraction to make the combination acceptable. The human head of the Aegina sphinx is disturbingly naturalistic. The next step is represented by the sphinxes on the lid of the Lycian sarcophagus in Istanbul (ca. 400 b.c.) (Fig. 54), which have developed prominent feminine breasts: the human element is increasingly encroaching on the beastly and will ultimately cause the end of the type.

One type which, on the contrary, receives added impetus and vigor in the Severe period is the Nike. The humanization process, rather than hampering, infuses new life in this creation of archaic times, invented, if we believe literary sources, by the sculptor Archermos from Chios (Fig. 55). The Sixth century, if so much relevance can be given to a minute detail, conceived a Victory as a creature closer to a monster than to a human being, since the hairstyle of extant Nikai resembles that of sphinxes rather than that of contemporary korai. But from the very beginning the body was treated in fully human fashion; the Severe sculptor, with his sober tendencies, had only to relegate entirely to the back of the figure the very decorative wings that the archaic master endeavored to make visible also from the front. The contrast between the human and the nonhuman was therefore minimized and Nikai received prominent place in the Severe and then in the classical repertoire.

Original Nikai are here represented by an unusual example from Paros (Figs. 56, 58). O. Rubensohn, in his general account of the island, dates the statue to the decade 490-480 on purely historical grounds. Those years, during which the island was notably successful in her resistance to Miltiades and in her alliance with the Persians, were particularly prosperous for her and could have given good cause for the setting up of a trophy. The good preservation of the statue seems to imply that it did not stand for long, and it may have been taken down by the Athenians after Salamis. The years after 480, though more productive in terms of sculpture found within the island itself, do not seem to justify the erection of a victory monument. If, however, Rubensohn's chronology is accepted, the island would seem to lead in the introduction of the peplos, a rather surprising fact since the garment is Doric par excellence, and its widespread adoption is usually one of the reasons why the whole Severe period is considered under strong Peloponnesian influence. Recently J. Dörig has more plausibly dated the Parian Nike to 470-460, although no historical connection is suggested. It should not be forgotten, however, that a Nike is also a symbol of victory in the games, and though examples of Nikai connected with military victory can be found earlier, in official sculpture the concept is not definitely associated with war and battles until the time of the Nike Balustrade in Athens, where Nikai are shown setting up trophies.

The Parian statue has been rightly called the predecessor of Paionios' Nike (Rubensohn) (Fig. 57), in that here too the feet seemingly do not touch the base, yet this effect has been obtained without recourse to the archaic *knielauf* pose, where the drapery, dipping low between the legs, functioned as a support and held the figure aloft. The Nike from Paros has her feet on the sloping surface of a high plinth, which rises in the back to connect with the drapery as a support for ankles and feet. The plinth must have risen well above the surface of the base, thus giving the impression that the Nike was alighting, or in any case did not touch ground: an impression heightened by her bent knee. The costume emphasizes this rendering of forward motion by clinging closely to the fully shaped legs, while the fullness of the material gathers in the back in long vertical folds. The cloth thus appears thin and heavy at the same time, though here somewhat incongruously, while the conflict is brilliantly resolved in Paionios' Nike.

Compared with other Severe peplophoroi, however, the Parian Victory strikes a peculiar note. The peplos, partly because subordinate to concepts of modeling and movement, has lost all tectonic quality, and the overfold, with its irregular edge, entirely fails to establish a strong accent on the figure. The costume, though Doric in character, is entirely Ionic in appearance and almost looks like a chiton/himation combination, with long catenaries scattered all over the front as clear reminiscences of the long curves created by the traditional pulling aside of the chiton. Yet these very catenaries, the peplos itself despite its unusual appearance, and the progressive compositional traits which link the Parian Nike to the work by Paionios, are sure indications of Severe style;[5] the selvedge (detail, Fig. 58) predicts the high classical.

What conclusions can be derived from the monuments examined above? By a peculiar chance, many of the important originals in the round come from Athens, and almost all those we possess seem to belong to the early years of the Severe period; this may partly be due to errors in chronological assessment, but it may also confirm the fact that most works of the Severe period were in bronze,[6] and have therefore survived mainly

[5] A typical example of the spreading of the peplos is provided by the peplophoroi from Xanthos (Fig. 59), most recently discussed by H. Metzger (*FdX* 2 [1963] 51, pls. 35-36 and reconstruction at fig. 28), who attributes them to a parapet around the most elaborate Heroon on the Acropolis (Building G). These Xanthian peplophoroi closely resemble the Parian Nike in the unarticulated, chiton-like treatment of the peplos, covered with catenaries. By contrast, another example from a peripheral region seems fully "Doric," the peplophoros from Thrace: G. Bakalakis, *Proanaskaphikes Erevnes sti Thraki*

(Thessalonika 1958) pls. 3-6, pp. 19-28, with good bibliography of the type. Other peplophoroi are illustrated by Buschor and Hamann, figs. 14-25. That the loose, almost inarticulated peplos is, however, not limited to the Ionic area but spread into Sicily and Magna Graecia is proved by a small bronze statuette in Reggio Calabria (Fig. 60) as well as by a marble peplophoros in Naples: *BdA* 26 (1932) 284-86 figs. 2-3 and bibliography.

[6] On the prevalence of bronze over marble see *Dedications*, p. 479: "The use of island marble, and of marble in general for the making of statues, was

in copies. It is thus somewhat hazardous to affirm, for instance, that the kore type, as such, seems to disappear in the Severe period, to be replaced by representations of specific women or goddesses. Though by and large the statement may be valid, the lack of large-scale works, seen in general perspective, makes the inference tentative.

In cross-reference to architectural sculpture, Angelitos' Athena, the Kritian Boy, and the Propylaia Kore should be contemporary with the Aegina Pediment East II; the Delphi Charioteer and the Aegina Sphinx should precede the Olympia sculptures, and the Nike from Paros should be contemporary with them. The Aeginetans, because of their narrative context, can be compared with the Acropolis statues only in general terms. The pedimental Athena, had it survived in its entirety, might have provided a good parallel for Angelitos' dedication, yet the need to balance the earlier West pediment probably imposed an "archaizing" costume which must have minimized affinities. The surviving heads reveal similar stylistic traits, and Herakles the Archer fortunately retains enough of his chitoniskos to warrant comparison with the drapery of Angelitos' Athena.

This latter introduces a specific version of the peplos, appropriate to women of action, and as such is not strictly comparable with the Olympia peplophoroi. Yet the experimentation with balance through drapery is the same, and tentative enough in the Athena to confirm the early date of her stage. Typologically, both the Athena and the Kritian Boy find their continuation in the Olympia figures, since also the male statues express the same concern with musculature and balance felt by the sculptor of the Acropolis youth.

The Delphi Charioteer seems somewhat removed from this main line of development, since it is not involved in problems of stance, like the naked male figures, nor does it wear its drapery like the female figures. Its composition is closer to an abstract formula than any of the block-like Olympia peplophoroi. Nonetheless the steep folds of its skirt resemble those of Angelitos' Athena more closely than any rendering at Olympia: an indication of time or of schools? Since the Charioteer is the most closely dated of all the originals in the round here discussed, and since its creation cannot postdate 470 B.C., it is perhaps safer to assume a chronological affinity, which thus coherently places the bronze between the Acropolis statue and the Olympia pediments.

The Nike from Paros is, however, impossible to reconcile in terms of sheer chronology and, like the reliefs from Xanthos, should rather be stressed as a further example of the diffusion of the Severe style despite the obvious vitality of previous stylistic currents.

Of the monuments considered, two represent the end and two the beginning of a series: the Aegina Sphinx and the Propylaia Kore are closer to the past than to the future and, as types, shall have no future in the major arts. The Parian Nike and Angelitos' Athena establish entirely new formulas for traditional types: a more human Victory in fully frontal pose and partly in mid-air, and an Athena differentiated from a common kore by a specific attire, in a pose of quiet authority. Finally the Kritian Boy represents the most perfect link between archaic and classical, being the logical development of the one and the true precursor of the other. The Severe period therefore appears represented in all the various forms suggested by scholars: as end, continuation, and beginning.

---

discontinued at Athens some years after 480 B.C. The numerical decline of marble sculpture, however, already begins a whole generation earlier and it is accompanied by an increase in the number of statues made of bronze."

1. *Head of Athena* (Athena Vogüé), in the Louvre, presumably from Aegina. The main study remains the original publication: M. Collignon, "Une Sculpture d'Egine—Tête d'Athéna en Marbre," *MonPiot* 13 (1906) 167-74, pls. 16-17; see also Langlotz, *FrühBild*, pl. 56 (p. 99 no. 12); *TEL* III, pl. 158; Lippold, *Handbuch*, p. 100. It is interesting to note that this head has bronze eyelashes, though the eyeballs are not inserted separately, as commonly done when metal eyelashes were added. Forehead curls must have appeared only at the temples, more or less like the roundels of the Athena from Aegina West Pediment, and presumably overlapped the edge of the helmet. Since the neck is broken and the present appearance is due to restoration, it is impossible to tell whether the head originally belonged to an akrolithic figure, as the bronze eyelashes might perhaps suggest. Collignon dates the head ca. 460-450 and sees in it Athenian influence; Lippold believes it reproduces the Athena of Aegina East Pediment: both positions are questionable.

2. *Female Head from Cyrene*: Besides Paribeni, *Catalogo* no. 15, consult the article by L. Polacco in *Sculture Greche e Romane di Cirene* (Padua 1959) 29-53. The head is perhaps closer to the sculptures from Selinus, especially the isolated heads from Temple E, than to those from Aegina, though it should be admitted that all resemblances are at best vague. It is interesting, however, to stress once more the strong affinity existing between works from Asia Minor/North Africa and those from Magna Graecia.

3. *Colossal Female Head* (*Hess Head*) in Schloss Fasanerie; Schefold, *Meisterwerke*, no. (and fig.) 244 on p. 218 and text on p. 59. Presumably from Tarentum, dated by Schefold ca. 470 B.C. Notice the pouting mouth, which so strongly resembles Euthydikos' Kore. Also the thick-rimmed eyes are reminiscent of an Acropolis kore: 688. The hair is still in the archaic tradition, though the forehead is strongly triangular.

4. *Head of Athena in Tarentum*: Langlotz, *Magna Graecia* pls. 98-99. Unusual for the soft rendering of the flesh around the eyes. What Langlotz considers Venus' rings on the right side of the neck are perhaps produced by a slight turn of the head or the raising of the shoulder on that side.

5. *So-called Leonidas in Sparta*: Lippold, *Handbuch* pl. 32:4; *BrBr* 776-778 with text, and *BSA* 26 (1923/24-1924/25) 253-66 (A. M. Woodward). The *BrBr* text has an extensive bibliography up to 1939. For the helmet see *Olympia-Bericht* 8 (1967) 131-32, 163-83. This over life-size warrior is remarkable in that it was carved entirely of marble, including the shield of which a fragment was found. Since it seems to have been a free-standing monument, not part of a pedimental composition, it is surprising that its maker risked the difficulty of carving all the weapons in stone while metal additions would have been plausible and easier to make. Yet the sockets for inserted eyes suggest familiarity with bronze casting techniques and practices. That the warrior, shown in a position of attack with arms outstretched, represents a Spartan is proved by the clean-shaven upper lip, contrasting with the prominent beard; but the identification of the personage represented is still uncertain. Though usually called Leonidas, the statue could as well portray King Pausanias, the victor of Plataia. For a recent attempt to rehabilitate the memory of that king see M. Lang, "Scapegoat Pausanias," *CJ* 63:2 (1967) 79-85.

Though Pausanias (the periegetes) mentions single statues or groups of warriors, none has come to us in its entirety, the closest parallel being perhaps the approximately contemporary cuirassed torso from the Acropolis, Schrader no. 307 (Akr. 599), pls. 130-31, which however represents a shooting archer. Entirely of marble was also another warrior from Olympia, the so-called Phormis, whose head has often been compared with the "Leonidas," but the parallel is not too convincing. The Phormis was moreover part of a group, from which the head of another warrior has survived (see text to *BrBr* 779-80). In the "Leonidas" notice not only the ram's heads decorating the cheekpieces, but also the bearded serpent adorning a leg greave. All these warrior statues are important as evidence for marble groups even during the Severe period, which was the bronze-casting era par excellence.

6. *Head of Apollo* (Apollo Townley) in the British Museum. The most extensive discussion of this impressive piece is in K. A. Pfeiff, *Apollon* (Frankfurt 1943) 73-75, pls. 19-23; but the work is little known. Generally considered Sikyonian, it is called by Lippold (*Handbuch*, p. 122 n. 8)

a copy of the Apollo Klarios at Kolophon, presumably on the basis of the alleged similarity between the Townley head and a terracotta from that site. Pfeiff also believes that the head is a Roman copy after a bronze original, but some scholars have (orally) expressed the opinion that the head is an original itself, from Magna Graecia. In either case, the date of the type is placed ca. 470-460.

The disturbing feature of this head—whether original or copy—lies in its forehead locks. The striking difference between the plastic curls and the engraved strands over the dome could perhaps be imputed to the copyist, but it is difficult to blame him for the entire coiffure. Yet the peculiar ending of the forehead locks and their wide spacing recall the "Augustan" treatment of the Munich terracotta plaque discussed infra, pp. 111-12. A similar arrangement, in a definitely archaistic work, occurs on a head of Silvanus from a double-herm trapezophoros in Verona (G. Riccioni, "Sculture del Museo del Teatro Romano di Verona," *ArteAntMod* [1960] 138 pls. 37c-d and 38a). That such hairstyle however occurred also in the Severe period seems proved by a coin of Leontinoi, ca. 466-460 B.C., with a head of Apollo (C. M. Kraay and M. Hirmer, *Greek Coins*, pl. 7). No convincing parallel for the Townley head exists in large-scale sculpture; Beyen's comparison with the Pisoni Kouros and the Piombino Apollo (*Argos et Sicyone*, pp. 55-61) actually endangers his theory that the Townley Apollo's original was by the same master of the Artemision Bronze.

7. *"Kouros" torso from Miletus*, Louvre MND 2792. This monument presents a problem. Some scholars (e.g. J. Charbonneaux, *MonPiot* 45 [1951] 47-50) consider it late archaic, made before the destruction of Miletus in 494 B.C., while others would make it contemporary with the Tyrannicides (Kunze and Schleif, *Olympia Bericht* 3 [1938/39] 130 and n. 1). Richter includes it in her *Kouroi*, but as part of the "Epilogue," ca. 485-460 B.C. (no. 192, figs. 579-81). The torso displays a powerful musculature, with right hip and buttock higher than the left and arms perhaps raised or at least not in the typical kouros position along the sides. Since the torso is of colossal scale, I wonder whether it might not be a Roman copy of a Severe bronze, or perhaps a Roman rendering in Severe terms to serve as body for a portrait statue. The excel-

lent quality of Asia Minor sculpture even during the Roman period may have prompted the interpretation as a Greek original, with the consequent difficulty of the forced *ante-quem* demanded by the destruction date and the added discrepancy that over life-size proportions are unusual for simple kouroi of late archaic times. The find spot—the theater of Miletus—supports my suggestion of an honorary monument, since it is unlikely that the statue was transported there, perhaps from the sanctuary of Apollo, in later times.

BRONZES

8. *The Apollo Chatsworth*, in the British Museum: usually considered an original of the Severe period, it has recently been called a creation of the Hadrianic classicism (W.-H. Schuchhardt "Zum Akrolithkopf von Cirò," *AJA* 66 [1962] 317-18). Again, the head in question has no close parallel in any other extant monument. The distinctive character of the piece could, however, be attributed to its origin: Cyprus. For an account of its provenience see O. Masson, "Kypriaka, Recherches sur les Antiquités de Tamassos," *BCH* 88 (1964) 212-13; for the history of the discovery of the statue and its subsequent demolition by peasants, see E. Gjerstad, "The Story of the Chatsworth Head," *Eranos* 43 (1945) 236-42. The technical account by A. B. Wace in *JHS* 58 (1938) 90-95 is superseded by D. Haynes, "The Technique of the Chatsworth Head," *RA* 1968, 101-12. (Could the "closed" eye-sockets point to a late date?) Cf. Langlotz, *FrühBild*, pl. 36a for the hairknot.

9. *The Poseidon from Kreusis* (modern Livadhostro) in Boeotia. Athens, Nat. Mus. 11761 (Lippold, *Handbuch*, pl. 37:1). Unfortunately this important ancient bronze has not been accessible for many years and therefore is omitted by most recent picture books. However, the National Museum plans to display it soon. The original publication (*ArchEph* [1899] cols. 57-74, pls. 5-6) still has the best detailed photographs, especially of the head, which is much better preserved than the torso. Notice the roll of hair at the nape and the peculiar "tongue" within the beard. See also J. Charbonneaux, *Les Bronzes Grecs* (Paris 1958) 72-77.

10. *The Selinus/Castelvetrano Youth*, stolen in 1962; this half life-size statue was recovered by Italian authorities in March 1968. For the best

illustrations see Langlotz, *Magna Graecia* pl. 81 and Miré Brothers, *Sicile Grecque* (Paris 1955) pls. 162-65 and fig. 27 on p. 309. This work is so definitely a provincial work that it adds virtually nothing to our knowledge of the Severe style in Sicily despite its similarity to the Aktaion of the metope from Temple E. In particular, its proportions are peculiar and its hair roll heavy, almost as if it were in marble.

11. *Bronze head of a youth from the Athenian Acropolis*, Boardman/Dörig/Fuchs/Hirmer, pl. 182; cf. C. Saletti, *ArteAntMod* 1960, 248-62, for a comparison with the Apollo Citharode from Pompeii (Mantua type). The head, with its low forehead and relatively short chin, gives almost an impression of brutality. The treatment of the eyebrows is unusual for the groove that detaches them from the top of the upper lid.

TERRACOTTAS

12. *Zeus and Ganymede, Olympia*: this imposing group, because of size and technique well deserves to be included among sculptural works (Lullies and Hirmer, pl. 105 and color pl. v, with bibliography). For interest, contrast it with the late archaic marble group of Theseus abducting Antiope from the pediment of the temple at Eretria, *ibid.*, pls. 66-68. Notice that Zeus wears his mantle so that his chest remains uncovered, like the Zeus of the East Olympia pediment. His hairstyle, despite the snail-curls over the forehead, has been gathered up at the nape, in the new fashion. The remarkable shelf-like coiffure of the Ganymede finds some parallels in small bronzes. Notice in particular the clinging of the drapery over the left forearm, which again recalls the marble Zeus.

41

FOR PAGE 29

The standard work on the archaic sculpture from the Acropolis is H. Schrader, E. Langlotz, and W.-H. Schuchhardt, *Die archaischen Marmorbildwerke der Akropolis* (Frankfurt 1939), cited as Schrader. Of the three authors, Langlotz discusses the female figures, Schuchhardt the remaining sculpture in the round and the votive reliefs, and Schrader the architectural sculpture. In this book, Angelitos' Athena (Akr. 140) is discussed by Langlotz as no. 5, pp. 48-49. For Raubitschek's attribution to Euenor's apprentice (Pheidias?) see his *Dedications*, pp. 497-98; also *ibid.*, no. 22, pp. 26-28; for the connection of the statue with column and capital see *BSA* 40 (1939-40) 31-36: figs. 36, 38, 43 in pls. 12-13; fig. 37 on p. 32; fig. 39a on p. 36; and fig. 41 on p. 32.

FOR PAGE 30

For representations of Athena in small bronzes see G. Niemeyer, "Attische Bronzestatuetten der spätarchaischen und frühklassischen Zeit," *Antike Plastik* 3 (1964).
For examples of a hair mass not directly centered on the back of late Archaic figures see e.g. Akr. 594 (Schrader, pls. 76-77; *Korai*, figs. 398-400) or the marble kouros torso from Pioraco in Ancona, G. de Luca, "Kouroi in italienischen Museen," *Antike Plastik* 3 (1964) pls. 54-57, pp. 52-59 and especially 55-56.

FOR PAGE 31

For a photograph showing the Athena with the other monuments from the same locality, see Schrader, p. 345, fig. 405.
The Kritian Boy, Akr. 698, is discussed by Schuchhardt in Schrader, no. 299, pls. 120-23 figs. 182-86.
For other examples of slanted hips see, e.g. the fragmentary torso attributed to the Blond Boy, Schrader no. 302, pls. 125-27, figs. 187-88, to be discussed infra, pp. 56-57. For feet held at an angle see e.g. Akr. 499, Schrader no. 303, figs. 189-90, p. 199.

FOR PAGE 32

For inscribed statue bases with similar traces, see the so-called Leagros base from the Athenian Agora, most recently mentioned by Harrison, *Agora* 11 (1965) 10, no. 61 with bibliography.

For kouroi with both knees bent see e.g. Akr. 692, Schrader no. 300, pls. 118-19.
For an interesting photographic commentary to the three-dimensionality of the Kritian Boy see the "rotating camera" experiment by Alscher, *Griechische Plastik* 2:1, folding plate.
The Kritian Boy has been compared with the Tenea Kouros on the one hand, the Doryphoros on the other, by Guido von Kaschnitz Weinberg, "Formprobleme des Übergangs von der archaischen zur klassischen Kunst," lecture delivered at Frankfurt University in 1948, published in *Kleine Schriften zur Struktur: Ausgewählte Schriften* 1 (Berlin 1965) 156-74.
For Aristodikos, see Ch. Karouzos, *Aristodikos* (Stuttgart 1961), or G. M. A. Richter, *Kouroi*² (London 1960) no. 165 figs. 489, 492-93.
For the Doryphoros see P. Arias, *Policleto* (1964) pp. 21-25 and passim.
For Carpenter's comments on measured heads see *Greek Sculpture*, pp. 92-98.

FOR PAGE 33

For a comparison between the Kritian Boy and the Delphi Charioteer see F. Chamoux, "L'Aurige," *FdD* 4:5 (1955) 78-80, and its review by R. Hampe in *Gnomon* 32 (1960) 60-73, who still believes that the Charioteer is Boeotian. Archaic draped youth Akr. 633: Schrader no. 308 pls. 128-29, pp. 204-7 figs. 202-3.

FOR PAGE 34

On the reliability of ancient sources about animal sculptors, see e.g. Pollitt, p. 61 and n. 21, contrasting Paus. 6. 12. 1 with Pliny *NH* 34. 71. Late archaic kore Akr. 684, Schrader no. 55 pls. 78-81, dated ca. 490; *Korai* no. 182, figs. 578-82 dated about 500-490.
Propylaia Kore, Akr. 688, Schrader no. 21, pls. 30-32, dated ca. 480 though considered probably post-Persian; *Korai* no. 184, figs. 587-90, ca. 480, "Beginning of the early classical style."

FOR PAGE 35

For intricate Severe hairstyle see, e.g. W.-H. Schuchhardt, "Köpfe des strengen Stiles," *Festschrift Carl Weickert* (Berlin 1955) 59-73.
Head in Athens Nat. Mus. 1949: Langlotz, *FrühBild* p. 140 no. 7 pl. 87b.
Aegina sphinx: good illustrations of the head in E. Homann-Wedeking, "Zu Meisterwerken des

strengen Stils," *RömMitt* 55 (1940) pl. 24 and p. 207 with n. 2.

Akropolis sphinx 632: Schrader no. 372 pl. 164 and p. 260.

FOR PAGE 36

The Cyrene sphinx is partly published (without the newly found head) in *Libya Antiqua* 3-4 (1966-67) 190-96 pls. 70-71. See the brief mention in the summary of a Paper presented to the 69th Meeting of the AIA, *AJA* 72 (1968) 174.

For a sphinx in the round, dated to the end of the Fifth century, see C. Blümel, *Die klassisch griechischen Skulpturen der staatlichen Museen zu Berlin* (Berlin 1966) no. 21 (K 32) pl. 28 pp. 29-30.

Lycian Sarcophagus from Sidon: Lullies & Hirmer, pl. 193.

Nike from Paros: O. Rubensohn, *RE* 18:4 (1949) s.v. Paros, cols. 1815-16 and 1864. For Dörig's suggestion see the caption to fig. 183 left, in Boardman/Dörig/Fuchs/Hirmer (cf. also p. 281).

FOR PAGE 37

On the significance of Nike as personification, and on possible meanings, see F. W. Hamdorf, *Griechische Kultpersonifikationen der vorhellenistischen Zeit* (Mainz 1964) 58-62 and catalogue on pp. 112-16 nos. 449-65. For specific reference to the Parian Nike see p. 60.

For another Severe Nike see the statue in the Conservatori, *BrBr* 263, most recently discussed by W. Fuchs in Helbig[4], no. 1509, who considers it a Magna Graecian original. See however also infra Ch. 9, App. 8.

CHAPTER 4

Greek Originals: Reliefs

THE SUBJECT of Severe reliefs is so complex that it would suffice for a book in its own right. Athens in this period yields only some votive reliefs. The grave stelai, which formed such conspicuous part of its archaic production, seem to have been stopped by a possible anti-luxury decree, or by some unknown factor not yet fully assessed, and do not reappear until the time of the Parthenon, or possibly even a decade later. A few earlier gravestones, from the neighborbood of Athens rather than from the city itself, may be imported and in any case still fall after the middle of the Fifth century, outside the Severe period proper. Archaic funerary sculpture, be it monuments in the round, stelai, or decorated bases, has been found mostly incorporated within the Themistoklean walls, built in great haste and with any material at hand, as so vividly described by Thucydides. This procedure has saved for us works which might otherwise have been hopelessly lost. Since no such emergency occurred in later times, one could speculate whether the lack of Severe gravestones may be attributed not to a specific prohibition against luxury monuments, but rather to the same natural causes that have caused the disappearance of so many originals of the Severe period, or of classical art in general, especially since grave reliefs would not have had enough appeal to be copied in Roman times. Since, however, funerary monuments survive from the end of the Fifth century, and are amply preserved for the following as well, it is perhaps absurd to assume that just the Severe stelai should have suffered so drastically from the passing of time. A passage in Cicero's *De Legibus* indeed mentions an anti-luxury decree issued "some time after Solon," but the reference is so vague and the phrasing so controversial, that no complete agreement has as yet been reached as to its interpretation.

One more possibility remains, that the Attic stelai of the Severe period were made of perishable material, presumably of wood with metal ornaments. This theory may find rather vague support in representations on white-ground lekythoi, showing tall and narrow, sometimes perhaps even cylindrical, gravestones topped by sharply dentated acanthus leaves. Since these representations differ from previous renderings on similar vases, the suggestion has been made that an actual change in funerary customs and burial monuments may correspond to the shift in pictorial formulas. Be that as it may, a wooden stele crowned by metal leaves,[1] even if important for the history of funerary art, cannot be relevant to a study of the Severe style, and we ought to accept the fact that Athens cannot provide much information on funerary relief during the Severe period.

[1] Even a marble stele, but with a plain shaft and perhaps only a painted picture or inscription, would be likely to go unrecognized today. A glance at any modern cemetery will allow us to visualize how easily such slabs could be reemployed, as steps, thresholds, drain covers, etc., without betraying their original function. Since any anti-luxury decree is aimed at the complexity but not at the very existence of funerary monuments, it is logical to assume that some form of simple grave-marker must have existed in Athens even in the Severe period. A cursory search through L. Jeffery's selected catalogues in *Local Scripts* shows that several inscribed gravestones were set up for foreigners in Athenian cemeteries during the crucial period: p. 169 no. 30 (for Argive allies who fell at Tanagra, ca. 458-457); p. 206 no. 14 (for Sko(t?)eas of Messene, ca. 500-450?); p. 275 no. 10 (for Anaxagoras of Syracuse, ca. 450?); p. 369 no. 7 (for Mikkos of Torone in Chalkidike, 475-450?); p. 371 no. 38 (for Pythagoras of Selymbria, ca. 450).

By way of compensation, as it were, the production of grave reliefs increases considerably all over the Greek world, just at this time. It has indeed been postulated that Athenian artists, free from commissions in their own territory, had moved elsewhere to satisfy the demands of other patrons, thus spreading abroad the typical Athenian format for grave stelai. Yet evidence, though scanty, exists to prove that funerary relief was already familiar to non-Attic Greeks, and the representations on these Severe gravestones seem so typically non-Attic in content, and perhaps even in style, as to support the belief in a local development. As already stated, the problem is so complex that here it can only be mentioned but not analyzed in any detail. We shall, therefore, examine these Severe stelai mainly in terms of their style, and only incidentally for the iconographic and typological problems they present.

When this part of the problem is removed from the picture, the rest of it appears surprisingly unified. The traits of the Severe style are unmistakable, and follow the general pattern of sculpture in the round. As for architectural sculpture, one basic distinction is here needed: metopes and friezes, though also in relief, have to be seen from a considerable distance, being placed usually quite high on a building. By contrast a votive or a funerary relief is set at a convenient height for examination, and can usually be inspected at close quarters. Thus while architectural relief needs strong contrast of light and shadow to assert its composition even at a distance, votive or funerary relief can be quite low and depend purely on color and soft modulations of surface to be completely intelligible. As such, its dependence on pictorial tradition is stronger than for architectural relief, not in the sense of retaining a pictorial relationship to its background, of being steeped in space, or of using landscape and other pictorial elements in the composition, but in the sense of being firmly based on strong outline drawing and of remaining virtually just raised silhouette, as contrasted with metopal sculpture which also originates from drawing, but technically, with its deep undercutting, more resembles sculpture in the round.

Most reminiscent of vase painting is the stele from Nisyros in Istanbul (Fig. 61). The relief is low and some details are only engraved against the background, to be picked out in paint. The deceased, a youth, is characterized as an athlete by his equipment: a javelin and a discus faintly engraved against his left foot. Because of the profile pose, the emphasis on the strong chin and massive head is all the more apparent. The hair, undoubtedly once enlivened by color, is basically a solid mass against which the ear appears almost inserted. Despite the sinewy modeling of the strong musculature and the characteristic indication of the veins, the artist has stressed smooth surfaces, with a resultant solidity and unity typical of the Severe style. The bent leg of the Nisyros youth suggests the experimentation with balance of free-standing figures, while the shoulders and torso imitate somewhat awkwardly the foreshortening of painting.

The youth is shown in a three-quarter pose, with only legs and head in complete profile. Small details emphasize the change from one position to the other; for instance, the transition between torso and legs is made clear by the slanting of the linea alba which graphically suggests torsion. In the chest, the left nipple carved in profile against the arm is made much more prominent than the frontal right. The right hand is fisted against the thigh, but the index finger was once extended, though now damaged and chipped, and perhaps even the thumb. Since the stele relied on color for several details, possibly the hand once held a painted object, perhaps a strigil or an aryballos, to complete the athletic equipment and emphasize the characterization.

Even more eloquent, because the figures are widely spaced against the neutral background, is the so-called Banquet Relief from Thasos (Figs. 62-65). The motif is oriental and ultimately goes back to the famous Assyrian representation of Assurbanipal in his garden, attended by servants and in the company of his wife. This image of the potentate surrounded by the comforts of life frequently appears in the Asia Minor repertoire, whence it must have passed on to Greece and more specifically to Corinth, where it was adopted as a subject for vases. Characteristically, in Ionia the reclining man became also part of the repertoire of sculpture in the round. The Thasian relief is only an early example in a long series of representations where the dead man is depicted not only in the midst of his earthly possessions, therefore as if alive, but also enjoying particular pleasures, with allusion perhaps to the funerary banquet or life in the Elysian Fields: a heroizing connotation.[2] The Severe style is here obvious, again and especially in the hairstyles, the correct foreshortening of the bodies, the smooth surfaces, the lack of elaboration of details. The lady of the house still wears chiton and himation, but the former garment is smoothed of all crinkly folds and the latter is wrapped around her legs in the new fashion and with the new doughy rendering of cloth.

This association between life and death, this ambiguous representation which tries to characterize the deceased by his home environment, has been called typically Ionian, as contrasted with the more neutral Attic portrayal. A young person can, for instance, be shown with his pets, mostly birds, not because the bird in particular alludes to the soul but because quite probably a bird was the favorite pet of young people. The typical example of the Severe style is the Girl with Doves in New York, from the Island of Paros (Fig. 66). It has all the salient traits of the Severe style: the type of costume, the basic simplicity of the lines, the clear contour of the body with the bent leg and the drapery clinging to the thighs, the large (perhaps over-large) head with the massive jaw and the linear fluent hair loose over the shoulders. The tectonic approach of the style is also obvious in the rendering of the garment which, with the almost straight lines of its opening, appears to support rather than to accompany the body. The awkward profile rendering of the chest is skillfully hidden behind the birds.

It is interesting to compare the Girl with Doves to the so-called "Adoration of the Flower" relief, which came from Pharsalos, Thessaly, and is now in the Louvre (Fig. 68). The lower part of the Thessalian relief is missing, but it is now usually accepted that both women should be restored as standing, and not one standing and one sitting, as once postulated on the basis of other compositions. The stele, as Biesantz has pointed out, conforms to a specific type of Thessalian gravestones, with the only difference that it is of better quality than most because it comes from one of the major centers. Though the objects held by the two women and the relationship of the figures are still open to question, the scene obviously represents a moment of intimacy and companionship, such as will become popular in Attica toward the end of the Fifth and the beginning of the Fourth century. Since Athens is empty of grave monuments at this period, it is logical to assume that the motif reached her from other areas, when her production

---

[2] Hausmann, *Gr. Weihreliefs*, p. 25 and p. 29, emphasizes the "otherworldly" connotation more than the purely human, though admitting a mixture of both elements.

of funerary reliefs was resumed.[3] The presence of the companion in the Pharsalos relief carries approximately the same emotional implications as the pet of other stelai, or the small servant boy often introduced into reliefs of athletes or young men, sometimes together with a dog.

Stylistically the Louvre stele seems less advanced than the New York stele, though presumably they are approximately contemporary. The profile of the woman on the right, with her protruding breast, is awkward, and in both faces the almond-shaped eyes appear fully frontal, as contrasted with the large triangle of the New York girl's eye. But the heavy chins are similar, and so is the treatment of the hair, which in the Pharsalos stele adds the contrast of the scarf to the pattern of the strands. The costumes are the same in both reliefs, though different approaches are used. The artist of the Girl with Doves is more interested in revealing the body, to the point that the open peplos becomes an opportunity for introducing the outline of the girl's buttock. The relief is sufficiently high for a slightly diagonal point of view to reveal more of her body than a purely frontal approach. The Pharsalos artist, on the contrary, exploits the flat panel and the graduated folds which form at the vertical edges of the apoptygma to create decorative effects and suggest greater depth than the carving actually possesses.

Between the two stelai, typologically, falls the so-called Giustiniani relief in Berlin (Fig. 67). The girl represented, though perhaps slightly younger than the Pharsalos maidens, is older than the child in New York. Accordingly, she holds not a pet but a box, whose lid she has just put down on the ground in order to lift some item of jewelry, perhaps a necklace, from the container. Like the New York girl, she bends one leg, but this time it is the one nearer to the foreground, so that the other leg is hidden behind it, and the skirt of the peplos has free play to create long vertical folds. Since the position is straighter, the pleats are also more regular, and rather than suggesting a material support for the body, as in the New York stele, they clear the ground and hang from the shoulder, yet at the same time provide a strong vertical accent at the edge of the composition. The foreshortening is good and the garment is fully understandable, though so little of the body is actually shown: the curving folds around the neck of the figure recall the similar rendering in the Pharsalos stele and so do the hairstyle and the general outline of face and chin. The inclined position of the head, common to all three reliefs, is typical of the new climate of introspection and concentration of the Severe style. It is not a sign of mourning, but simply an indication of absorption which contrasts with the straight-headed aloofness of Attic funerary representations in archaic times. While this concentration may seem further to separate the dead from the living, at the same time it emphasizes their interest in the purely physical activity they are performing, whether choosing a jewel, playing with a pet, or sharing gifts with a friend, and therefore makes them seem alive, again as contrasted with the passive images of the archaic gravestones, usually devoid of any action.

Though the Giustiniani relief, with its careful rendering of folds and overfold, comes

[3] A type of heroizing relief with seated woman and standing worshiper exists also in Athens during the archaic period (G. M. A. Richter, *Archaic Gravestones of Attica*, Excursus 2, pp. 55-56). But the standing figure is obviously subordinated to the seated, and therefore the relationship is different from that expressed in the Pharsalos relief although Richter includes this work also in her enumeration of extant examples of the type.

close to it, none of the reliefs examined until now, whether in low or in fairly high relief, has presented that doughiness of drapery so typical of the Olympia figures and of sculpture in the round. Could this basic difference stem from the fact that relief, originating from a drawing, did not require experimentation with clay models, as postulated for free-standing sculpture?

A relief from Athens seems to belie this supposition, and ascribe the difference to regional trends (Fig. 69). Yet ultimately the "Mourning Athena" from the Acropolis is so close to Angelitos' dedication (Fig. 39) that it might simply be a transposition in relief of a monument in the round, and therefore reflect the same plasticity of the prototype.

The nickname is, course, valid only for mnemonic purposes. It derives from the belief, now superseded, that the goddess was depicted reading the names of the Athenian dead engraved on the small stele in front of her. But the pose with head bent does not necessarily indicate sorrow, and nothing else in the composition supports the mourning theory. Recent suggestions have interpreted the stele in the relief as a sanctuary boundary stone (Athena looking at the confines of her own domain, the whole relief either votive or a stone-marker itself), or as a palaestra pillar, as often shown in vase painting, on which athletes can throw their cloak before exercising. The relief would then be the dedication of a winner in the Panathenaic games. The interpretation of the subject is, however, not of primary concern, and the stele is much more important as an example of Athenian relief at this period than as pure representation.

The Athena seems the mirror image of Angelitos' dedication (Fig. 39): the position of the arms is approximately the same, but right and left have been reversed. One leg is definitely bent, but in this case it is removed from view, being the one farther from the foreground, and the peplos freely falls in front of the body, hiding it entirely. Only the retracted left foot suggests the position of the legs under the cylindrical abstraction of the skirt. If it is legitimate to establish a chronological sequence among works geographically so unrelated, the Athenian relief should come first, perhaps representing the stage of the Delphi charioteer, around 470 B.C.: balance is of concern, but the garment predominates. The second step in development (ca. 460?) would be represented by the Giustiniani stele (Fig. 67): the artist wants to show the position of the body through the outline of the legs, but by bending the forward one he eliminates the problem of the garment's appearance over the other leg, which remains left to the imagination in the background; the garment can still assert itself with long vertical folds somewhat divorced from the complexity of the body beneath. Finally (around 450?), the Girl with Doves in New York (Fig. 66): the body is now winning over garment, the free leg is the farther, and the skirt gathers in between the thighs revealing both, while the opening of the peplos further uncovers the body in the back. With a certain amount of exaggeration it could perhaps be affirmed that the New York girl is an ancestor of the Aphrodite of Frejus, and of comparable renderings of the late Fifth century.[4] In any

[4] This subordination of garment to body cannot be considered solely a characteristic of Ionic (Parian) art since the Giustiniani stele, which presents an entirely different treatment of drapery, probably comes from the same environment. Of particular interest in this respect, and for the relationship between the Giustiniani and the New York stele, is the article by Ch. Karouzos, "Eine Mädchenstele kimonischer Zeit in Skyros," AthMitt 71 (1956) 245-53 Beil. 133-38, publishing the lower part of a relief strongly resembling the Girl with Doves. Karouzos, pp. 246-47, dates the Giustiniani stele ca. 465-460, the Skyros stele ca. 450, and the New York stele ca. 440 or shortly afterwards.

case, of the three reliefs, the Athenian surely is the earliest, though of better quality than the others. Notice the uncertainty of the master in carving the cloth over the left ankle, the impossible course of the folds in the skirt, which, because of the law of gravity, should be truly vertical and not oblique like the body, and finally the correct but de-emphasized rendering of the opening of the peplos over the right side. The lack of aegis is perhaps partly due to the artist's desire to show his ability in rendering the torso through folds, in an incipient understanding of V-patterns as modeling lines, both above and below the breasts.

As a votive relief, the "Mourning Athena" defies comparison with earlier examples from the Acropolis. In the archaic period the goddess was usually represented fighting, mounting a chariot, or receiving offerings from a family of worshipers. The climate of contained aloofness of the Mourning Athena is new and attributable to the Severe style— a reflection in votive relief of the contemporary development in funerary art elsewhere. Morphologically, the type set by Euenor and his workshop has won over even the conservative field of votive offerings, and helmet and spear, in combination with the belted apoptygma, are considered adequate to identify the goddess. The "capricious" quality of Athena as an over-size kore, so apparent in the relief with the family of worshipers, though a mannerism of the very late archaic phase, finds no continuation in the Severe period, except perhaps in the archaistic works of vase decorators like the Pan Painter.

Another relief usually interpreted as the votive offering of a victorious athlete is the so-called Sounion stele in the National Museum in Athens (Fig. 70). The votive nature of the work is usually postulated on the basis of its provenience and the fact that no other gravestone is known from Attica at this time. The relief was found in the sanctuary of Athena at Sounion, but within an area artificially filled, and therefore no great reliance can be placed on the find spot, since the carving was obviously not *in situ*. The second argument, the lack of Attic funerary reliefs at this period, carries more weight but seems effectively counterbalanced by the fact that athletic votive reliefs are equally scarce.[5] Since Sounion was an ancient harbor, the relief could have marked the grave of a foreigner who did not need to abide by Athenian laws. The style of the relief, admittedly, seems Attic, but obviously a local artist would be employed for the task if the death was accidental and the burial unplanned. It could also be assumed that, away from the capital, observance of the law was more relaxed, and that contact with the islands, at this period leading in funerary reliefs, might have prompted at Sounion a resumption of grave monuments earlier than in Athens proper. Typologically the relief would fit well within the repertoire of contemporary gravestones: an athlete, characterized by the metal wreath of victory which he is placing on his head, and perhaps also by some piece of athletic equipment in his missing left hand, presumably accompanied by a young servant or a dog carved in the portion of the slab now lost. The type is well known through the examples in Delphi and the Vatican.[6]

[5] I personally know of no other. The "Mourning Athena" could perhaps qualify, but its interpretation is still controversial. Even a much later example is disputed: the relief Akr. 1329, dated by J. Miliadis ca. 420 B.C., could represent Nike crowning a victorious athlete in the presence of Athena, or Herakles-Nike-Athena, or even Nike leading Hebe to Herakles.

For an illustration of this relief see *EncArAn* 5, p. 462 fig. 600.

[6] The missing portion of the slab could easily have accommodated a young servant figure. Notice the height of the companion in both the Delphi and the Vatican stelai in relationship to the pelvis of the major personage. (Delphi stele: Lippold, *Hand-*

The Sounion stele should belong fairly early within the Severe period: the lids around the youth's eyes are still as heavy as rims, the chin is massive, the foreshortening good but still exposing a great deal of the body in an almost frontal pose. The person represented is probably a boy rather than a youth, as suggested by the rather long hair, probably knotted over the forehead. This is the Severe style at its best, with all the connotations typical of contemporary sculpture in the round, with the same massiveness and simplicity of form, the same seriousness of content, the same subdued rendering of anatomy. Though later in time, the Sounion youth is the relief counterpart of the Kritian Boy.

Besides votive and funerary stelai, other reliefs can be dated to the Severe period, though their function has not been clearly determined. The most important of these monuments is perhaps the Ludovisi "Throne" (Fig. 71) with its companion piece, the so-called Boston Counterpart. The recent analyses of the Boston Museum of Fine Arts Laboratory have convincingly demonstrated the antiquity of the piece in America, but its exact date cannot be determined; it seems safe to assume, at least, that it must be later than the Ludovisi triptych since it was made to match it. Where, why, and when this manufacture took place are problems beyond the scope of this survey. As for the Ludovisi "Throne," the problems are equally serious: though its authenticity has never been in doubt, nor its date within the Severe period, its iconography has proved difficult to explain, and no hypothesis advanced until now has met with complete approval. The purpose of the monument is also undetermined. That it was found in Rome does not necessarily imply a Western manufacture, though some place in Magna Graecia has been most often advocated as the origin of the piece on stylistic ground. Recently the Thessalian attribution has been revived, but an Ionian workmanship is also possible. The entire controversy is an excellent demonstration of the difficulties encountered in trying to assign a specific origin to a work of unknown manufacture.

In terms of style, the Ludovisi relief undoubtedly belongs around 460 B.C., though strikingly different in some ways from the Olympia sculpture. The explanation of this difference as due to pictorial prototypes can, however, be supported by so many parallels in vase painting as to be convincing.[7] Notice how the artist managed to eliminate the intrinsic difference between peplos and chiton by dressing the two attendants of the central panel with these dissimilar garments, yet treating the folds of the peplos as if it also were a chiton. The engraved detailing of the front contrasts with the more massive simplicity of the sides and attests the presence of conflicting trends within the work, perhaps the best justification for placing the manufacture of the Ludovisi Throne in an area peripheral to the mainland of Greece.

Two major difficulties stand out in this brief review of original Greek reliefs of the Severe period. The first, and more important, is the lack of any valid chronological cor-

---

buch, pl. 38:2, Vatican stele, *ibid.*, pl. 58:4, or *Studies Robinson* 1, pl. 59, with addition of the lower fragment.)

[7] See, e.g. Richter, *Sculpture and Sculptors*, figs. 288-89 (detail of a kylix by Makron in the Metropolitan Museum); the naked flutist of the short side has often been compared with the flutist on a psykter by Euphronios in Leningrad, see E. Pfuhl, *Malerei*

und Zeichnung 3 (1923) pl. 122 fig. 394; the central figure of the main panel strongly resembles the Penthesileia of the name-piece by the Penthesileia Painter in Munich (Arias & Hirmer, pl. 169).

The peculiar trait of the ear emerging from the hair mass is repeated in the so-called Humphry Ward head in the Louvre, *TEL* III, pl. 151 B)

relation with historical events and thus the absence of absolute dates of any kind. The second is the mingling of techniques, that affinity between low relief and drawing which makes analysis in purely sculptural terms somewhat one-sided. A survey of reliefs also points out the difficulties of assessing cross-currents: funerary stelai stop in Attica, but spread elsewhere in the Attic format. Yet the content, with its intimacy and its representations from real life, seems in direct continuation of Ionic traditions, or at least alien to earlier Attic production. When such gravestones are examined in isolation, the contrast with Athenian monuments of the previous century is obvious and striking, and the assumption is logical that motifs must have come to Athens from abroad when Attic funerary art was resumed. Yet, when reliefs such as the "Mourning Athena" and the Sounion stele, be it votive or funerary, are examined together with these non-Attic monuments, they reveal the same "introspection," the same quiet tone of the others. Should the answer be found in the style rather than in the geographical origin? Can this intimate, "human" tone be considered typically Severe rather than Ionic or more simply non-Attic? The outward signs of the style are unmistakable, regardless of content. All the reliefs examined have displayed the same costumes, comparable hairstyles, similar anatomical treatment, and that most typical of all facial features, the heavy chin. The block-like structure of the peplophoros type is not so readily apparent in reliefs as in sculpture in the round, and the deviations from the vertical caused by the bent legs are more apparent because outlined against a solid background; but the basic tectonic principles remain unchanged. The wide geographical range of the works, from Thessaly to Macedonia, to Thasos, to the Cycladic islands, and finally to Attica and perhaps also to Magna Graecia, prove once again the great diffusion of the Severe style and its basic homogeneity.

Not all originals of the Severe Period have been discussed, for obvious reasons, and not even all *major* originals, some of which will be included in future chapters. But the selection made should be fairly representative, and should be adequate to train our eye to the Severe style in its variety of forms and expressions. The basic traits outlined in the first chapter have appeared, either together or singly, in all the monuments examined. The contrast with the archaic, even with some classical monuments of comparable type, has been pointed out, and from this firm foundation we can now turn to the examination of copies, hoping to discern what was part of the original prototype and what was added by the later maker of the replica. Yet a few more comments should be made about the originals just surveyed.

Among all of them, the most informative are the firmly dated Olympia sculptures. The other works come either from the early years of the period, or from outlying areas, which makes them more difficult to evaluate. This is especially true of sculpture in the round. Within the reliefs, the range in time is greater and presumably spans the entire Severe phase, but no absolute chronology is available and only relative dating can be suggested, on the subjective basis of style. The consequent picture appears somewhat slanted, with a greater concentration on the decades 480-460 and little evidence for 460-450. Architecturally, there is no way to fill this gap since no major decorated building seems to have been erected at this time in Greece proper; nor can we expect ancient architects and sculptors to have worked systematically as if to leave each decade of development documented: temples were built only when the demand for them arose, not by decades. We can demand more, perhaps, from sculpture in the round, since dedications and free-standing monuments must have continued to be erected, and the difference in time should be visible between works made ca. 480-470 and those produced ca. 470-450. The answer, however, seems to lie not with the originals, no longer extant, but with the copies: since most of the sculptural production must have been in bronze, we should now turn to the Roman replicas to fill in the gap.

1. *Melian Reliefs*: though of terracotta, the series of these reliefs is so well defined in time as to deserve mention in a work on the Severe style. They seem to have been made exclusively in the years between 480 and 440/430 B.C. and therefore reflect the Severe style of the period, coupled with a strange lankiness of figures typical of the series alone. The major study is by P. Jacobstahl, *Die melischen Reliefs*, 1931, and remains fundamental. See also the recent summary by W. Fuchs in *EncArAn*, s.v. Melici, Rilievi.

The reliefs enjoyed wide distribution and are found in a variety of sites, but the majority come from the Island of Melos, hence the conventional name. Their purpose seems mostly funerary, either as adornment of wooden coffins or as tomb gifts, but one example comes from the Sanctuary of Demeter and Kore in Kos. They represent various mythological or epic subjects, or sometimes simply mythological monsters. The so-called "Penelope type" (see infra pp. 101-05) appears in these à-jour plaques in a definite Odyssey context.

Representations of heroes show the same braided hairstyle discussed in Ch. 5. The closest stylistic affinities are to be found in the Locri reliefs (see infra, p. 96) though these latter were made for a local cult, not for funerary purposes.

2. *Marble disc with head of Selene*; Athens NatMus 3990. This fragmentary disc with the partially preserved head of a woman was found on the Island of Melos in 1936. It is published in a thorough article by Ch. Karouzos, "An Early Classical Disc relief from Melos," *JHS* 71 (1951) 96-110, with discussion of other examples of Severe style from the islands. Karouzos tentatively identified the goddess as Aphrodite and suggested that a flower might have occupied the remaining portion of the disc. F. Brommer ("Selene," *AA* 1963, cols. 680-89) has proposed that the head represents Selene, and his arguments are convincing. He prefers a hand to a flower, as shown by a similar head-tondo on a vase. I wonder whether a star or a moon sickle would not be possible, reinforcing the interpretation. Mrs. S. Karouzou, (*Sylloge Glyptōn*, Athens 1967, p. 33) returns to her husband's identification as Aphrodite, goddess of life and rebirth.

3. *Relief with dedication to the Priest Pausanias, Cyrene*. This monument has been greatly discussed, because its carving seems Severe in style while the dedication was written in the year A.D. 2. G. Becatti (*Critd'Ar* 5 [1940] 49-57) assumed that the piece was reemployed; H. Fuhrmann (*AA* 1941, cols. 706-14) insisted that relief and inscription were contemporary and classicizing; F. Chamoux (*Studies Robinson* I, 694-701) suggested that only one side of the double relief was Severe, and that the other had been carved at the time of the inscription. E. Paribeni, *Catalogo*, no. 24, pl. 31, emphasizes that the inscription is complete while the relief compositions are not, on either side. He therefore supports Becatti's contention.

The double relief, with a reclining banqueter on one side and various personages, seated and standing, on the other, is of difficult interpretation, but interests most for its hard and linear contour and the superficial treatment of the drapery.

4. *Relief of Charioteer on a quadriga, Cyrene*. I know this plaque only from an illustration in the *EncArAn* 2, p. 364 fig. 525 (article on *carro*) and one in G. Becatti, *The Art of Ancient Greece & Rome* (1967) 13 fig. 119. It comes from the Agora of Cyrene and should be in the local museum, but it is not included in Paribeni's catalogue. Becatti places the illustration within his discussion of the Severe period, as an echo of the bronze chariots erected during the early Fifth century to victors in the races. He also mentions (in the Italian edition, 1965, p. 134) that the many inscriptions on the relief were added "later"; and the letter forms seem to place them in the First century B.C./First century A.D. I am assuming that Becatti considers the relief carved during the Severe period, and indeed the regularity of the folds in the charioteer's skirt recalls the Delphi Charioteer. However, the three-quarter rendering of the chariot wheels might suggest a later dating, despite the strict parallelism of the four horses to the background. Cyrene was famous for her charioteers; it is interesting to note that a charioteer torso in the round was also found in Cyrene: Paribeni, *Catalogo*, no. 460 pl. 198—no date suggested. F. Chamoux, in his book on the Delphi Charioteer (*FdD* 4:5 [1955] 69-70 and n. 1), mentions sev-

eral charioteer reliefs from Cyrene as being still unpublished. Paribeni (*Catalogo*, Introduction p. VIII) refers to "bases with quadrigae" as subject for a future monograph by some other author.

5. *Relief from Xanthos, with Flying Nikai*; found in 1957, it is illustrated in *RA* 1968, p. 85 figs. 1-8, by P. Demargne who dates it to the period 470-450, which he considers one of the most important phases in the history of the town. "Lingering archaism" is suggested by the tiny folds of the chitons, but the way in which the Nikai wear their mantle has only classical parallels. The coiffures recall those of the sphinxes on the British Museum pediment from Xanthos, Building H, discussed supra, p. 25. The block with the Nikai may have formed part of a door lintel. Demargne suggests that Ionic sculpture of the Severe period was strongly influenced by Attic pottery rather than by Athenian or Peloponnesian statuary, largely inaccessible. This dependence on vase painting may explain some "archaizing" traits in Lycian works.

BIBLIOGRAPHY 4

FOR PAGE 44

For a recent discussion of Cicero's passage and the problems involved in its interpretation, see, e.g. Ch. Karouzos, *Aristodikos* (1961) 41-43.

On the subject of funerary reliefs the best sources up to date are:

for the archaic period, G. M. A. Richter, *The Archaic Gravestones of Attica* (London 1961)

for the Severe period (non-Attic Stelai), E. Akurgal, "Zwei Grabstelen vorklassischer Zeit aus Sinope," 111 *BerlWinckPr*, 1955, with list of stelai on pp. 26-28.

On funerary reliefs in general, K. F. Johansen, *The Attic Grave-reliefs of the Classical Period* (Copenhagen 1951).

On the subject of votive reliefs, see, e.g. U. Hausmann, *Griechische Weihreliefs* (Berlin 1960).

For the theory of metal crowning leaves see A. Schott, "Akanthus," *ÖJh* 44 (1959) 54-79, who refers, however, to Periklean times and does not expand on the nature of the stelai themselves.

FOR PAGE 45

On the differences between architectural and votive/funerary relief see Carpenter, *Greek Sculpture*, pp. 112-13 and also pp. 60-65.

On the Nisyros stele, read the good description by G. Mendel, *Catalogue des Sculptures* 1, (1912) no. 11 pp. 73-76.

FOR PAGE 46

On the Thasos banquet relief see, e.g. Hausmann, *Gr. Weihreliefs*, p. 28; B. S. Ridgway, "The Banquet Relief from Thasos," *AJA* 71 (1967) 307-9. Funerary banquets in general: N. Firatly, *Les Stèles funéraires de Byzance Gréco-Romaine* (Paris 1964) 20-22, reviewed by C. Clairmont, *BCH* 91 (1967) 455-56; and R. N. Thönges-Stringaris, "Das griechische Totenmahl," *AthMitt* 80 (1965) 1-98, the Thasos relief Catalogue, no. 34 and passim.

For an archaic example of the type see Athens, N.M. 55, N. N. Svoronos, *Das Athener Nationalmuseum* (Athens 1908) no. 5 pp. 100-1 pl. 2 from Arkadia; Thönges-Stringaris, *op.cit.*, cat. no. 34 and passim.

On the Girl with Doves see G.M.A. Richter, *Catalogue of the Metropolitan Museum* (Harvard 1954) no. 73 pl. 60a pp. 49-50, dated just after the middle of the Fifth century.

On the "Adoration of the Flower" see, recently, H. Biesantz, *Die thessalischen Grabreliefs* (1965) 22 no. K 36 pl. 17 and bibliography.

FOR PAGE 47

On the Giustiniani Relief see C. Blümel, *Klassisch griechischen Skulpturen der Staatlichen Museen zu Berlin* (1966) no. 2 (K 19) pp. 12-14 figs. 2, 4, 6, 9. Blümel suggests that the girl lifts from the box a fillet for the grave, but the shape of the box is different from those shown on white-ground lekythoi as containers for fillets.

FOR PAGE 48

On the "Mourning Athena" and its interpretation as a victory monument see F. Chamoux, "L'Athéna mélancolique," *BCH* 81 (1957) 141-59, with summary of previous positions and bibliography. Carpenter, *Greek Sculpture*, p. 144, supports the Athena Horia interpretation.

FOR PAGE 49

Archaic votive reliefs: Athena fighting, Akr. 120, Schrader no. 423 pl. 174 and fig. 349 a; Akr. 121, Schrader no. 425, fig. 350.

Athena mounting a chariot: Akr. 290, 290a and 3532; Schrader no. 426 fig. 351. Athena receiving offerings from a family of worshipers: Akr. 581, Schrader no. 424 pl. 175.

On the Sounion stele, Athens Nat. Mus. no. 3344, see, e.g. Hausmann, *Gr. Weihreliefs*, p. 23. My comments are largely based on E. R. Young, *The Stele Found at Sounion*, unpublished M.A. Thesis, Bryn Mawr College, Bryn Mawr, 1967, though Mrs. Young leaves the purpose of the relief undecided.

FOR PAGE 50

The bibliography on the Ludovisi Throne is enormous. For a recent attempt at interpretation see, e.g. Ch. Kardara, "Some Remarks on the Ludovisi Relief," *AthMitt* 76 (1961) 81-90.

On the Boston Counterpart see, e.g. L. Alscher, *Götter vor Gericht* (Berlin 1963—Supplement to *Griechische Plastik* II:2).

For the analysis of the Boston Museum of Fine Arts Laboratory, see *BMFA* 66:346 (1968) 124-66.

On the revival of the Thessalian-Origin theory, see H. Biesantz, *Thessalische Grabreliefs*, pp. 107-8.

FOR PAGE 51

For further bibliography on the question of influences on Attic funerary reliefs, see also infra, pp. 97-98.

CHAPTER 5

Roman Copies: The Problem of Schools

IN APPROACHING the numerous Roman copies of Severe works, some basic system should be established and followed. In the past, some authors have preferred what could be called a philological approach, trying to group works around the name of a great master, first on the basis of literary evidence, and then of affinities. Others have selected the division into schools, so that works which do not bear the unmistakable imprint of a great sculptor would still be grouped with comparable ones on the basis of local styles. With either method a mingling of originals and copies has resulted, but little positive evidence has been gained. Both systems are open to difficulties, though both have value. We shall examine first the problem of schools, though strictly speaking a clear division between the two methods is impossible, and one approach will often lead into the other.

Schools can be understood in two ways: either as workshops working in a local style, and therefore the location of the school is all important, or as students of different origins gathered around a major leader and working in his style. In either case the mobility of artists makes distinctions difficult, and the popularity of famous monuments must have made their imitation common and therefore somewhat independent of local peculiarities. Ancient literary sources seem to imply that some basic stylistic trends had geographical connotations since Pausanias, at least, often makes distinctions between the Aeginetan and the Attic style, but it is difficult for us to determine on what his judgment was based since our main original basis for an Aeginetan school, famous for its bronzes, is limited to the marble sculpture from the Aphaia temple.

TYPOLOGICAL GATHERING

The method of attributing works to regional workshops can be called "typological gathering." An illustration of its dangers can be seen in the wide geographical distribution of certain statuary types. If a certain rendering is considered typical of, say, a Sikyonian workshop, what conclusions should be derived from the fact that similar renderings appear in entirely different areas? Can all the pieces be considered imports from the main workshop, or the product of traveling Sikyonian artists? Is it not more logical to assume that they were local imitations of important works? In this case, there is little validity in trying to distinguish local schools since the range of external influence is so wide. One could still attempt to arrange all available specimens of a certain type in a progressive order based on their respective artistry, and determine the origin of the type from the find spot of the best example. This procedure too is open to question since, again, the piece could be imported, the artist who made it could have come from elsewhere and, finally and most important, the law of chance might have eliminated a great deal of the evidence and left only poor specimens in the center of origin because the best monuments were either taken away or made of bronze and therefore melted down. A case in point is the diffusion of what may conveniently be called the Blond Boy Head Type.

The name-piece of this group, Akr. 689 (Figs. 72, 74), was found on the Athenian citadel to the NE of the modern Museum, an area which, as several authors have pointed out, does not seem to have been filled with Persian debris. The date of the work is therefore controversial; Schuchhardt prefers to place it between 490 and 480, while others date it after the Tyrannicides. The fragment of a torso and a right foot attributed to the Blond Head on the basis of marble, workmanship, scale, and style, seem to support a date in the third decade of the Fifth century. The torso shows clear differentiation between weight and free leg, and has powerful but simplified musculature; only the toes of the foot rest on the plinth: a wedge has been inserted under the heel, at a pronounced slant which seems to indicate that the foot was not only raised but placed at a definite angle to the other foot. Schuchhardt calls it a forerunner of Polykleitos' Doryphoros and advocates an Argive master.

We cannot, at present, fully judge the revolutionary importance of the body, in its fragmentary state. The head is indeed remarkable. As often pointed out, it is built with strong asymmetry, the right cheek being flatter and the whole right half of the face seemingly sloping down toward the ear. In keeping with this rendering the head turns toward the right shoulder, with a corresponding strong compression of the powerful neck on that side. A great deal of color must have added considerably to the general appearance of the piece; even now the eyes retain traces of the painted pupils and the hair is faintly red, thus giving the piece its nickname. More difficult to discern are the painted locks on the nape, rendered as if escaping from the tight braids, and the fine whiskers which suggest that the Blond Boy is more of a youth, a typical athlete as they appear on some Attic vases of the period.

In terms of style the Blond Head is fairly unique. Traditionally he is compared with Euthydikos' kore, to the point that the two pieces are sometimes called Brother and Sister, the brother perhaps slightly younger than his sibling. But the difference between them is not one of age: next to the youth the kore appears cold and lifeless, unsatisfactory if seen from any but the frontal view, while the asymmetry of the Blond Head results in a different appearance from different angles, making the face seem warm and alive. Also the Apollo of the Olympia West pediment (Fig. 73), another standard comparison, or Herakles the Archer of Aegina East (Fig. 6), cannot compete with the complexities of the Blond Boy. The youth has been called Attic influenced by Ionian work, or typically Peloponnesian. His features are not even typical of the Severe style; if the eyes are heavily lidded, the asymmetrical cheeks break the smooth contour of the face; the chin is strong but almost pointed; the mouth appears serious and has a longer upper lip, but the lips themselves are fairly thin; the skull, in profile, does not have the high-swinging dome of Severe works, though the general structure of head and neck is massive and cubic. Carpenter uses the Blond Boy as a typical example of the new *symmetria*, of measured heads, and dates it about a decade earlier than the Kritian Boy (therefore ca. 480), but the difference between the two pieces, as he notes, is not merely of chronology, or even of authorship. Carpenter calls it a difference in "epochs of sculptural understanding," but if the Blond Boy is to be dated after the Persian invasion, as I believe, the difference from the Kritian Boy, in terms of actual years, may be minimal indeed.

The Blond Boy must have been considered a masterpiece in its own time, and must have greatly influenced the production of different areas. Several works bear a strong resemblance to the Acropolis head, another indication that it, or a similar work, must have been accessible for imitation after 480. Surprisingly enough, or perhaps under-

standably in terms of mediocre sculptors, the heads after the Blond Boy look more definitely Severe than their prototype, not simply because later but presumably because
translated in generic terms of familiar style.

The closest resemblance is perhaps in a head in Volo, Thessaly (Figs. 76-77). The
connection is not based exclusively on the hair style; in point of fact, there are several
differences in the way in which the braids originate and cross the nape in the two
pieces, and the basket-weave pattern is more accurately rendered in the Thessalian
head than in the Blond Boy, where the hair within the braid is left undetailed, in contrast with the fine engraving of the strands in the Volo head. The similarity in hairstyles
diminishes even more over the front, where the Blond Boy sports loose bangs covering
the ends of the braids, while the long locks of the Volo head fall over a wide fillet which
covers the upper part of the forehead. What creates the resemblance between the two
pieces is the basic structure of the head, the slightly asymmetrical face,[1] the proportions
of neck to head, the difference in thickness between upper and lower lip, all translated
into more "Severe" terms in the Thessalian head, noticeably in the area of the eyes.
Brommer and Biesantz classify the Volo head as local work with Ionic influence from
the islands, the former adding also that the slight differences in hair rendering of all
these braided heads might be due to local variants of the fashion.

The second comparable head was found in Cyrene, North Africa (Figs. 80-83). The
strange asymmetry of the face is retained, and the peculiar contour of the cheeks, but
the beauty of the Acropolis youth is only a vague reminiscence in this almost grotesque
Cyrenaican head, with its thick lids, and high-set parted mouth. The hair, though different in details, follows the same arrangement of the braids originating behind the ears
and crossing over at the nape, but while in the Blond Boy they disappear under the forehead curls, in the Cyrene head they end above them, and the strands beneath appear
as a thick mass terminating in spiral locks. In the back, a smooth raised area terminating
in a point (indistinguishable in the photograph under the shadow of the braids) was
probably painted to suggest escaping wisps of short hair. Paribeni calls the piece a
Peloponnesian work of ca. 480 B.C.

Even more asymmetrical is a head in the Cyprus Museum (Figs. 84-87), with a
strongly articulated chin and a hairstyle similar to that of the Cyrene head. Dikaios
dates it ca. 475-450 and considers it an import into the island. Its place of origin is not
certain since it was found in private hands in Nikosia, but together with material that
came from Lapithos. It is, in any case, quite different from local work, and perhaps a
clear case of traveling sculpture.

This type of hairstyle, with the braids tied over, rather than under the front locks,
seems to be more popular than the true Blond Boy's style. There is one more example,
poorly preserved because of later reworking, under life-size and presumably of Naxian
marble, in the Capitoline Museum (Figs. 78-79). The curls over the forehead seem to
have been, at least partly, inserted in metal, since a few tenons remain in some of the
holes which dot the hair over the forehead. The braids do not cross each other at the
nape, but run just above each other, in almost parallel course, as in the Thessalian head.

---

[1] This asymmetry has prompted Biesantz to suggest (p. 130 n. 154) that the figure might have been
part of a group, but I believe this surmise is unnecessary.

The traits of the Severe style seem fainter in this last example than in all the others mentioned previously, though a date around 480 can still be supported.

Finally a head that might still be archaic, perhaps earlier than the Blond Boy and a possible ancestor: it was found in Corinth in 1964 and is still unpublished except for brief mentions in newsletters (Fig. 75). Approximately half life-size, and made of coarse island marble, it has a strong tapering facial structure, with heavy chin and highly set mouth. The lids are also heavy, and the eyes appear quite high in the face. The hair, brushed forward from the crown, ends over the forehead in a line of solid snail curls; the braids are finely engraved and originate behind the ears; it is impossible to tell how they crossed over the nape since that part of the head is broken off, but they terminate in a fillet which runs over the strands of the snail-curls. The head has a slight turn to the right, like the Blond Boy to which it must be chronologically close. It has been suggested that the Corinth head is of local, or of Argive, manufacture.

If this last example stands perhaps at the beginning of the series, another head, in Cleveland, might stand at the end, as a variant rather than a true representative of the "Blond Boy Type" (Figs. 88-91). The work, slightly under life-size and made of island marble, seems to have suffered heavy weathering and the blurring of some features suggests that it might have been under water for some time; therefore some details are difficult to read. The frontal view emphasizes the cubic structure of head and neck, while the profile shows the powerful line of the jaw and the surprising squareness of the neck at the nape, despite the projection of the right trapezium muscle, presumably caused by a slight turn. This surmise is supported not only by the general Severe tendency to break the law of frontality, but also by the fact that the features on the left half of the face appear to lie on a more superficial plane than those on the right. The hair at first glance seems to repeat the traditional pattern, but though the forehead curls compare well with those of the heads from Cyrene and Cyprus, in the Cleveland head the braids have been replaced by an angular, ledge-like roll which encircles the entire skull tapering in the area above the forehead. It is formed by the long strands of the back tightly looped around a fillet, but while other such rolls usually stop at the level of the ears, as in the Agrigento kouros (Fig. 92), or continue uninterrupted over the forehead, as for instance in the Kritian Boy (Figs. 43-44), the Cleveland coiffure is unique in that the roll over the front behaves like braids and overlies the forehead bangs.[2] The strange

---

[2] I know of only one other example of this rendering, and its state of preservation is such as to render interpretation difficult: the head Akr. 657, Schrader no. 324, pl. 152 and p. 246. The work appears almost unfinished, with the left side largely undetailed. The hair roll, which encircles the head completely, is left plain except for the indication of three twisted strands above the right ear; it is broken off in the area of the forehead. The hair calotte is left smooth, with a tongue-like projection stretching under the roll at the nape. Temples and forehead display a series of holes for the insertion of metal curls. Schuchhardt dates the work after 480 B.C. and attributes it to Kritios' workshop, per-

haps as part of a metope or high relief.

A most interesting arrangement of hair bound at the nape, also almost ledge-like in its appearance and seemingly limited to Sicily, occurs on a head in Hannover and its two parallels in Dresden and Vienna: W. Amelung, "Archaischer Jünglingskopf in Hannover," *JdI* 35 (1920) 49-59; W. Fuchs, *RömMitt* 65 (1958) 2-3. For a peculiar and very linear stylization of the hair-roll over the forehead, wound around *two* fillets, see the statue of a seated male from the Nekropolis of Cabecico del Tesoro in the Murcia Museum, Spain. This presents a curious mixture of Greek and Hispanic traits (A. García y Bellido, *ArchEspArq* 14 [1940-41] 350-52, dated

dichotomy between the roll and the finely engraved hair over the skull recalls the Kritian Boy, but the flatness of the rendering, with the deeper lines at intervals marking irregular groupings, as if the skull were sectioned into slices, is more closely paralleled in the so-called Selinus/Castelvetrano Youth (Fig. 93). In the latter, however, the roll is broken into clearly spaced loops around the fillet. The compact winding of the Cleveland Youth's hair is closer instead to the hairstyle of the Agrigento Kouros (Fig. 92), which even displays a comparable crossing and diverging of strands on the axis of the nape. Since the Cleveland head was bought in Rome, it is plausible to assume that, like the work last cited, it was made around 470 B.C. in Magna Graecia, and in later times found its way to the capital. That the more traditional hairstyle with crossing braids was, however, familiar to Southern Italy is attested by the statue of Apollo the Archer, also found in Rome in the area of the temple of Apollo Sosianus and attributed to Tarentine art.[3]

In summary, of the works listed above, the name-piece (the Blond Boy) was found on the Athenian Acropolis, one comes from Corinth, one from Cyprus, one from Cyrene, and one from Thessaly. The Cleveland head and that in the Capitoline Museum were found in Rome and may possibly come from Magna Graecia. These heads were chosen as belonging to the type not only on the basis of the hairstyle, which actually in some of them differs considerably from the name-piece, but mostly because of their facial structure which differentiates them from other presumably contemporary Severe works. The type in general is considered Peloponnesian, mostly because of the alleged similarity between the Blond Boy and the Olympia Apollo; yet of all the examples, only one, though perhaps the earliest, was found in a Peloponnesian site: Corinth. The wide distribution of the others should caution us against facile attributions to local schools. Two factors add to the interest of the type: one, that the hairstyle seems more suitable for bronzes, and therefore we might possess only a few scanty examples of an otherwise rich series; two, that it must necessarily have been a type limited to the beginning of the Severe period, yet it enjoyed a wide diffusion, despite this chronological restriction. The early date of the type is suggested not only by the style, but also by the fact that long hair for mortals became obsolete in the 470's.

STYLISTIC GATHERING

The second method of defining schools might be termed "stylistic gathering." It tries to group works on the basis of their affinities, on the assumption that they stem from

---

second half of the Fifth century after earlier prototype; R. Mendez Pidal, *Historia de España* 1 [Madrid 1954] pl. 494 fig. 399, pp. 503-4 "probably second half of Fifth century," though Nekropolis continues till Roman period—3rd c. B.C.).

When first published, the Cleveland head was considered a Roman copy rather than a true original, and similar doubts have been expressed orally by some scholars. However the very ledge-like nature of its roll speaks against a date in the Augustan period, when copyists had considerable skill and tended toward plastic rather than glyptic renderings. The appearance of the Cleveland head suggests that it was carved by a sculptor acquainted with bronze work but unable to translate into stone the ductile appearance of a metal coiffure. The tiny drill holes marking the transition between the ribbon-like strands and the spiral curls are purely a technical feature present in some of the Acropolis korai, and prominent in the hairstyles of figures on the Harpy tomb.

[3] For a comparable though "classicizing" example, see the so-called Pisoni head of a kouros in Naples, presumably after a Magna Graecian prototype: C. Saletti, "Il Kouros Pisoni," *Athenaeum* 38 (1960) 310-27 pls. 1-7 with extensive bibliography on p. 310 n. 1.

one major master and his pupils. This approach can be illustrated by the "Omphalos Apollo group" (Figs. 94-97).

The Omphalos Apollo is the first Roman copy as yet considered in our discussion (Figs. 94-95, 97). The original behind this work was obviously a superb bronze by a great sculptor and was famous in antiquity, as attested by the large number of extant replicas. Only marble copies have come down to us; the most important, probably made in the Second century A.D., has given the name to the type, since it was found in the Theater of Dionysos in Athens next to an omphalos which had once served as the base of a statue. It was later noticed that the Apollo, because of its stance and size, could not have stood on that omphalos, but the nickname was retained. Among the other replicas, the most complete is in the British Museum, the so-called Choiseul-Gouffier Apollo (Fig. 96), bought in Istanbul, but there are a great number of more or less preserved torsos and heads, some of which have come to light as late as 1960. The examination of all extant replicas would form a good study on methods of copying, since vast differences exist from one specimen to another, though the type is clearly recognizable in all. Even the two best replicas, the Omphalos and the Choiseul-Gouffier Apollos, though both of excellent workmanship, vary considerably in general appearance and in individual details, the British Museum statue being mostly harsher and colder; in particular, the face of the former is narrower.

The most distinctive feature of the Apollo is his hair: it is combed forward over the forehead, where the loose bangs part approximately in the center and otherwise arrange themselves in seemingly casual but well-planned disarray (Figs. 94-95). Over the nape the long strands are tightly woven into two braids which originate behind and above the ears, and run one above the other (as in the Thessalian and the Capitoline heads of the "Blond Boy Type") until they meet over the forehead bangs and are tied together with a Herculean knot. The fine engraving of dome and braids, the small wisps of hair escaping from under the braids over the nape, the fluffy appearance of the bangs with their small curly ends are typical of bronze work, and indeed they are the most difficult feature of the statue to translate in stone. Many replicas only roughly block out the forehead bangs, often fuse them together, enlarge the central part and otherwise neglect the intricacies of the strands over the dome, where they are absorbed into the braids.

The statue, or more precisely its prototype, has been called a cornerstone in our knowledge of the Severe style, and should be briefly examined as a whole. We are immediately struck by its longilinear proportions and relatively small head, a canon which will reappear only with Lysippos and the early Hellenistic period, but, in contrast with late Fourth century renderings, the elongated general appearance is not the result of slender forms: the massiveness of upper torso and shoulders is quite distinctive. The stance, with both feet flat on the ground, is basically that of the Kritian Boy; it produces the same shift in the level of the hips, but the balancing motion loses itself before reaching the shoulders, which remain strictly horizontal. In contrast with the Acropolis statue, the Omphalos Apollo clearly appears more mature and powerful, with ample musculature and prominent rib-cage; the head turns toward the side of the supporting leg, thus being closer to the scheme of Angelitos' Athena than to that of the Kritian Youth. The date of the original and its authorship are highly controversial. The more traditional chronology places the Omphalos Apollo around 470, the more radical around the middle of the Fifth century. As for the artist, the following Severe masters have been suggested: Pythagoras (Waldstein), the young Myron (Poulsen), Kleoitas of Sikyon (Beyen), Hageladas (Robinson), Onatas of Aegina (Picard, Lippold, Dörig), Kalamis (Richter, Orlandini, Paribeni, *et al.* First attributed by Conze), this last sharing with Onatas the greatest number of votes. Great variety of opinions exists also as to the possible association of the Omphalos Apollo with the statue from Cape Artemision.

This spectacular bronze original (Figs. 98-99), found at sea near the northern tip of the Island of Euboea, is controversial even in its identification, since some scholars consider it Zeus and others Poseidon. The answer, in the case of two divine brothers who were iconographically very close, lies with the attribute once held by the statue: if a trident, Poseidon, if a thunderbolt, Zeus. Arguments in favor or against either theory can be easily advanced, but the point is not crucial for an aesthetic appreciation and evaluation of the piece. It is perhaps more important to point out that the composition relies mainly on a system of triangles (between the legs, between each arm and the body) and therefore should be seen from the point of view which reveals these triangles most emphatically. Attempts to turn the statue in a three-quarter position, stressing the three-dimensionality of the work, seem unnecessary, because, as in a metope, the statue must have been created to be intelligible from a distance. One can easily imagine it standing on a promontory, in the open air, silhouetted against the sky, with its definite "battle pattern" once rendered complete by the presence of the weapon. As a cult statue[4] the composition is inconceivable: first, because a figure in action is not compatible with what we know of cult statues in the Fifth century; second, because the action is such as to frighten, not merely to impress, the beholder; third, because a cult image at this period would probably be frontal, to establish a direct relationship with the worshiper, while the Artemision bronze, even if turned somewhat sideways, would never fully face the spectator. But the most compelling reason, to my mind, is the need for an open air setting, as required by the composition. Surely the fact that the statue was found near Cape Artemision does not imply that it once stood there,[5] but neither does it exclude a

---

[4] See: W. Schwabacher, "The Olympian Zeus before Pheidias," *Archaeology* 14 (1961) 104-9; "Olympischer Blitzschwinger," *AntK* 5 (1962) 9-17; "Nochmals der olympische Blitzschwinger," *RömMitt* 72 (1965) 209-12, in answer to objections by W. H. Gross, "Kultbilder, Blitzschwinger und Hageladas," *RömMitt* 70 (1963) 13-19. Schwabacher has advanced the interesting theory that the original cult statue in the temple at Olympia, before the Pheidian Zeus, must have been of the "striding god" type. The theory stems from two considerations: 1) it is unlikely that the temple stood without a cult image from the time of its completion in 457 B.C. until the erection of the Pheidian colossus, in the 430's; 2) the striding-god type appears on coins of Elis since archaic times and is reproduced in a variety of bronze statuettes from the geometric period to the Severe period: it seems therefore to be the traditional portrayal of the Olympic Zeus and as such appropriate for the cult statue. Schwabacher supports his theory with the argument that the type existed in monumental size (not only in statuettes or coins), as proved by the Artemision bronze, and that the Zeus Ithomatas by Hageladas is described by literary sources as being also in a striding position.

Gross argues that cult statues of the early Fifth century are likely to have been seated figures, and that the Zeus Ithomatas does not qualify as a cult statue since it stayed in the house of the priest and was moved from place to place periodically.

For further discussion of the Artemision bronze in connection with Hageladas' Zeus see also C. A. Robinson, Jr., "The Zeus Ithomatas of Ageladas," *AJA* 49 (1945) 121-27. For a fragmentary marble herm of Zeus found in Olympia and attributed to the Hadrianic period after a large-scale bronze original of the "Blitzschwinger" type, see *Olympia-Bericht* 6 (1958) 200-4.

[5] Some suggest that the statue represents Poseidon striking at the Persians on behalf of the Greeks, and that it was a thank-offering for the decimation of

similar, if not that very same, location. Though the argument may seem somewhat circular, the emphatic pattern visible when the bronze is properly set is a typical example of the stylizing tendencies of the Severe style and of the Severe concept of a statue in action, basically two-dimensional and eloquent only in outlines, despite the apparently far-flung pose.

The discrepancies in the rendering of the action are visible from the back, where the right gluteus is seen to collide almost at right angle with the left, as if the legs of the figure were disjointed and one could be frontal while the other turned almost to full profile. The position of the legs, moreover, does not imply any subtle balancing; the weight of the body should rest mostly on the advanced foot, which alone is flat on the ground, but the vertical axis of the torso coincides with the center of the space between the legs, and thus the figure is perfectly balanced, with no displacement of weight, musculature, and hip level. From this point of view the statue is less advanced than the Omphalos Apollo, and in comparison with the Aristogeiton of the Tyrannicide group (Fig. 115) it reveals that it retains somewhat the character of an apparition, or at least that it portrays a more sedate action.[6]

The strongest reason for relating the Omphalos Apollo to the Artemision bronze is the treatment of the hair in both figures (Figs. 94-95, 99); and indeed, when seen in metal, the hairstyle looks more plausible and more effective. Yet, for all the superiority of the medium and of the original creation, the Artemision coiffure is more regular, and therefore less natural: what, in a copy, would perhaps be termed more mechanical. This characteristic is perhaps most noticeable in the short hairs over the nape, under the braids,[7] which in the Omphalos Apollo are of different lengths and group themselves variously, while in the bronze they are more uniform and neatly arranged; also the forehead part is more accurately centered in the original work, and it creates more of a pattern than the disorderly bangs of the Apollo. Yet, though the copyist of the latter might have

---

the enemy fleet at the time of Xerxes' invasion and the battle of Cape Artemision. If this theory is correct, the monument could indeed have stood on the Euboean promontory near which it was found. Indeed R. Lullies believes that the similarity in pose between the Artemision bronze and the Zeus-hurling-the-thunderbolt type derives from the surname Soter, usually applied to Zeus, which the Greeks bestowed upon Poseidon after the events off Cape Artemision in 480 B.C. (Herod. 7 192; Lullies in Lullies & Hirmer, p. 75, notes to pls. 130-32).

Yet the bronze statue was found in the context of a shipwreck, which implies that it was being transported somewhere and was therefore away from its original location. The wreck still appears under the mud, and definitely deserves further attention, in order to determine its date.

Karouzos (*Deltion*, p. 94 n. 1) dates to the middle Hellenistic period the sherds found together with the statue; Robinson (*AJA* [1945] 125) believes the sherds "are nondescript and can date

from practically any period at all, Fourth century before Christ to Fourth century after Christ." G. F. Bass (*Archaeology Under Water* [New York 1966] 77-78) writes that "pottery finds date the shipwreck to about the time of Christ." An early date for the shipwreck would explain the lack of Roman copies of such an excellent work.

[6] The possibility that the figure is shown in a "Myronian moment," that is, an instant of pause in between two actions, should not be excluded. Poulsen indeed believes that the bronze represents the Erechtheus by Myron (*ActaA* 11 [1940] 41-42).

[7] It should also be noted that in the Artemision bronze the braids cross over the nape, while in the Omphalos Apollo they run parallel around the head. But this is a minor difference, comparable to the variations in the Blond Boy type. For the detail of the Artemision bronze see Karouzos, *Deltion*, 82-83. A well-documented discussion on the various forms of the krobylos is given by Stucchi in *Bull-Comm* 75 (1953-55) 17-18 n. 36.

somewhat "improved" or updated the style of his model,[8] it is unlikely that he might have improvised in the arrangement of the hair, which seems most accurately imitated.[9]

On the basis of stance, balance, anatomical details, and hair treatment, it could perhaps be assumed that the Artemision statue is simply earlier than the Omphalos Apollo. On the other hand some scholars have strongly, and probably correctly, opposed the attribution of the two works to the same master.

Already, this all too brief summary of scholarly discussion about two major Severe works must have given some indication of the difficulties inherent in the "stylistic gathering" method. But the question becomes more complex as more works are added to this original nucleus of two. A common attribution is the sphinx from Aegina (Figs. 51-52), already mentioned in Chapter 3. Indeed, the presumed similarity between this statue and the Omphalos Apollo is mostly responsible for the attribution of the latter to the Aeginetan school, and therefore to Onatas, its most famous sculptor. Yet the rather flat face and shallow eyes of the sphinx, and the almost impressionistic treatment of her hair, seem quite different from the fine detailing of the Apollo's coiffure and his fleshy face.

The similarity between the Apollo and the so-called Conservatori Charioteer (Figs. 172-73) is, on the other hand, undeniable and unanimously acknowledged, but with different results. Indeed, those who advocate the closest resemblance point out that the Charioteer is but a Roman re-elaboration of the Apollo itself, made into a different personage and with minor changes in hairstyle (see *infra*, pp. 134-35).

A similar combination might exist in a head which looks remarkably like a Roman portrait (Figs. 100-2). It was found on the Acropolis in Athens and was at first published as copy of a work by the young Pheidias, presumably a Poseidon. Recently an attempt has been made to identify it as the Hermes Kriophoros by Onatas, again on the basis of the similarity with the Artemision bronze and the Omphalos Apollo, mostly confined to the braided hairstyle.

The coiffure and the serious, almost pouting face are responsible also for the attribution of the so-called Hestia Giustiniani to the group (Fig. 103). The figure could be Demeter, Hera, or perhaps even Hestia, as the type is commonly named, though this identification is based only on vase painting. The veiled goddess stands with her left foot retracted, but the pose is understandable only from a side or the back view, since the heavy peplos entirely covers the lower part of her body with an effect similar to that of the Delphi Charioteer. The position of the hand on the hip recalls Angelitos' dedication and the relief of the Mourning Athena, but despite its similarity to Attic works, the Hestia is usually considered Argive and brought forth as an example of Peloponnesian influence on Attic art during the Severe period. The original, obviously of bronze, has been sometimes attributed to Hageladas, a name also mentioned in connection with the Artemision bronze by those scholars who believe it might portray the Zeus Ithomatas. Another common connection is with the master of the Blond Boy.[10]

---

[8] Poulsen (SS, p. 139) suggests that in order to recapture the appearance of the original, one should put together the Omphalos Apollo and Choiseul-Gouffier replica and produce an ideal cross-section of the two.

[9] It could, of course, be argued that greater regularity implies a later rather than an earlier date,

but I favor the opposite point of view, more in keeping with the intentional asymmetries of the early Severe style.

[10] For the opinion that it is the work of an Argive artist (Hageladas?) in collaboration with the Sikyonian master of the Omphalos Apollo, see Beyen & Vollgraff, *Argos et Sicyone*, pp. 87-88. The Hestia

As for the date, the simplicity of the pose, the lack of differentiation in the folds, the abstract contour, the block-like structure with its horizontal divisions into smaller rectangles, the rather early mannerisms of the hand on the hip, would place the original around 470 B.C., a most important monument for our evaluation of female statues in bronze during the Severe period.

If the hairstyle were such a determining factor, another attribution should be rightly made to this group: that of the so-called Penelope (Figs. 104, 139-40). The type presents "one of the most nebulous and evasive problems of monumental sculpture in the Severe period," and will be discussed below (Ch. 7, p. 101). Here it suffices to point out that though most scholars would consider the master of the Penelope an Ionian, they do so mainly on the basis of the drapery, and perhaps because unconsciously influenced by the fact that the most important replica of the type was found in Persepolis. Of the heads preserved, only the ones in Berlin and Copenhagen are reliable, and it is the latter which strongly resembles the hair treatment of the Omphalos Apollo: indeed an early opinion had attributed the Penelope to Kalamis.

Finally one last attribution:[11] a monument which must have indeed been famous in antiquity, to judge from the number of extant replicas, the so-called Aspasia. The most complete treatment of the subject, with list of replicas up to 1950, is by Orlandini who recognizes in the type the famous Aphrodite Sosandra by Kalamis, dedicated by Kallias on the Athenian Acropolis; this nickname will be used here for practical purposes, though other identifications of the type have been suggested (for instance Demeter-Europa because of an inscribed statuette),[12] as well as other masters, notably Onatas and Kalon.

Because of its date, Orlandini's study could not take into account two important additions to the replicas: the unfinished statue from Baiae (Figs. 106-8), and the youthful head from Gortyna (Fig. 105). This last piece comes perhaps closest to the fleshy treatment of the Omphalos Apollo replica in Athens, while its slightly pouting expression (a truly "hidden" smile!) is perhaps most comparable to the Choiseul-Gouffier replica. The hairstyle this time cannot be held responsible for the attribution of the prototype to the Omphalos Apollo Group since it differs basically from the male coiffure; it is, on the

---

would be a Demeter, the "Aspasia/Sosandra" would be Kore, and a third unidentified statue would have represented Triptolemos.

[11] Other attributions to the Omphalos Apollo group have been made by various authors but cannot all be mentioned here; one may see the list of attributions in Beyen and Vollgraff, p. 61, and summary of career at pp. 87-88; a different grouping is suggested by Homann-Wedeking, *RömMitt* 55 (1940) 196-218. As echoes or imitations of the Artemision bronze see also the Zeus in the Hieros-Gamos metope, Selinus, Temple E (Langlotz, *Magna Graecia*, pls. 105 and 107); some elders on the North Parthenon frieze (slab 10 fig. 41: EA 728; Homann-Wedeking, *loc.cit.*, fig. 1); a head on the antiquarian market (Poulsen, SS, p. 140 and fig. 74 on p. 141); a head in London (*BrBr* 517), and even some Fourth century grave reliefs. For a braided hairstyle in a

herm see Harrison, *Agora* 11, nos. 156 and 159, pls. 40 and 42.

Another important attempt at grouping works by the same master has been made by W.-H. Schuchhardt, "Köpfe des strengen Stiles," *Festschrift Weickert* (1955) 59-73, who attributes the so-called Candia type and other female statues to a Corinthian bronze-caster of the Severe period.

[12] E. Langlotz (*JdI* 61-62 [1946-47] 104) suggests that because of the turn of the head the type must have belonged to a multi-figured group, perhaps of the Muses; but the turn of the head seems a typical Severe attempt to break the Law of Frontality, without further implications.

More convincing is M. Robertson's attempt to identify the personage as the Europa kidnapped by the bull of Zeus, on the basis of similar representations on vases (*JWarb* 20 [1957] 1-3).

other hand, quite representative of the linear tendencies of the Severe style, and with its "ogival canopy" motif is the true predecessor of the Amazonian hairstyle fashionable in the 430's.[13] Like the identification and the attribution, the date of the Sosandra is in dispute, though oscillating within a decade: Orlandini places it ca. 465, Beyen as high as 470, von Steuben down to 460. The type was greatly favored in Roman times, when it was used as a stock body for portrait statues: three replicas have a Hadrianic, an Aurelian, and a Commodian head respectively.

If the traits of the Severe style in the Sosandra are unmistakable, nonetheless the statue remains a most original creation and a truly unusual masterpiece. The scheme is basically very simple: the figure stands with its weight on the left leg, the right knee slightly bent, and the right foot forward and somewhat to the side, though flat on the ground. The body is entirely enveloped in a voluminous mantle which covers also the head: one tip of the himation has been thrown back over the left shoulder, capturing the right arm within its folds; the other arm emerges from the opening on the left side, holding an attribute now lost. The subject of a veiled woman was known to Greek sculpture since the archaic period, especially in Ionia: the typical example is the Hera of Samos, which resembles the Sosandra in the abstraction of its contours and its textural contrast, much more drastic, however, in the Severe work and with totally different results. The Samian figure also shares with the Sosandra the rendering of one arm through cloth, though the pose of the earlier figure is simpler and her right hand is partly revealed. Since the Hera is headless, a parallel for the veiled head must be found elsewhere, such as the charming head from Miletos where, however, the tight clinging garment practically fuses with the contours of the skull. In the Sosandra, the mantle is used to create a niche around the head (hence its value as a stock body for portraits), the long drooping lines of the cloth emphasizing the oval of the face.[14]

No other extant statue wears the mantle in quite the same fashion as the Sosandra: certainly not the archaic korai with their shorter diagonal himation so decorative in its zigzag edges, not even the early classical figures, such as the Propylaia kore, with her cloak worn symmetrically over the shoulders and open on the front (Fig. 46). The

---

[13] Follow the softening of this pattern, for instance, on a female head in a private collection, Basel (K. Schefold, "Agorakritos als Erbe des Pheidias," *R. Boehringer* [Tübingen 1957] 545 fig. 1; E. Berger, *AntK* 11:1 [1968] 78-81, pl. 20:4); the head of the young servant in the so-called Cat Stele (Lullies and Hirmer, pl. 182); a female head attributed to the same master (N. Himmelmann-Wildschütz, *MarbWinckPr* [1956] 3-6, pls. 1 and 8) and other monuments. The arrangement is typical for long hair.

A slightly different development from the same initial pattern can be followed through the so-called Cherchel Demeter, the Barberini Suppliant (both illustrated in detail by Dörig, "Kalamis," *JdI* 80 [1965] figs. 83-84 on p. 241 and figs. 19, 21, 23 on pp. 174-76), the Laborde Head (Brommer, *Parthenon-Giebel*, pl. 132) and the female head from the Argive Heraion (Richter, *Sculpture and Sculptors*, fig. 165). The lateral waves over the forehead become progressively more frequent, rounder, more undercut, and from the edges move gradually inward toward the dome until they give way to the wavy furrows of Praxitelean hairstyles, almost at right angle to the forehead. It is interesting to note instead that the hairstyle with "bangs," which characterizes the Hestia Giustiniani and the Penelope, finds no obvious development in later times, perhaps because it was basically adapted from a male coiffure, and it only reappears in classicizing works, when distinctions between male and female renderings were no longer clear.

[14] Entirely different is the effect of the head covering in other more or less contemporary works, such as the Hestia Giustiniani, or the Cherchel Demeter (Boardman/Dörig/Fuchs/Hirmer, pl. 216: there considered the Aphrodite Sosandra by Kalamis).

closest parallel is perhaps to be found in a male figure, a bronze mirror support from Locri, however with head uncovered (Fig. 110). The very voluminous mantle of the Sosandra is used by the artist as if it were a challenge to his ability to show the position of the body underneath. The great simplicity of surfaces made possible by the all-encompassing size of the garment favors abstract contours and a block-like rendering of the body, but this vast expanse has been broken at three salient points by the projection of the left breast, the right arm, and the right knee, with the consequent formation of folds which lead the eye to these crucial points and emphasize the three-dimensionality of the structure. None of these projections, in fact, lies quite in the same plane with the others, and the statue is remarkably appealing from various points of view, with that discreet but definite breaking of the law of frontality, which seems to have been a special pursuit of the Severe artist. Yet there is no denying that the composition is basically frontal: what makes it remarkable is the amount of depth achieved through so little penetration into space. It is the same principle employed in the Herakles Archer of Aegina, as contrasted with its West counterpart, or the difference between the Aristodikos and the Kritian Boy. If one could express this principle in diagrams and geometric terms, one could say that an archaic statue should be viewed from a position at right angles to it: full front, full back, and perhaps from the sides, though those are obviously secondary viewpoints. Severe statues, and the Sosandra in particular, command a visual field of 180 degrees, while the back forms a screen, as it were, a backdrop to the main aspect of the composition.

The most interesting views of the Sosandra are directly from the front and diagonally toward her right side. From this latter point of view one can distinguish patterns not obvious from the front, and lines otherwise only imaginable. From both points of view the composition is revealed as a basic system of triangles, combined in a variety of positions within the rectangular bulk of the draped body: one goes from right shoulder to enveloped hand to left shoulder; another, mostly visible from the side, links the three main projections of the right arm: shoulder, elbow, and hand; a more linear, open version of this pattern is formed by the bending of the opposite arm. The largest and most impressive triangle goes from left shoulder to right elbow to projecting knee, while a right profile view uses one side of this same triangle, takes in the right shoulder and replaces the focus on the left shoulder with one on the right foot. The major diagonal lines linking these focal points are skillfully balanced by straight, or almost straight, verticals, such as the long fold which starts somewhat uncertainly from the left shoulder and ends emphatically over the left foot, as if to call attention to the hidden leg. Another important group of vertical lines is the mass of folds created by the bent left arm, while the whole base of the composition is reinforced by the closely spaced ridges of the undergarment. Finally, a third type of line comes into play: catenaries, long oval curves like chains hanging from two suspension points (hence the name), which indeed depend from the same focal sources as the main triangle but spread out within it like the ripples of water in a pond when a stone has been dropped in its center.

Other statues of later period incorporate the same basic principle of establishing triangular patterns within the main composition, with folds serving as guide-lines to direct the eye. One of the best known, also quite popular in antiquity as a stock body, is the so-called Great Herculanensis, which however destroys the effectiveness of the pattern with the complexity of its folds. Though the basic scheme and pose are the same as in the Sosandra, the result is entirely different and, next to the Severe statue, less pleasing, though quite successful in its own right and for its time, at the end of the Fourth century.

A slightly later statue, the Tyche of Antioch by Eutychides, a pupil of Lysippos, though seated, employs the same principle of points projecting in different planes, this time with a thoroughly three-dimensional effect compatible with the experimentations of the period. But harsh triangular effects are emphasized over verticals and catenaries, and once again the pattern is too complex to be as immediately perceived as in the Sosandra. Closer, though also in Hellenistic terms, is the so-called Baker Dancer (Fig. 109), a bronze statuette of a veiled woman in a twisted position, convincingly dated to the late Third century B.C. The right arm is enveloped by the garment and serves basically the same function of creating a prominent triangle, while similar patterns are visible all over the composition. Here, however, the main difference lies in the fact that the triangles have turned into pyramids and invest the whole structure of the work, as partly true also for the Tyche of Antioch. The spiral motion of the body is therefore infinitely more prominent than the static draping of the mantle, which itself has changed from the heavy cloak of Severe times to the thin material of the Hellenistic period through which the vertical lines of the undergarment can still assert themselves.

These Hellenistic works increase our comprehension of the Sosandra by pointing out the different results achieved with basically the same patterns; among them, it is quite clear that the Severe statue strikes an entirely different note. Yet even works of the same period emphasize the originality and aesthetic value of the Sosandra. As already mentioned, only a mirror support from Locri provides a comparable arrangement of the mantle (Fig. 110), but though the pose is similar, including the stance with the bent right knee, the treatment is entirely different, since the bronze stresses contours rather than inner planes, and the cloak adheres to the body to a point of almost total flatness.[15] Moreover, the right hand emerges from its wrappings at the neck, and its awkward fingers match the diagonal folds of the mantle border, establishing a contrasting pattern of diagonals high in the figure and centered on its vertical axis; conversely the composition of the Sosandra has no central axis and even seems intentionally to deviate the glance of the observer to the periphery in a centrifugal pattern. Equally ineffective is the motif of the wrapped hand in another mirror support, this time a young peplophoros who hides her left hand under the apoptygma and bends such a pointed left knee that it seems to pierce the skirt of the peplos.

Near the Sosandra one can perhaps group the so-called Eleusinian attendants in the Conservatori (Fig. 112) or the "Phokion" in the Vatican (Fig. 113), probably a Hermes restored with an unrelated head, also after an original of ca. 460-450 B.C. Though compositionally the "Phokion" is obviously more sophisticated than the Eleusinian youths and closer to the Sosandra in its use of triangular motifs, it does not attain the same degree of plausibility as the female figure, in that no clear reason is given for the origin

[15] Langlotz (*Magna Graecia*, pp. 276-77) sees in this treatment an example of Ionian influence, as contrasted with the Doric treatment of the Sosandra. For the Hellenistic version of the pose, see the Aeschines in Naples (Fig. 111) (Lippold, *Handbuch*, pl. 108:3) and the Eretria Youth (*BrBr* 519).

The type has recently been discussed by F. Hiller, who dates the prototype ca. 320 B.C. ("Zur Neapler Äschines," *MarbWinckPr* [1962] 53-60, pls. 12-14). It is interesting to note once more this correspondence between Severe and Hellenistic *schemata*, despite the great elaboration of the latter.

and course of its diagonal folds, and the pattern establishes focal points which do not correspond to clear anatomical features.

Only one work seems to come close to the Sosandra in its high quality: the so-called Boy from Tralles (Fig. 114). This remarkable statue has been considered a Greek original of the Hellenistic period, either a representative of the quiet style of the late Fourth–early Third century or of the classical revival of the early First century B.C., though recently it has been tentatively suggested that it might be a Roman copy of such a Greek original rather than the prototype itself. Its similarity with some figures of the Daochos dedication has often been pointed out, but the affinity seems to lie more in the type of garment worn than in the manner of wearing it and in the style of the composition. In its basic simplicity, its emphasis on projecting points created by the arm wrapped in the mantle, its basic frontality with only minor deviations encouraging a diagonal point of view, even the curling of the mantle at the opening, which recalls the Locrian mirror support, the body of the Tralles Youth seems compellingly Severe in style. Yet the position of the crossed legs is incompatible with a dating within the Severe period and more plausible in the Fourth century B.C. The head, with its tightly engraved locks, at first glance seems Polykleitan, but the strong Michelangelo bar of the narrow forehead and the peculiar shape of the face, with the deeply and closely set eyes, the parted mouth, and the hollow temples, obviously belong to a later period. Rather than any of the traditional dates, perhaps a chronology within early imperial times should be accepted, not as the date of the copy, but of the creation of the work, which is not a pastiche in the traditional sense, but rather a complete re-elaboration of motifs from different periods, eclectically fused in a surprising masterpiece. If Fuchs' interpretation is correct, as I believe, the Tralles statue is a funerary monument, and it would seem surprising to have it copied, as indicated by the Terme replica. The piece in Rome, however, does not seem to have been leaning on a pillar, and therefore the whole composition must have been different. Eclectic creations adapted to a variety of arrangements are well attested, as we shall discuss below, and some of them even for funerary purposes.[16] Therefore neither the function nor the reproduction of the Tralles Boy argue against the proposed chronology.

This chapter seems to reflect a position of extreme skepticism: the problem of schools remains unsolved, and neither the "typological" nor the "stylistic gathering" have been accepted as satisfactory methods, the first because of the international character of the period, with the consequent wide diffusion of motifs and formulas, the second because of the inevitable disagreement among scholars, which partly stems from different understanding of each monument, but is mostly caused by the difficulty of assessing Roman copies, the scarcity of Greek originals and the lack of information.[17] This is not to deny

[16] For instance, the Orestes/Elektra group in the Terme and the so-called Ildefonso group in Madrid, both works of the School of Pasiteles (see infra, p. 136). It is, however, not improbable that the type of the Tralles Boy had already been inspired by funerary art: see, e.g. the (not too close) stele in Cyrene (Paribeni, *Catalogo* no. 52 pl. 51; L. Beschi, in *Sculture Greche e Romane di Cirene*, Pubblicazio-

ni Università di Padova, Facoltà di Lettere e Filosofia, Vol. 33, 1959, fig. 40 and pp. 143-45) dated to the Hellenistic period.

Another related work, from Rhodes, has not yet been extensively published (*BCH* 91 [1967] 768 and fig. 6 on p. 769, undated).

[17] As a random example, read the summary of opinions on the so-called Apollo Citharode from

that local schools existed, and that some artists were more influential than others or had a more original style: it is simply to emphasize that at the present state of our knowledge, so pitifully incomplete, it is extremely risky to venture attributions to schools, or even to masters, should they be called Kalamis and Onatas or simply "the Master of Olympia" or "the Master of the Omphalos Apollo." It seems also of relative importance to determine whether a work was created in Argos or Sikyon when there can even be some question whether the work belongs at all to the Severe period or simply reflects Severe style. Much more important is to provide answers to such questions, to be able to evaluate the Severe style wherever it appears, whether within or without the Severe period; only when a basic agreement has been reached on this point, can one hope to proceed to a more refined subdivision and attribution of the truly Severe works.

Pompeii, which might not even be a true copy of a Severe prototype but a classicistic creation (infra, p. 136): C. Saletti, "L'Apollo Citaredo di Pompei," *ArteAntMod* (1960) 248-62 and especially pp. 250-51. Also the book by Beyen and Vollgraff, *Argos et Sicyone*, is highly instructive in this respect.

1. *Head in Berlin—Blond Boy Type*: C. Blümel, *Römische Kopien griechischer Skulpturen des fünften Jhrdt v. Chr.* (Berlin 1931), K 135 pl. 18. It is the head of a youth turned downward and to the left, with spiral curls over the forehead and braids crossing over the nape. It lacks the heavy features characteristic of Severe originals, and chronologically would seem to go back to a later prototype than the Blond Boy or his associates. But the differences may be imputable to the copyist. Blümel suggests that the original was probably in bronze, and made in Magna Graecia during the second quarter of the Fifth century.

2. *The Tiber/Cherchel Apollo*: Paribeni, *Sculture V Sec.* no. 13, with list of replicas. It must be later than the Omphalos Apollo and represents the god in a more youthful stage. The replica in Rome has undoubted classicistic traits, but the original in bronze was probably Severe. The latest discussion (Dörig, *JdI* 80 [1965] 230-36) dates it ca. 450 and attributes it to Kalamis.

3. *The Cyrene/Perinthos type*: It has been recently discussed by L. Polacco (*L'Atleta Cirene-Perinto*, Rome 1955) and Paribeni (*Catalogo*, no. 445, pls. 192-93), but the finding of a new replica from Side, of excellent quality, will probably alter our conception of the prototype. Prof. Jale Inan recognizes in it a Hermes and attributes it to Kresilas: to be published in the forthcoming catalogue of the Sculptures from Side, Pamphylia. Notice the unusual triangular hairline over the forehead, which Prof. Inan rightly compares with the Diomedes supposed to be by Kresilas. Yet a similar hairline (perhaps due to the copyist?), appears on the Lancellotti Diskobolos, obviously Myronian. Poulsen (*ActaA* 11 [1940] 29), though believing the Diomedes to be by Lykios, attributes the Perinthos type to Kresilas on the basis of the similarity with the head of Perikles. Polacco ascribes it to Pythagoras. Paribeni favors a Myronian environment. The date of the prototype is also in dispute, and (as for the following type) oscillates between 460 and 440.

3a. *Youth Monteverdi/Cleveland Type*: W. Amelung, *JdI* 41 (1926) 263-74, ascribed it to the group of the Omphalos Apollo and connected it with the Perinthos head, now known through other replicas (see supra). But the shape of the

hair over the forehead differs so strongly in these two types that they must go back to different originals, as recognized by Poulsen, *ActaA* 11 (1940) 28-33. He attributes the Monteverdi/Cleveland type to Myron's son, Lykios. The type is known through several replicas, the most complete of which is in Cleveland and looks fairly classicistic. The replica in the Terme (Paribeni, no. 30) is the closest to the Severe original, while the head in Corinth (F. P. Johnson, *Corinth 9* no. 4) appears too narrow in the lower part of the face. The date suggested for the type oscillates between 460 and 440.

4. *Anakreon Borghese*: Strictly speaking this statue no longer belongs within the Severe period, since it was probably made around 440 B.C. It is interesting, however, to compare it with the Oinomaos of the Olympia pediment, of which it represents, as it were, the further development. Both figures wear the mantle in the same fashion, rolled around the right arm for variety, and the stance of the poet is the mirror image of that of the king, with added freedom and differentiation in the musculature. A striking trait in the Anakreon is the pronounced tilt of the head, to suggest poetic inspiration.

The most recent and comprehensive discussion of the Anakreon type is in G. M. A. Richter, *The Portraits of the Greeks*, 1 (London 1965), 75-78, figs. 271-90. The only complete statue is in Copenhagen (inv. no. 491), formerly in the Borghese collection, which gives the name to the type (Richter, figs. 278-79, 283, no. 5). The inscribed bust in the Conservatori (Richter, no. 1) is discussed by H. von Heintze in Helbig⁴, no. 1770. An interesting article by Hafner (*JdI* 71 [1956] 1-28) compares the Anakreon Borghese to the so-called Capaneus of the Athena Parthenos shield. The Anakreon has been attributed to Pheidias, Kresilas, Kolotes, and Pythagoras, but without certainty, simply on the assumption that the statue was dedicated by Perikles because it stood on the Athenian Acropolis near the portrait of Xanthippos. Anakreon lived ca. 572-487 B.C.

5. *Goddess Corinth/Mocenigo type*: the best illustration in Boardman/Dörig/Fuchs/Hirmer, pl. 169 right, p. 276 and n. 12 on p. 586. Dörig attributes the prototype to Kalon of Aegina, who is known to have made a statue of Demeter or

Kore which stood under a giant tripod in the Amyklaion near Sparta. E. Homann-Wedeking (*RömMitt* 55 [1940] 208-14) recognizes in the type the Demeter Melaina by Onatas because a replica of the type in Venice (Mocenigo replica) stands near a horse head. But the statue by Onatas was presumably a seated figure and therefore the attribution is doubtful. Poulsen (*SS*, p. 133) considers the statue a classicizing creation, and indeed the peculiar mannerism of the peplos fastened over only one shoulder looks surprising before the Parthenon pediments. Also the way in which the peplos is worn over the chiton, leaving much of the latter uncovered at the hem, is not easily paralleled in Severe works unless a mantle, not a peplos, is worn over the chiton. Yet the statue is so impressively cubic, the treatment of folds so consistent with the Severe period, the stance so similar to that of the "Aspasia/Sosandra" that a Severe prototype is hard to dismiss. Furthermore, an excellent parallel exists in Attic vase painting: an Athena on a RF krater by the Kadmos Painter in the Metropolitan Museum, New York (G. M. A. Richter, *Red-Figured Athenian Vases*, no. 127 pl. 126, dated ca. 440). However, see also the discussion in F. P. Johnson, *Corinth* 9, no. 7 pp. 14-15.

This statue type is usually associated with another, supposedly representing the second Eleusinian goddess (see infra). The theory is strengthened by the fact that the two types were found together in Corinth, though perhaps there the bodies were used for portrait heads. E. Paribeni has tried to associate with the Corinth/Mocenigo body the head Barracco/Budapest, of which a replica exists in the Terme (Paribeni, *Sculture V Sec.* no. 92; *Bolld'A* 40 [1955] 97-102) but the attribution has not met with much favor. The same head-type has been grouped by Schuchhardt with other similar works which he attributes to a Corinthian master, maker of the so-called Candia-type (see infra; Schuchhardt, "Köpfe des strengen Stiles," *Festschrift Weickert* [1955] 59-73). More recently G. Hanfmann has compared the same head-type to that of the Watkins Aphrodite statuette in the Fogg (*AJA* 66 [1962] 281-84; see also infra p. 117 n. 8). The replica of the head in the Barracco collection is discussed by von Steuben in Helbig⁴, no. 1870 and attributed to a NE Peloponnesian master.

If this head (Barracco/Budapest) goes with the Corinth/Mocenigo body, the statue should represent Kore, and the hairstyle would be comparable with that of the Goddess on the Great Eleusinian Relief in the National Museum in Athens.

6. *Goddess Corinth/Conservatori*: A body of this type was found in Corinth together with the previously discussed monument (F. P. Johnson, *Corinth* 9, no. 5, with extensive discussion of previous bibliography). The statue in the Conservatori preserves its head, with rather short corkscrew locks and a youthful appearance (Helbig⁴, no. 1758—von Steuben), but a replica of the same head in the Antiquarium Palatinum (Helbig⁴, no. 2093—see also Paribeni, *Bolld'A* 40, and Becatti, *The Art of Ancient Greece and Rome*, fig. 116 on p. 132) seems definitely elderly and sorrowful. The comparison of the coiffure with that of Demeter on the Great Eleusinian Relief seems to confirm that short locks (in mourning) are appropriate to the Mother rather than the Daughter. But obviously copyists took great liberties with the type. Poulsen (*SS*, p. 133) considers this type (as well as the previous one) classicistic and eclectic, and this opinion is partly shared by Homann-Wedeking (*RömMitt* 55, p. 214). K. Lehmann-Hartleben discusses the head in connection with the Spinario and the Madrid Youth, both of which are not truly Severe, thus endangering his conclusions (*Die Antike* 5 [1929] 85-106). He also believes that the statue derives from an earlier prototype of which the relief in Eleusis with Persephone and an attendant boy (see infra Ch. 7, App. 2) gives another echo. Yet this inference is based on his chronology: ca. 450 the Corinth/Conservatori type, ca. 460 the relief, a dating which has been questioned.

Dörig dissociates this type from the Corinth/Mocenigo (*loc.cit.* no. 5), though he assumes that both originals stood in the Amyklaion. He sees in the Corinth/Conservatori type a replica of the Aphrodite by Gitiadas, and connects it with a third type, of which a replica was also found in Corinth (Corinth-Hierapytna type).

7. *Goddess Corinth/Hierapytna*: The main study of the type is by E. Schmidt, "Zwei Vorläuferinnen der Sappho Albani," *Antike Plastik*, Festschrift W. Amelung 1928, pp. 222-27. The replica in Corinth is discussed by Johnson, *Corinth* 9, no. 6. Dörig (*loc.cit.*) believes this type reproduces the Artemis by Gitiadas which

stood in the Spartan Amyklaion: and indeed the replica from Hierapytna has a quiver strap to confirm the identification. But the replica in Corinth has a wheel next to the right foot, which suggests a Tyche or a Nemesis. A relief in Athens from Megara, which perhaps reproduces the same type (NatMus 1442, Schmidt, *op.cit.*, fig. 5) shows the woman holding a bird, and is tentatively identified as Aphrodite. The most complete replica of the statue (in the Museo Torlonia) and the torso in the Antiquario Comunale have no attribute preserved. It would seem that the type was used for a variety of purposes, and its connection with a famous monument seems to me questionable. More specifically, I should question its "Severe" date: the elaboration of the mantle is more in keeping with a late Fourth century date, and it is only the apparent block-like treatment of the himation hem that vaguely recalls Severe works. Johnson has already doubted that the type is the forerunner of the Sappho Albani (*BrBr* 255).

8. *Peplophoros Ludovisi = Candia Type*: The type is named after a statue found in Kisamos, Crete, and taken to the Herakleion Museum (it is therefore also referred to as "Kisamos type" or "Herakleion type") (Fig. 168). The best replica, though headless, is in the Terme Museum (Paribeni, *Sculture V Sec.*, no. 89) and is restored with a cast of the head after the replica in the Lateran (Helbig⁴, no. 1085, Fuchs; see also no. 1498, replica in the Conservatori, von Steuben). The head-type has been discussed by Schuchhardt, "Köpfe des strengen Stiles," *Festschrift Weickert*, 59-73. The head in New York (G. M. A. Richter, *Catalogue MMA* no. 26 pl. 24 c-d) is a variant, presumably from a statue in chiton and himation. The headless statue in Santa Barbara, California (M. Del Chiaro, *The Collection of*

Greek and Roman Antiquities at the Santa Barbara Museum of Art, 1962 S-3; Idem, "Greek and Roman sculpture in Santa Barbara," *CJ* 60 [1964/65] 113-15 fig. 4) is considered a Graeco-Roman version from Sicily. A small-scale replica of the head was excavated in Ephesos (*AJA* 70 [1966] 157).

The type is the epitome of the Severe peplophoros with hair waving linearly over a high triangular forehead, heavy peplos with kolpos and apoptygma and columnar skirt. The right leg is free, but barely disarrays the fall of the vertical pleats. The apoptygma is distinctive because of the shallow catenary linking the breasts and the two sharp ridges originating from the left shoulder and curving abruptly under the breast to disappear at the edge of the overfold. The metallic appearance of such ridges, as well as the treatment of the skirt, suggest a bronze prototype.

9. *Kneeling figures in Detroit and Naples* (a third specimen in Stockholm, EA 4973, is heavily restored): It is not known whether both or either of these kneeling figures are Greek originals, but probably they are both copies of the same prototype, and might even have been grouped with the statue in Stockholm as a special monument of the perirrhanterion type, perhaps supporting a colossal cauldron. The Naples maiden is illustrated in EA 532, the one in Detroit in *Art in America* 15 (1926) 26 and figs. 3-4; *Bulletin, Detroit Mus. of Art* 4:8 (1923) 65. In later times, both the Naples and the Detroit statues were used as fountains. These figures are remarkable for the linear treatment of their folds crossing over the thighs and gathered in between the legs; the kneeling position is also unusual. They are little known and have been only superficially studied.

FOR PAGE 56

On the mobility of artists see the anecdote related by G. M. A. Richter, *Ancient Italy*, pp. 40-41 (taken from Philostratos the Elder, *Life of Apollonius* 5) and her comments in n. 24.

The ancient allusions to the Attic and Aeginetan styles have been collected by J. J. Pollitt, pp. 225-26.

Blond Boy, Akr. 689: Schrader, no. 302 pls. 125-27, figs. 187-88, pp. 197-99, with the inclusion of the bodily fragments.

FOR PAGE 57

For a list of authors who date the work after the Tyrannicides see L. Alscher, *Griechische Plastik* 2:1, p. 260 n. 7a, text at p. 173.

For an example of whiskers in vase painting see, e.g. Arias and Hirmer, pl. 119 (Kalyx krater in Tarquinia by the Kleophrades Painter).

Attic manufacture with Ionic influence is advocated by M. Bieber, *AthMitt* 37 (1912) 158; Peloponnesian not only by Schuchhardt, but, more recently, Alscher and others.

Carpenter on the Blond Boy: *Greek Sculpture*, pp. 90-96.

FOR PAGE 58

Head in Thessaly: it is usually cited as coming from Halmyros but its provenience is actually Meliboia and it is now in the Volo Museum, inv. no. 532. A recent discussion in H. Biesantz, *Die thessalischen Grabreliefs*, L 17, p. 29, pl. 35, discussion on pp. 128-30. Better illustrations in F. Brommer, *AthMitt* 65 (1940) 63-66, text on pp. 105-7.

Cyrene head: E. Paribeni, *Catalogo*, no. 14 pp. 14-15 pls. 20-21.

Head in Cyprus: M. Markides, *JHS* 33 (1913) 48-49, pl. 1; *AA* (1934), cols. 97-98 fig. 12 and text at col. 99; P. Dikaios, *Guide to the Cyprus Museum*, p. 101, pedestal 27, pl. 20:2.

Head in the Capitoline Museum: E. Paribeni, "Una scultura Greca di Stile Severo dai magazzini del Capitolino," *BdA* 33 (1948), 193-96; L. Alscher, *Götter vor Gericht* (Berlin 1963) fig. 62 a-b; W. Fuchs, in Helbig[4], no. 1692 p. 479.

FOR PAGE 59

Head in Corinth: *BCH* 90 (1966) 749 fig. 1, considered Argive; *AJA* 71 (1967) 297 and pl. 90 fig. 9; *Deltion* 19 (1966) Vol. B:1, p. 128.

Head in Cleveland: no. 28.195; *Cleveland Mus. of Art Bull.* 16 (1929), frontispiece illustration and pp. 7-8; *Art News*, Feb. 9, 1929, p. 22; *Deltion* 13 (1931) 91-92 figs. 32-33; E. Kukahn, *Anthropoide Sarkophaqe in Beyrouth* (Berlin 1955) 34-35 and fig. 12: B. S. Ridgway, "A Greek Head of the Severe Period," *Cleveland Mus. of Art Bull.* 56 (1969) 121-27.

Agrigento Kouros: Richter, Kouroi[2] no. 182 figs. 547-49 (Fig. 92).

FOR PAGE 60

Selinus/Castelvetrano Youth: Langlotz, *Magna Graecia*, pl. 81. This statue was stolen in 1962 but was recovered by Italian Police in March 1968 (Fig. 93).

Apollo Sosianus: Langlotz, *Magna Graecia*, pls. 115-17. See also additional bibliography infra, p. 91, 106.

FOR PAGE 61

For lists of extant replicas of the Omphalos Apollo see Poulsen, SS, 136-39 no. 16, who in 1937 knew a total of 19 items and Paribeni, *Sculture V Sec.* no. 16 pp. 20-21, who in 1953 lists 23; a head was found in 1960 and is now in the Conservatori Museum: Helbig[4], no. 1776. See also *ibid.*, no. 1385 pp. 191-93, for a recent discussion of the subject with a short bibliography (von Steuben). Another interesting summary in G. Mansuelli, *Uffizi, Sculture* 1 (Rome 1958) no. 4 pp. 31-32.

For a date around 470 see Paribeni, *op.cit.*; ca. 450 is advocated by Beyen, in Beyen and Vollgraff, and, most recently, by S. P. Karouzou, *Sylloge Glypton* (Guide to the National Museum, Athens 1967) p. 43 no. 45.

FOR PAGE 62

The Artemision Bronze. Italian scholarship tends to call it also the Zeus of Istieia, from the name of a village near the place where it was found. For bibliography up to 1947 see Beyen and Vollgraff, *op.cit.*, p. 41 n. 1. The most important studies remain that by Ch. Karouzos, "O Poseidon tou Artemisiou," *Deltion* 13 (1930) 41-104; and that by G. Mylonas, "The bronze statue from Artemision," *AJA* 48 (1944) 143-60, where the identification as Zeus is defended.

FOR PAGE 64

Against the association of Omphalos Apollo and Artemision bronze see, e.g. E. Homann-Wedeking, "Zu Meisterwerke des Strengen Stils," *RöMitt* 55 (1940) 196-218.

Against the attribution of the Aegina Sphinx to the Omphalos Apollo School is, e.g. Karouzos, *op.cit.*, p. 91.

Head from the Athenian Acropolis, Akr. no. 2344: G. Dontas, "Un'opera del giovane Fidia?," *ASAtene* 37-38, N.S. 21-22 (1959-1960) 309-20.

For the attribution of this head to Onatas see Dörig, in Boardman/Dörig/Fuchs/Hirmer, p. 278 and pl. 173 left.

Hestia Giustiniani: recently discussed by von Steuben in Helbig⁴, no. 1772 (replica in the Museo dei Conservatori). The similarity to the drapery of the Delphi Charioteer is also pointed out by von Steuben and others.

FOR PAGE 65

For the quote on the Penelope see Paribeni, *Sculture V Sec.*, p. 48 no. 78.

For the attribution of the Penelope to Kalamis see P. Orlandini, *Calamide, Bibliografia e sviluppo della questione dalle origini ai nostri giorni* (1950), passim, and index, p. 110 s.v. Penelope del Vaticano.

"Aspasia"/Sosandra: P. Orlandini, *Calamide, 1°, Le Fonti, 2°, Ricostruzione della Personalità di Calamide attraverso le fonti, 3° Il Problema della Sosandra* (1950).

The statuette inscribed Europé is in the Metropolitan Museum, New York. G. M. A. Richter (*Catalogue*, 1954, no. 30 pl. 29, pp. 25-26) leaves the question of identification open, but other scholars have accepted the inscription at its face value: cf. n. 12 to this chapter, and infra.

Unfinished Sosandra from Baiae: M. Napoli, "Una nuova replica della Sosandra di Kalamis," *BdA* 39 (1954) 1-10; reproduced also in Boardman/Dörig/Fuchs/Hirmer pl. 170, where it is attributed to Kalon.

Youthful head from Gortyna: U. Jantzen, "Meidiama semnon kai lelethos," *Festschrift M. Wegner* (Münster 1962) 17-20. For the type in general see, recently, von Steuben in Helbig⁴, no. 1197, with the tentative suggestion that the type represents Demeter Europa worshiped especially at Lebadeia in Boeotia, homeland of Kalamis.

FOR PAGE 66

Hera of Samos: see, e.g. E. Akurgal, *Die Kunst Anatoliens* (Berlin 1961) 235, fig. 201: *Korai*, no. 55 figs. 183-85. Veiled head: Akurgal, *op.cit.*, pp. 258-59 figs. 221-22; *Korai*, no. 95 figs. 293-95.

FOR PAGE 67

Mirror support from Locri: Langlotz, *Magna Graecia*, pl. 91. Back and side views in Mussche, *Monumenta Graeca et Romana* 5:1, C. Rolley, *Bronzes* (1967) no. 77 pl. 2.

For a similarly large mantle on a female figure cf. the Hera of the Hieros Gamos metope, Selinus Temple E, Langlotz, *Magna Graecia*, pl. 105 (Fig. 35).

Great Herculanensis: Lippold, *Handbuch*, pl. 86:1.

FOR PAGE 68

Tyche of Antioch: Bieber, *Sculpture of the Hellenistic Age²*, fig. 102.

Baker Dancer: D. B. Thompson, "A Bronze Dancer from Alexandria," *AJA* 54 (1950) 371-85. Peplophoros-Mirror support in Copenhagen, Langlotz, *FrühBild* pl. 17b; cf. also pl. 25b for a similar support in Athens.

Eleusinian Attendants in the Conservatori: Beyen and Vollgraff, pl. 11. The most recent discussion by von Steuben in Helbig⁴, no. 1503: three replicas of the Second century A.D. after a prototype of the Severe period (perhaps with some archaistic elements?).

Phokion in the Vatican: Beyen and Vollgraff, pl. 12; W. Fuchs in Helbig⁴, no. 502.

FOR PAGE 69

Boy from Tralles: H. Sichtermann, "Der Knabe von Tralles," *Antike Plastik* 4 (1965) 71-85, pls. 39-52: considered eclectic, early First century B.C.

For the suggestion that it is a copy of a work from ca. 275-250 B.C. see W. Fuchs in Boardman/Dörig/Fuchs/Hirmer, p. 506 and the caption to pl. 282.

Daochos dedication: T. Dohrn, "Die Marmorstandbilder des Daochos-Weihgeschenks in Delphi," *Antike Plastik* 8 (1968) 33-53, pls. 10-37; the statue most closely comparable to the Tralles Boy is Daochos I, discussed on pp. 38-39 and illustrated on pl. 29.

"Tanagra" terracotta figurines, mentioned by Sichtermann (p. 73) as examples of the continuity of fashions, look considerably more complex in the arrangement of their drapery. See, e.g. R. A. Higgins, *Greek Terracottas*, pl. 41 D (Attic, ca. 330-200 B.C.), or S. Mollard-Besques, *Figurines et Reliefs de Myrina*, II (Paris 1963), pl. 154 e-f and pl. 155 f (children).

CHAPTER 6

Discussion of Copies: The Artists

TWO MAIN CRITERIA dominated the production of Roman copies: availability and demand. Obviously a famous original could not be reproduced unless it, or a replica, was available from which to take points for a mechanical reproduction. In some cases pitch was used to make re-casts in bronze, when the original to be copied was accessible and could be touched (or even smeared!) without consequences. In other cases, the monument was not approachable (for instance, the famous chryselephantine statues displayed behind barriers), but could be observed from a distance and a general impression could then be converted into stone. Undoubtedly plaster casts of famous works traveled freely in artistic circles, so that even if a famous original was no longer available, or perhaps happened to be in a different country, a certain workshop could still secure a representation of it from which to make its copies.

As for the second criterion, demand, this was also a necessary prerequisite, since no artist would have made an expensive and time-consuming copy, no matter how mechanical, if he had not believed that there would be a market for it. We know through Pausanias that at least as late as ca. 170 A.D. a good many Severe originals were still available for inspection, many of them donations of famous athletes or wealthy victors in the Olympic games of the early Fifth century B.C., and several dedicated after a victory in more or less private wars among city states. Obviously the subject matter or the historical importance of such pieces could only seldom have had a specific appeal for the Romans: the logical assumption is that if the statue of a victorious athlete was copied, it was not for the renown of its dedicator but for that of its maker.

Artists must have been well known in their own times since they were called upon from far-away places to execute specific monuments: for instance, Theopropos of Aegina made the Corcyran Bull in Delphi (Paus. 10.9.3), and Kalamis executed a group of praying boys in Olympia for the people of Akragas (Paus. 5.25.5). Even when excavation of a specific site has yielded considerable amounts of sculpture made locally, literary sources tell us that a famous master from elsewhere was employed to make a special dedication. For instance, the Thasians had adorned their city gates with sculpture and could boast a native artist as famous as Polygnotos the painter, who was also a bronze caster (Pliny, *NH* 34.85); yet they commissioned Onatas of Aegina to make for them a colossal bronze Herakles to be set up in Olympia (Paus. 5.25.12). Similarly, a monument set up by the Argives in Delphi after the battle of Oinoe in 456 B.C. (?) was made by Hypatodoros and Aristogeiton of Thebes (Paus. 10:10.3-4) although many Argive sculptors of renown existed at that time and are attested through signatures found in Olympia.

Another indication of the mobility of artists is given by the "schools" they attended. For example, Synnoon and his son Ptolichos of Aegina, a site famous for its sculptors, were the pupils of Aristokles of Sikyon (Paus. 6.9.1), and Askaros of Thebes was their fellow pupil (Paus. 5.24.1). Often two masters belonging to different schools collaborated in one monument: e.g. Simon of Aegina and Dionysios of Argos executed the dedication of Phormis in Olympia (Paus. 5.27.2). At times, these dedications involving more than one sculptor were groups, for which it is plausible to assume that each master contributed one figure (e.g. as specifically stated by Pausanias in the above instance, when each artist made a horse and a man). In the case of a single bronze statue it has been suggested that one master might have been the sculptor who made the model and the other the technician who melted the bronze and executed the actual casting, as for example in the case of Kritios and Nesiotes' joint signatures on single-statue bases (see infra, p. 79), or the case of the Hermes Kriophoros dedicated by the Arkadians at Olympia, where both Onatas and Kalliteles are named as the makers (Paus. 5.27.8). But we even have mention of two sculptors working together at a single *marble* statue (e.g. Sokrates and Aristomedes of Thebes, who made of Pentelic marble the statue of the Mother Dindymene dedicated by the poet Pindar: Paus. 9.25.3), and it is difficult to visualize the division of tasks in such cases, or to assess which of the two determined the style and appearance of the work.

It is also interesting to find that artists worked in more than one medium. We have already mentioned Polygnotos who was at the same time painter and bronze-caster, though his first activity overshadowed his second. Another such artist was Mikon of Athens (Paus. 6.6.1; Pliny, *NH* 34.88). Other masters worked in marble and bronze, but also in wood: Kanachos of Sikyon, for instance, made a cedar-wood statue of Apollo for the Ismenion in Thebes (Paus. 9.10.2); and Kallon of Aegina made a xoanon of Athena for her temple on the Troezenian acropolis (Paus. 2.32.5). The akrolithic and the chryselephantine techniques were also in vogue during the Severe period: Menaichmos and Soidas of Naupaktos made a gold-and-ivory statue of Artemis for Kalydon (Paus. 7.18.9-10) and Pheidias' statue of Athena Areia at Plataia, built from the spoils of Marathon, had a wooden body and extremities of Pentelic marble (Paus. 9.4.1).

Pheidias is so well known for his work on the Parthenon that he seems almost synonymous with high classical sculpture; yet the beginning of his career must date well back into the Severe period, and an attempt has even been made to attribute to him one of the earliest statues in the new Severe style, Angelitos' Athena. The same must apply to the famous Polykleitos, though a recent study would place his birth around 460 b.c. and the beginning of his career around 435, therefore well out of the Severe period. Conversely some sculptors, for instance Ageladas of Argos, Kanachos of Sikyon, and Onatas and Kallon of Aegina, must have been active in the late archaic period, though several of their works were probably created after 480 b.c. This state of affairs obviously emphasizes the difficulty of confining the Severe style to the thirty years span 480-450 b.c.

Other difficulties are created by the discrepancy between information and evidence. J. J. Pollitt's Introduction to his *Art of Greece* admirably summarizes the nature and reliability of ancient literary sources, and his main points can be repeated here with profit. Besides the many drawbacks caused by lacunose text, variants in the readings or faulty transcriptions, there are the problems connected with the very nature of extant ancient sources, chiefly that their authors lived much later than the artists about whom they wrote and that most of them were not dealing intentionally and directly with art as such but mentioned monuments and masters only parenthetically, digressionally, or with ulterior motives. The authors themselves have been classified by Pollitt as: *compilers of tradition*, who related "popular criticism" and anecdotical information; *literary analogists*, who were far more interested in producing a well-turned epigram, a startling image, or an hyperbolic metaphor than in describing a work of art; and *moral aestheticians*, who investigated art only for its potential impact on man. The most important group, that of the artists themselves, has left its literary echoes only in works of other writers. The one "professional critic," Xenokrates, who seems to have been Pliny's main source of information, lived in the early Third century B.C. He therefore evaluated earlier artists by Hellenistic standards, which emphasized naturalism and technical ability, and thus his aesthetic judgment is bound to be vitiated by this fundamental, if unintentional, bias.

Difficulties exist also with the most objective and impersonal of ancient sources: the purely factual account of Pausanias in his travelogue of Greece. He mentions many works which have disappeared without trace, and names many artists who are otherwise unknown to us. In general, it can be stated that many monuments, allegedly famous through their mention in literary sources, either were not copied extensively in Roman times or have not been recognized among the extant replicas. Similarly many artists are known only because named by ancient authors: the signature of Kanachos of Sikyon, for instance, has not survived on any ancient monument, and even the prolific Kalamis is only represented epigraphically by a fragmentary base from the Athenian agora. Conversely, other masters are known to us only because their names are inscribed on some of the extant statue bases; one of them is Sotadas of Thespiae, whose signature appears on a block sometimes attributed to the monument of the Delphi Charioteer. Other such masters are Diopeithes of Athens, and a whole group of Argive sculptors: Argeiadas, Atotos, and Asopodoros, who together with Athanodoros of Achaia erected a large monument in Olympia.

Finally, even when both literary sources and epigraphical monuments preserve the name of a sculptor, they often differ in its spelling, and sometimes so drastically as to suggest different individuals. The ethnic of the artist may also vary, and in some cases chronological discrepancies arise between the letter forms of the preserved signatures and the floruit given by Pliny or the date related by Pausanias.

Modern scholarship has dealt variously with the available information. On a factual basis, extant artists' signatures have been collected, first by E. Loewy in his pioneering work, *Inschriften griechischer Bildhauer* (1885), and now by J. Marcadé, *Recueil des Signatures de Sculpteurs Grecs*, of which two volumes have appeared to date (1953 and 1957 respectively). The author follows the method of cataloguing artists' signatures by sites: the first book deals with the inscriptions at Delphi, the second with those on Delos; but once a master is represented by an inscribed monument at either site, a complete dossier of all his other preserved signatures and general information are included. A similar work, though limited to the finds on the Athenian acropolis, and to the Sixth and Fifth centuries B.C., has been compiled by A. Raubitschek (*Dedications from the Athenian Acropolis*, Cambridge 1949), who supplements the catalogue of the inscriptions with a general discussion on the individual masters represented by the finds.

More numerous are the works concerned with literary sources, beginning with the fundamental sylloge by J. Overbeck, *Die antiken Schriftquellen zur Geschichte der bildenden Künste bei den Griechen* (Leipzig 1868). Various critical translations of ancient sources have followed: K. Jex-Blake and E. Sellers, *The Elder Pliny's Chapters on the History of Art* (London 1896) is perhaps the best known, but quite important is also S. Ferri's *Plinio il Vecchio* (1946). J. J. Pollitt expands Overbeck's initial scheme by including Architecture among the arts and enlarging the time bracket (*The Art of Greece 1400-31 B.C.*, Sources and Documents in the History of Art Series, edited by H. W. Janson, 1965).

Finally there are the various encyclopaedias: the most specific for our purpose, though including artists of all periods and areas, is U. Thieme and F. Becker, *Künstler-Lexikon* (1907-1950). Important articles under the individual artists' names are to be found in A. Pauly and G. Wissowa, *Realencyclopädie der klassischen Altertumswissenschaft* (Stuttgart 1894, to date), and in the *Enciclopedia dell'Arte Antica* (1958-1966).

The realm of monographs and individual articles on single masters is too vast to be reviewed here; important works have already been mentioned and some will be cited in conjunction with what follows. It is impossible to give a comprehensive summary of evidence and attributions for all the masters known to have worked in the Severe period. We shall attempt here to outline briefly only a few representative careers, and some of the problems connected with attributions to such masters.

In roughly chronological order, the most frequently mentioned artists of the Severe style are Kanachos of Sikyon, Ageladas of Argos, Kallon and Onatas of Aegina, Hegias (or Hegesias, probably the teacher of Pheidias), Kritios and Nesiotes, Pythagoras of Samos/Rhegion, Kalamis and Myron. Pheidias and Polykleitos, though they must have started their career, or at least their training, during the Severe period, are best left out of this account. Of these masters we shall discuss Kritios and Nesiotes, Pythagoras, Myron, and, very briefly, Kalamis.

KRITIOS AND NESIOTES

There is a certain basic agreement in reconstructing the activity of these two masters, famous principally because of the Tyrannicide group they made in replacement of the original monument by Antenor, which had been taken away by the Persians in 480 B.C. Since the *Marmor Parium* dates the replacement group to 477-476 B.C., the activity of the two artists must have started before that period, but their great popularity must postdate that important monument and was probably determined by it. Pliny (*NH* 34.49) places their *akme* in the 83rd Olympiad, 448-444 B.C., but both Fuchs and Bieber agree that this date can only represent the lowest limit of their career. Raubitschek ventures a birth-date also: ca. 510 for Kritios, ca. 525 for Nesiotes, since this latter was already active around 500 B.C., if he can be identified with the master who signed the dedication of Alkibios, a cithara player (Raubitschek no. 84).

We do not know why the two masters collaborated in all their signed works, though it has been speculated that one was the sculptor and the other the caster. But other examples, already mentioned, indicate that artists collaborated even in the making of a marble statue, and therefore the association might have been determined by other factors which escape us. Very probably it was only a matter of economics, time, and convenience.

The ancient sources mention Kritios and Nesiotes solely in connection with the Tyrannicide group; only Pausanias (1.23.9) gives a brief description of a statue on the Athenian acropolis which he attributes to Kritios alone. The base of this work has, however, survived and shows the typical joint signature (Raubitschek no. 120). We therefore know the two masters' range of activity only through the epigraphical evidence, which comes exclusively from Athens, and it should be emphasized, more than it is currently done, that this by necessity results in a somewhat slanted picture. It should be a logical assumption that their popularity brought them outside commissions. On the other hand, attempts to connect the two sculptors or their workshop with extant statuary in different areas (such as Chamoux's attribution of the Delphi Charioteer), are based exclusively on stylistic criteria and therefore bound to be controversial. The two masters' popularity might have remained purely local.

Of the six signed bases from the Acropolis, one carried the statue of a hoplitodromos and has been dated after 480, mostly because it was seen by Pausanias. A bronze statuette in Tübingen is considered a forerunner of this work, but since it is earlier (Bieber, Fuchs), and perhaps even Aeginetan (Fuchs), it can hardly be used in an evaluation of the masters' style. The other five statue bases carried: 1) a bronze statue in an active pose (i.e. with footprints wide apart) dedicated by Ekphantos and Hegelochos in obtaining Athenian citizenship; it might have been an Athena of the Promachos type (Fuchs) or a warrior (Raubitschek); 2) a bronze statue of some size, possibly a horse and horseman, dedicated by Aristokles; 3) a statue standing quietly with feet close together, either an Athena like Angelitos', or a kore, since a kouros is unlikely as a dedication to Athena by two men, Aristeas and Ophsios (Raubitschek); 4) and 5) are too fragmentary to suggest the composition of the statues they supported but presumably these were also of bronze. Two more bases have been tentatively connected with the masters by Raubitschek on the basis of the similarity in the letter forms, but they carry no signatures and add nothing to our knowledge. Conversely, the base connected by Raubitschek with the Kritian Boy (no. 21) has letter forms of an entirely different type from those used on the signed works.

It is important to note that two of the signed statue bases (nos. 1 and 2, Raubitschek nos. 121 and 123) were re-employed in Roman times; Raubitschek plausibly assumes that only the inscriptions were changed, and not the statues, since the Greeks often honored the Romans by rededicating to them famous statues of a much earlier period. This forceful presentation to the Romans of works in the Severe style must have increased their interest in the art of that period.

With the archaeological evidence as a guide, we can say that the two masters worked exclusively or mainly in bronze, and adhered to a fairly traditional repertoire of statues in quiet poses as well as in action: the Tyrannicides group constituted an exception since it reflected contemporary historical events and can, therefore, be considered an unusual theme. On the other hand, this work was simply a replacement of an earlier monument with the same subject, and, as it is known to us through later copies, it made use of action motifs already employed in vases and the minor arts. This group is safely identified in Roman full-scale replicas, and must be our only criterion in evaluating the sculptors' style. All other attributions are unsafe: they range from the "forerunners" (the statuette in Tübingen) to some of the earliest Parthenon metopes. The most insistent tradition, that of assigning to the team the Kritian Boy, originated with Furtwängler, but it has nothing to recommend it except the general style and the obvious influence from bronze. Even the echoes noticed by Fuchs in the Selinus metopes can be called more appropriately Attic Severe than Kritian.

The Tyrannicides have been discussed in detail by S. Brunnsåker, and more recent studies have added little to our knowledge. Only two points deserve specific mention in

80

this context: the relative paucity of known Roman copies and the relationship of the second monument to the first.

Since the first group of Harmodios and Aristogeiton was taken away by the Persians in 480/479 B.C., all representations on vases or other objects prior to 330 B.C. must reproduce the replacement. Its popularity in antiquity is attested not only by these fairly faithful reproductions in the minor arts, meant to be recognized as replicas of the famous group, but also by the many echoes of the composition in architectural sculpture. After Alexander's victory over Persia, the first group was recovered and returned to Athens, where it was placed alongside the Kritian group, and was therefore available for copying in Roman times, yet ancient sources still mention only Kritios and Nesiotes in connection with their Tyrannicides (indeed, to the exclusion of all their other works), and it is perhaps plausible to assume that it is their group which continues to be copied. But surprisingly enough, there are few full-scale replicas of this very important monument.[1] Aristogeiton is represented by one statue (Fig. 117), two torsos and two heads (or maybe only one), while of Harmodios exist merely one entire statue, one torso, and two heads. Compared to the twenty or so replicas which the Omphalos Apollo and the Sosandra can boast, the number seems small indeed, even though only one each of the replicas belongs to a definite set and therefore the others can potentially represent a maximum of seven additional groups.

At least the entire Aristogeiton in Rome seems to date from the First century B.C. since it was found with fragments of Republican inscriptions, and the shape of its tree-trunk support corroborates this chronology. Why so few replicas in Roman imperial times? The conclusion is inevitably that the monument was not appreciated for its artistic quality but only for its subject, which therefore was too outspokenly "democratic" for an imperialistic regime. It may also be inferred, though very tentatively since available information is so scanty, that Kritios and Nesiotes were therefore not famous as great sculptors but only for the anecdotical value of their work, which would explain the silence of the sources as to the rest of their production. Their popularity in Athens might have been limited to their own time and perhaps even to their own environment, though Kritios is mentioned as head of a "school" (Pliny, *NH* 34.85; Paus. 6.3.5).

---

[1] The list of replicas, as derived from Brunnsåker, is as follows:

Harmodios (H)
1) Statue in Naples
2) Torso in Frankfurt am Main
3) Head in New York
4) Head, Rome, Terme Museum

Aristogeiton (A)
1) Torso in Naples (head is a cast)
2) Torso, Boboli, Florence
3) Torso, Rome, Conservatori
4) Head, Rome, Vatican/Conservatori
5) Head, Rome, Conservatori, Museo Nuovo
6) Head, Madrid (Pherekydes)

Among these works, the only definite set is in the Naples Museum (H 1 and A 1), and is supposed to come from Hadrian's Villa at Tivoli, though on uncertain evidence. The Aristogeiton (A 1) was once restored with a nonpertinent (Lysippan?) head, which has now been replaced by a cast of Head A 4. This latter was once in the Vatican Magazines, but in 1957 was given in exchange to the Conservatori Museum since it was noticed that it belonged to torso A 3 (Figs. 115-16), which may now therefore be considered a complete statue and seems to be of Republican date. F. Coarelli ("Le Tyrannoctone du Capitole et la mort de Tiberius Gracchus," *MélRome* 81 [1969] 137-60) has now advanced the interesting hypothesis that A 3/4 was erected in 52 B.C. to commemorate the assassination of T. Gracchus (in 133 B.C.). The group was set up on the Capitoline under the consulship of Metellus Scipio. Aristogeiton's head no. 5 has been attributed to Antenor: see infra, p. 82.

Raubitschek indeed suggests that they may have just copied, "though in their own style," the statues by Antenor. There is no question that Antenor was an important sculptor of the archaic period; since traits of the Severe style were already present before 480 B.C., the replacement group might have closely followed the earlier work and still appear to us as Severe. This could be especially true if the first monument was set up after Marathon, as it has been claimed; yet Antenor must have been dead by 477, or he would have been asked to replace the stolen monument. It is difficult to believe that an artist, at the end of his career, could work in the latest style.[2]

In 1956 E. Langlotz tried to throw some light on the problem by advocating that the Aristogeiton head in the Conservatori (A 5) was a replica of the statue by Antenor and not of that by Kritios and Nesiotes. Indeed the differences between the head once in the Vatican (A 4) and the Conservatori head are noticeable (Figs. 116-17): the very structure of the heads is different, as well as the treatment of hair, eyes, beard, and cheeks. Fuchs penetratingly pointed out these discrepancies, but concluded that they arise from the freedom with which the copyist of the Conservatori head reproduced his original, perhaps in the Third century A.D. This is a possibility not to be discounted, especially in view of the wide range of renderings noticeable in undisputed replicas of the same work; yet the difference between the two heads remains rather remarkable. What is particularly interesting is that, against Langlotz's argument, the Conservatori head looks more advanced than that generally assigned to Kritios and Nesiotes, while the attribution to Antenor should make it definitely earlier. The large eyes, the shape of the lids, the way in which the moustache frames the mouth, and especially the use of the drill in the center of the spiraling curls of the beard, strongly recall some of the centaurs in the Parthenon metopes and some of the renderings in the Olympia sculptures; the modeling of the cheeks, seemingly a point in favor of the earlier date, finds a good parallel in the face of the Artemision bronze. Nothing prevents an interpretation of the head as a replica of a different statue, not a divinity because of the short hair, and not the Aristogeiton of the traditional group because different, but perhaps another citizen, or, more probably, a herm, since neither the "true" Aristogeiton nor the Conservatori head can be considered portraits in the modern sense of the word but remain elderly types.

Stylistically, notice how similar the silhouette of Aristogeiton is to the Artemision bronze (Fig. 98), not because they may be by the same master, but because they are based on the same principle of eloquent contours. The system of triangles so effective in the deity is, however, less obvious in the Tyrannicide since his balance is different and the body is definitely thrust forward. Despite this emphasis on outlines one wonders how clearly they could be seen once the composition stood on its base: the fragments of the original pedestal in fact prove that the two Tyrant-slayers shared a single podium, though the replicas in Naples have individual plinths. Scholars still disagree as to the proper arrangement of the two figures in relation to one another, but the "eloquent silhouette" should be a major criterion in the reconstruction of the group. It is also sig-

[2] M. Robertson has indeed suggested to me that perhaps Antenor had not made a true group, but merely two statues of more or less Kouros type: "a late archaic Kleobis and Biton." This theory might explain our difficulty in recognizing the earlier Tyrannicides. J. Dörig ("La tête Webb, l'Harmodios d'Anténor et le problème des copies Romaines d'après des chefs-d'œuvre Archaïques," AntK 12 [1969] 41-50) believes that the Archaistic-looking Webb head is a Roman replica of Antenor's Harmodios.

nificant, as others have already pointed out, that the "victim" of the Tyrannicides' attack is not represented, not only because the subject of the representation is the goal and not the very action but also because it is typical of the Severe style to present only the "antecedents" of a fact, or else just those elements which allow the spectator to come to a complete mental reconstruction. This element of participation required from the viewer recurs again in the Hellenistic period and provides one more link between the styles of the two periods.

PYTHAGORAS

Pliny (*NH* 34.59-60) and Diogenes Laertius (8.46) distinguish two artists by this name, one of Samos and one of Rhegion. The one signature preserved on a statue base at Olympia, for the boxer Euthymos of Locri Epizephyri, is accompanied by the ethnic Samian. Pythagoras was probably one of those Samians who left their island in 496 B.C. and emigrated to Rhegion; this would explain the double ethnic and, given the coincidence in time and activity, it is improbable that there were two separate sculptors by the same name. The chronological range of Pythagoras' activity is based on the works attributed to him by the ancient sources, and goes from ca. 480 to ca. 448 B.C. He is said to have been a pupil of Klearchos of Rhegion (Paus. 6.4.4), and the teacher of Sostratos, Dameas, and Patrokles. He seems to have sculpted exclusively in bronze, and especially for victorious athletes: of the fifteen works attributed to him by the literary sources, eight represent victory monuments, seven of which were erected in Olympia and one in Delphi. He was otherwise active in the various cities of Sicily and South Italy, and does not seem to have been represented in Athens by any of his statues. Ancient sources praise him for his attention to the rendering of hair and veins, features typical of the Severe style in general, as already seen at Olympia. He was also famous for his "rhythmos" and "symmetria."

The range of his works is quite representative: the athletes he portrayed were runners, boxers, hoplitodromoi, wrestlers, pankratiasts, and even a charioteer, shown with his team and with a Nike standing by him on the chariot; though three out of the seven Olympic victors were from Magna Graecia, the others were two from Cyrene, and two from Arcadia (Stymphalos and Mantinea), and one wonders whether commissions for the great sanctuaries such as Delphi and Olympia were given to artists not only for their ability but also for their availability at the site. Of the mythological monuments we hear of a winged Perseus, Apollo killing the Python, Eteokles and Polyneikes killing each other, a limping man, probably Philoktetes, a group of male figures, of which seven were naked and one elderly (a puzzling description which has been interpreted to mean the Seven against Thebes), and finally his one reported female figure: Europa on the Bull. One more work is known through an anecdote: within the deep folds of a statue in Thebes, representing Kleon playing the lyre, somebody hid a treasure in gold and recovered it after thirty years, so that the statue earned the epithet "just" (Pliny, *NH* 34.59; Athenaion, *Deipn.* 1.19c quoting Polemon).

All this information is purely academic, even when supported by inscriptions on statue bases. A remarkable group of bronze statuettes (Fig. 118) has been attributed to the style of Pythagoras, but probably as reminiscent of the sculptor's manner rather than works of his hands. They show all the traits of the Severe style, and especially a certain massiveness of the head, with hair treated as a smooth cap, reminiscent of the athlete on the Nisyros stele. Since, however, these bronzes are all originals of the Severe period, they cannot be considered copies of famous large-scale works by Pythagoras; they can at best be only adaptations and are therefore rather questionable as a basis for stylistic judgments on Pythagoras, though useful for our knowledge of the Severe style in general.

A more likely attribution, though also partly based on comparisons with the statuettes, is the strange Diskobolos Ludovisi, a hip-herm now in the Terme (Fig. 119). That the original composition was a complete statue is proved by the recent find of another replica in Side, Pamphylia, of excellent quality, and it is surprising that a prototype of such vigor and potential motion was not more extensively copied in Roman times. Contrary to the pendulum-like pattern of Myron's Diskobolos, the Ludovisi athlete appears more self-contained, and his motion seems to expand upward rather than sideways, as is often the case in Severe action poses.

Of other works, the Delphi Charioteer has been attributed to the Magna Graecian sculptor simply because dedicated by one of the Deinomenids of Sicily. The Cirò Apollo (Fig. 158) (see infra Ch. 8) qualifies also, purely for its provenience. S. Stucchi had tried to connect an original marble Apollo in Rome with the Apollo shooting the Python made by Pythagoras for Kroton and represented on coins of that city; but the valid criticism that the original was of bronze destroys this attractive hypothesis. The Pythagorean Perseus has been recognized in two heads, one in the British Museum (Fig. 120) and one in Rome (Fig. 121). Only the latter betrays distinctive Severe style traits. This attribution, however, rests on the fact that the literary sources mention only Pythagoras and Myron as having made statues of Perseus, and in fact, with equal impartiality and more emphasis, the type has been also attributed to Myron. Carpenter has questioned the date of the original, which he would place at the end of the Fifth or the beginning of the Fourth century B.C., and also its identity since Hermes would be just as appropriate an identification as Perseus. On the basis of such tenuous evidence it is impossible to reconstruct what must have been a major personality in the Severe period.[3]

MYRON

He is perhaps the best-known sculptor of the Severe period, our first instinctive mental association when we think of the art of that time. Yet he is not better known than Kritios and Nesiotes, though many more attributions have been made to his name. The "Perseus" has already been mentioned in connection with Pythagoras, which in itself invalidates the Myronian candidacy for the work. Of all the many other sculptures mentioned by

---

[3] Mrs. Ch. Hofkes-Brukker seems to hint at a similar skepticism in the title of her article quoted in the bibliography; yet she reaches a definition of Pythagorean style as the "rhythm of unbound movement." This definition may perhaps be correct on the basis of the monuments considered (which indeed are all quite different from contemporary statuary in their rendering of motion), but it does not rest on any *proved* identification of Pythagorean works. Another trait sometimes advocated as a Pythagorean hallmark is the impressionistic rendering of the hair calotte; this however could be just a feature of the Severe style rather than of a specific master. Parallels can be found among the Olympia sculptures, but this evidence can be used in two ways: either to advocate the wide diffusion of the practice or to equate the Olympia master with Pythagoras, as it has indeed been suggested (see, e.g. L. Polacco, *L'Atleta Cirene-Perinto* [Rome 1955] 32). Theoretically, this possibility cannot be excluded, since the Magna Graecian artist was active in Olympia at the appropriate time, but the dangers of attributing sculptures purely on the basis of hair renderings are obvious.

the literary sources, the only definite identification is that of his Diskobolos (Fig. 122), so clearly described by Lucian (*Philopseudes* 18), and attempts are made periodically to define exactly which moment of the athletic activity is being portrayed. The marble translations of an original in bronze inevitably flatten and damage the composition, but the artificiality of the pose should not be entirely blamed on the Roman copyists. Other Severe works have already shown that the Severe artist relied on the "eloquent silhouette" and enjoyed the play of patterns and geometric forms within his composition. It is therefore somewhat superfluous to determine exactly which moment is chosen in the action of discus-throwing: it is obviously that in which the human body can more readily be expressed as a geometric formula: a zigzagging line topped by the arc of a pendulum. As in the Artemision bronze, a system of triangles is created around and within the figure, which is best appreciated from a single point of view. The "internal" anatomy is immobile, though the body strongly bends and moves: it is therefore a motion of outlines rather than of muscular masses, and the Omphalos Apollo, with his slanting hips, constitutes a more correct representation of movement than the "distorted" Diskobolos.

The other work most often attributed to Myron is the group of Athena and Marsyas. Pliny's passage alone (*NH* 34.57) is not sufficient to prove that the two figures were juxtaposed in a single composition; indeed, Pollitt's translation introduces a comma between the listing of the two works, thus breaking the connection. The original Latin text has no such punctuation as an aid to the interpretation, and the possibility of such a Myronian group must be left open; yet all other works within the same list seem individual entries. Apparent support for a joint arrangement is given by Pausanias (1.24.1) who describes a group of Athena and Marsyas on the Athenian acropolis without mentioning the sculptor, and representations of such a group appear on Roman coins and works of the minor arts. Yet all these depictions vary not only from the group as reconstructed, but also from each other in many details. The figure of Athena, in particular, appears in two versions, one definitely more advanced in style than the other, so that the possibility of two different groups has been mentioned.

The reconstruction of the group through extant Roman statuary copies took the initial move from the literary references; suitable types were found, which might fit the description, and the monument is now traditionally recomposed with the Frankfurt Athena and the Lateran Marsyas. The satyr has been questioned by Carpenter, who on the basis of the statue's anatomy and pose would date it in the late Fifth–early Fourth century B.C. The chronology of the original group is not established by external factors, but it is usually assumed that the myth was exploited to allude to the friction between Athens and Boeotia, which ended in open conflict between 457 and 447 B.C. Myron's activity is documented from ca. 480 to 440 B.C. since one of the athletic victories commemorated by a Myronian monument occurred in 444. Even if the Athenian group were considered one of his last works, Carpenter's dating of the Marsyas would effectively eliminate it from the composition.

Yet of the two statues the Lateran Marsyas is the one which more closely resembles the ancient reproductions in the minor arts. The Frankfurt Athena is more difficult to reconcile with them, either because the type was not copied with great fidelity, or because the image on the coins is poorly preserved; finally, in some, it appears entirely different in attire.[4] The Frankfurt type (Figs. 123-24) remains within the sphere of the late Severe style, though perhaps created shortly after 450 B.C.,[5] but there is no assurance that the original belonged to Myron or that it was part of a group. The lateral displacement of the foot occurs also in isolated statues, as well as the turn of the head, though (erroneously?) exaggerated in the Frankfurt replica. The face, especially the copy in Dresden, with its marked oval and heavy-lidded large eyes, is as closely related to the Diskobolos as, for instance to the "Aspasia" head in Crete; the hairstyle, especially in the profile view, recalls the Aegina sphinx (Figs. 51-52) on the one hand, the Iris of the Parthenon East frieze on the other. Finally, to my knowledge, never was the Athena type found with the Marsyas type, as to be expected if both were part of a famous composition. In view of all these problematical points, it seems best to eliminate the two statues from an evaluation of Myronian style.

Other attributions have been made, but with even greater difficulty. More information can be derived from the list of works mentioned in Pliny and other ancient sources, from which we learn that Myron worked also in wood (he made a wooden Hekate for Aegina, Paus. 2.30.2) and represented mythological subjects and deities as well as athletes. Poulsen has advocated that the Artemision bronze is Myron's Erechtheus fighting Immarados, a monument which stood on the Athenian acropolis, and that the Omphalos Apollo is one of two statues of that god mentioned among the artist's works. Most recently J. Dörig has recognized Myron's Erechtheus in a bust in the Boboli Gardens, Florence. Epigrams seem to bestow the greatest praises to Myron's cow as an example of superb naturalism. This rendering would be hardly in keeping with the style of the Severe period, and it is therefore logical to suspect that the writers were more interested in making florid poetry than in describing accurately. Also the realism of the runner Ladas appears to have been exaggerated by this poetic muse.

Echoes of Myron's style have been detected in the Parthenon metopes; the head of his Diskobolos has been judged under Polykleitan influence, and Pheidias' art is supposed to have had a great impact on the end of Myron's production. On the basis of the available evidence, the Roman copies of the Diskobolos, such judgments cannot fail to seem somewhat arbitrary.

[4] Carpenter has already noted that the Athena on the Finlay vase reproduces that of the Madrid Puteal, and therefore ultimately the Athena of the Parthenon East pediment; the red-figure oinochoe from Vari has an Athena impossible to match with a known statuary type.

[5] At first glance the complexity of the Athena's drapery, especially in certain replicas as the one in Reggio Calabria, may suggest a date well into the high classical period. But a comparison with the relief of the "Mourning Athena" may prove useful in this respect. In this latter the folds at the waist already tend to form a V-pattern, quite different from the perpendicular rendering in Angelitos' Athena. This V-motif is elaborated further in the Frankfurt Athena and will lead eventually to the pronounced effect of the Athena Parthenos. In the Frankfurt replica, the wide panel of the apoptygma below the belt may recall Fourth century renderings, for instance the Dresden Artemis Type (Rizzo, *Prassitele*, pls. 16-17); but other copies (e.g. the one in Reggio) break the smoothness of the area with additional folds. The left foot held sideways disturbs the over-all rectangular pattern, but not more so than in the Athena Parthenos, as exemplified by the Varvakeion statuette. Finally, and perhaps most convincingly, the straight accent at the waist and the almost completely exposed belt strongly contrast with high classical renderings, where the curve of the kolpos is emphasized, or the fullness of the cloth at the waist covers most of the belt on either side of the central knot.

KALAMIS

He shares with Pythagoras the dubious honor of being widely mentioned by ancient sources without being represented today by any definitely identified monument. He was obviously one of the great masters of the Severe period, probably a Boeotian but mainly active in Athens, where one of his signatures has perhaps been recovered. His problem is further complicated by the fact that a Younger Kalamis might have existed since some of the monuments and pupils attributed to the important master seem to belong to too late a period. Orlandini resolves the question in favor of two homonymous sculptors, a perfectly plausible supposition. Dörig, in a recent study, reconstructs an entirely different artistic personality and lowers the span of his activity to the period between 466 and 430, thus attempting to reconcile both early and late evidence. Despite their great scholarship, neither of these studies seems based on adequate and objective evidence. Every important monument of the Severe period has at some point been attributed to Kalamis—but also to Onatas or to other masters. It is simpler to admit that his name remains for us within the realm of academic information.

In conclusion it should be stressed once more that we possess many more names of artists than works attributed to them by the literary sources, and conversely many more works than is licit to attribute on the basis of available information. The modern tendency of assigning all available sculpture to a few great masters known through the ancient sources resembles the ancient tendency of assigning to Homer all the "Homeric" poems. Another factor, not often kept in mind, is the high competence and general ability of ancient Greek sculptors: many monuments of high quality may have been made by masters of little or no renown with the Romans. As already suggested, a commission might have depended on other factors than simply the fame of the sculptors, and perhaps the availability of an artist at a specific sanctuary might have been responsible for some of his contacts and orders. In view of the kaleidoscopic picture presented by our information on ancient sculptors of the Severe period, we should conclude again that the time for attributions to individual masters has not yet come, or at least that such pursuit should not take precedence over research on the period as a whole.

APPENDIX 6

The following accounts are outlines only, mostly based on the articles in the *EncArAn*, whose authors are named in parentheses at the beginning of each "sketch." The arrangement is in rough chronological order.

Kanachos of Sikyon (G. Carettoni)
Late archaic master (second half of the 6th c.), contemporary of Hageladas of Argos.

WORKS

1) Apollo Philesios for Miletos; taken to Persia by Darios (494 B.C., though Pausanias and Strabo say it was Xerxes), brought back by Seleukos I. In bronze, with mechanism to make deer on right hand rock.
2) Wooden replica of Apollo Philesios for Hismenion in Thebes
3) Boys playing ball
4) Chryselephantine statue of seated Aphrodite with apple and poppy, for Sikyon
5) Muse playing the pipes

Hageladas (Ageladas) of Argos (P. Orlandini)
Teacher of Myron, Pheidias, and Polykleitos (?). His activity is made to range from ca. 529 to 450; some scholars advocate two homonymous masters. (For other recent discussions see Amandry, *Charites* [1957] 73-74, and Donnay, *AntCl* 34 [1965] 457-58.)

Pliny's floruit in 432 B.C. is a chronological impossibility. His son Hargeiadas is mentioned in an inscription at Olympia of the beginning of the 5th century.

WORKS

1) Olympia—statue of Aniochos of Tarentum (ca. 520 B.C.)
2) Olympia—statue of Kleosthenes of Epidauros (ca. 516 B.C.)
3) Olympia—quadriga, Timasitheos of Delphi (ca. 507 B.C.)
4) Muse with musical instrument
5) Tarentine offering in Delphi: Messapian women with horses, before 474 B.C.
6) Zeus Ithomatas for the Messenian refugees in Naupaktos, ca. 460-455
7) Aigion: Zeus and Herakles *paides*
8) Herakles Alexikakos in the Athenian deme of Melites—plague of 430 B.C.

Echoes of his style are known only through coins. He has been attributed the Artemision Bronze and the Omphalos Apollo. Vollgraff ascribes to him also the Olympia pediments. The resultant picture would show a man capable of constant change and updating in his artistic production, and a most powerful personality.

Gitiadas of Sparta (G. Pesce)
Architect, sculptor, and poet of the late archaic period, contemporary of Kalon of Aegina.

WORKS

1) Statue of Athena Chalkioikos for Sparta; he also restored Athena's temple with bronze relief plaques
2) Amyklai, with Kalon: two bronze tripods, under which stood statues of Artemis and Aphrodite, dedicated with the spoils of the Messenian war (second?: end of the 7th century; third?: 464-459 B.C.)

Kalon (Kallon) of Aegina (A. Giuliano)
Pupil of Tektaios and Angelion, contemporary of Kanachos, collaborated with Gitiadas. One inscription with his name, on the Athenian acropolis dates from ca. 500 B.C.; two others are attributed to him on the basis of the letter forms, so similar to those used by Hegias that a possible association is postulated. (One base supported a tripod, the other a statue.)

WORKS

1) One of three tripods at Amyklai, with a statue of Demeter or Kore standing under it, in collaboration with Gitiadas (Giuliano places it after the first Messenian war.)
2) Xoanon of Athena in Troizen

Modern scholarship has attributed to Kalon some of the most important Severe types, including the "Aspasia/Sosandra" (Dörig, p. 276).

Onatas of Aegina (S. De Marinis)
Son of Mikon of Aegina, who was also a sculptor. Active in the first half of the 5th century, especially at Olympia, Delphi and Athens.
One inscription with his name comes from the Athenian acropolis, and is datable before 480 B.C. It was probably connected with a small bronze horse.

WORKS

1) Colossal Apollo in Pergamon (probably taken there from Aegina or the Peloponnese after conquest in 210 B.C.)
2) Delphi, Tarentine votive monument (together with Kalynthos?): warriors fighting

around body of King Opis, with Taras and the Spartan Phalantos and a dolphin

3) Phigaleia. Bronze statue of Demeter Melaina with horse's head, seated on a rock holding a dove and a dolphin

4) Olympia—Hermes Kriophoros dedicated by the Arkadians (in collaboration with Kalliteles)

5) Colossal standing Herakles for the Thasians

6) Achaian group of 10 Trojan heroes: 9 on one base (putting lots in a helmet, to decide who should duel with Hektor) and Nestor on a separate base

7) Votive group for Hieron of Syracuse to commemorate victory of 468 B.C. Bronze chariot and charioteer, probably made ca. 466-464 (Hieron died in 466, the dedication was completed by his son Deinomenes.)

Though no extant monument can be attributed with certainty to Onatas, modern scholarship has tended to ascribe to him works like the Omphalos Apollo, the Aspasia, the Aegina sphinx, the East pediment of the Aegina temple, the Artemision Bronze.

Hegias (Hegesias, Hagesias) (P. Orlandini)
Pliny: Floruit 448/444 with Pheidias, Alkamenes, Kritios and Nesiotes. Pausanias makes him contemporary of Onatas and Hageladas. Dio Chrysostomos says (though the text is emended by O. Müller) that he was the teacher of Pheidias. An inscribed base from the Athenian acropolis, with traces of fire, supported a bronze statue destroyed in 480 B.C. (the name is given as Hegias). He was probably active ca. 490/460 B.C., but more than one artist may be meant by the different names. Pliny's Hegias made a statue of Pyrrhos and therefore probably was not even a Fifth century man. Quintilian and Lucian compound the confusion between Hegias and Hegesias by grouping them with similar artists and passing the same judgment on their works: they looked almost Etruscan.

No definite work mentioned by ancient sources. Modern attributions include: the Sounion relief (Langlotz), the Great Eleusinian Relief (Anti), and the Dioscuri of Montecavallo (Della Seta).
Kritios and Nesiotes (W. Fuchs). See pp. 79-83.
Pythagoras of Samos/Rhegion (P. Orlandini). See pp. 83-84.

Myron of Eleutherai (Thebes?) (P. Arias). See also pp. 84-86.

WORKS
1) Diskobolos, ca. 460 (?); for Sparta?
2) Athena and Marsyas (for Athenian Acropolis?)
3) Many athletes (Pliny: Delphicos pentathlos, pancratiastas)
4) Runner Ladas
5) Wooden Hekate for Aegina
6) Two Apollo figures
7) a bronze Dionysos
8) Erechtheus fighting with Immarados
9) Athena/Herakles/Zeus (Introduction to Olympos) for Samian Heraion
10) Seated Herakles
11) Perseus
12) cows and bulls in Rome (Pliny: dog [?])

Kalamis (P. Orlandini). See also p. 87.
Probably from Boeotia, but active in Athens.

WORKS
1) Apollo Alexikakos in Athenian Kerameikos
2) Central Erinys in a group of three (the lateral ones were by Skopas) on the Athenian Areopagos
3/4) Aphrodite Sosandra—Aphrodite dedicated by Kallias near the Athenian Propylaia (These may be the same work.)
5) Zeus Ammon, dedicated by Pindar in Thebes
6) Marble Dionysos in Tanagra
7) Hermes Kriophoros for Tanagra
8) Olympia: bronze group of boys praying, dedicated by the people of Akragas
9) Olympia, two boys riding horses on either side of a bronze quadriga made by Onatas; dedicated by Hieron of Syracuse (cf. Onatas, no. 7).
10) Olympia, Nike Apteros dedicated by the Mantineians
11) Sikyon, Chryselephantine, beardless Asklepios
12) Delphi, statue of Hermione, given by the Spartans
13) Apollonia on the Black Sea: Colossal Apollo
14) Statue of Iphytos, a Phokeian hero
15) Statue of Alkmena (?) (text corrupt?)
16) many horses and chariots

BIBLIOGRAPHY 6

FOR PAGE 76

On the Hermes in the Agora being covered with pitch by the bronze workers see Lucian, *Juppiter Tragoedus*, 33.

On the general problem of plaster casts see Richter, *Ancient Italy* (1955) chs. 3 and 4 and especially pp. 41-43 with references.

FOR PAGE 77

On the career of Polykleitos, besides the monographs on the master (as, e.g. P. Arias, *Policleto*, ed. Barbera, 1964), see also P. Amandry, "A propos de Polyclète: Statues d'Olympioniques et carrière de sculpteurs," *Charites*, Festschrift Langlotz, ed. K. Schauenburg (Bonn 1957), 63-87 and chronological table on p. 87. According to this French author, there were three sculptors by the same name; the most famous, Polykleitos I, was probably born around 490 B.C.; his career began ca. 465 and ended ca. 425 B.C. Another Polykleitos, the second of that name, would have been born around 435/430 B.C., started his activity ca. 415/410 and ended it ca. 375/365. Polykleitos III would be primarily a Fourth century master. A different chronology is suggested by G. Donnay: "Faut-il rajeunir Polyclète l'Ancien?," *AntCl* 34 (1965) 448-63. In an attempt to reconcile chronological discrepancies, Donnay would place Polykleitos' birth around 460 and the beginning of his career around 435 B.C. Yet the unmistakable Severe traits of the Doryphoros' face argue against such a late start. Amandry's suggestion offers also the advantage of coherence in that Polykleitos I would then be responsible only for athletic statuary, while Polykleitos II would become the maker of the chryselephantine Hera at the Argive Heraion, the only divine image attributed to *a* Polykleitos by ancient sources.

FOR PAGE 78

On the Agora base with a probable signature by Kalamis, see Marcadé, *Signatures* I, 40, with references.

The latest discussion on Sotadas is in Marcadé, *Signatures* I, 102. For the specific attribution of the Delphi Charioteer, see supra, p. 42, and especially *FdD* IV:5 (1955) 34-38 with summary of previous literature. Cf. also Hampe's review of this work, *Gnomon* 32 (1960) 60-73.

On Diopeithes of Athens see Marcadé, *Signatures* I, 26-28.

On Argeiadas Atotos and Asopodoros, Argives, and Athanodoros of Achaia, see the base of Praxiteles' dedication at Olympia, L. Curtius and F. Adler, *Olympia* 5 (1896) nos. 266, 630 and 631; also *EncArAn* s.v. Argeiadas.

On spelling differences, see, for instance, the case of Kritios, quoted as Kritias in Pausanias and Lucian, Critias in Pliny: *Dedications*, pp. 513-17.

For an example of drastic spelling differences, see the case Hegias/Hagesias/Hegesias, mentioned by Pliny in separate passages (34.49; 34.-78), a statue base from the Athenian Acropolis preserves the spelling Hegias; *Dedications*, pp. 504-5.

On different ethnics, see the case of Myron, called Athenian by Pausanias (6.2.2; 6.8.4; 6:13.2) and Eleutheran by Pliny (*NH* 34.57); cf. *Dedications*, p. 517 s.v. Lykios son of Myron. See also the case of Pythagoras: Pliny, *NH* 34.59, speaks of Pythagoras of Rhegion, but a statue base found in Olympia bears the ethnic Samian; Loewy, *Inschriften*, no. 23. On this topic see infra, p. 91.

As an example of discrepancy between epigraphical evidence and literary sources see the one extant inscription with the name of Hegias. It was found on the Athenian Acropolis with obvious traces of fire and must predate the Persian attack; yet Pliny makes Hegias a contemporary of Pheidias and Alkamenes and sets his floruit in 448/444 B.C. (*NH* 34.49).

FOR PAGE 79

The Marmor Parium is an engraved marble stele with an account of local magistrates on the Island of Paros, which can be correlated with Athenian chronology. The reference to the Tyrannicides occurs in Epoch I, 54, cols. 70-71. Kritios and Nesiotes are discussed by W. Fuchs in *EncArAn* and by M. Bieber in Thieme-Becker, s.v.; by Raubitschek in *Dedications*, p. 516.

See also the very good account on Kritios in Richter, *Sculpture and Sculptors*, pp. 199-201.

On the nature of the masters' collaboration see S. Brunnsåker, *Tyrant-Slayers*, pp. 138-41 and refs.

FOR PAGE 80

On Chamoux's attribution of the Delphi Charioteer to Kritios' workship, see supra, p. 42.

For the Tübingen Hoplitodromos see *BrBr* 351b. On the subject of rededications of statuary in Roman times see H. Blanck, *Wiederverwendung alter Statuen als Ehrendenkmäler bei Griechen und Römern* (Cologne 1963), and especially comments on pp. 97-98, where he disagrees with Raubitschek's point of view; cf. also pp. 75-77 = B 27; p. 78 = B 30; pp. 80-81 = B 34.

For a brief mention of attributions to Kritios or his school, see the account by Fuchs in *EncArAn*; for a recently assigned torso see E. Paribeni, *Sculture V Sec.* (1953) 17 no. 10.

On the Tyrannicides see S. Brunnsåker, *The Tyrant-Slayers of Kritios and Nesiotes* (Lund 1955); a new edition is in preparation. A forthcoming issue of *Antike Plastik* will publish a monograph by W.-H. Schuchhardt and F. Eckstein, "Die Gruppe der Tyrannenmörder."

Among recent studies, worthy of mention are W. Fuchs in Helbig⁴, nos. 1646 and 1768; and B. Shefton, "Some Iconographic Remarks on the Tyrannicides," *AJA* 64 (1960) 173-79.

FOR PAGE 82

Raubitschek's suggestion as to the relationship between Antenor's and Kritios and Nesiotes' groups is to be found in *Dedications*, pp. 481 and 513; for the dating after Marathon, *AJA* 44 (1940) 53-59.

Langlotz: *AthMitt* 71 (1956) 149-52, "Aristogeitonkopf des Antenor?"

W. Fuchs, on the Conservatori Head A 5, Helbig⁴, no. 1768.

On herms, see the very informative account by Harrison, *Agora* 11 (1965) 108-41, and especially pp. 129-30 and comments to cat. nos. 156, 159, 161.

FOR PAGE 83

On the problem of Pythagoras' double ethnic see most recently A. Linfert, "Pythagoras—Einer oder Zwei?," *AA* 1966, pp. 495-96; A. de Franciscis, "Pitagora di Regio," *Klearchos* 5/6 (1960) 5-56.

On Klearchos, see A. de Franciscis, "Klearchos di Regio," *Klearchos* 1-2 (1959) 26-30.

The bronze statuettes most frequently cited in connection with Pythagoras are the Adernò Youth (Langlotz, *Magna Graecia* pls. 84-85); a diskobolos in New York (*EncArAn* 6, p. 574 fig.

664); and another in Stuttgart, once in London (G. Hafner, "Zwei Meisterwerke der Vorklassik," *AA* 1952 cols. 73-102 no. 1). Cf. also Ch. Hofkes-Brukker, "Pythagoras von Rhegium: ein Phantom?," *BABesch* 39 (1964) 107-14, where the typical Pythagorean trait is described as "der Rhythmus der unbegrenzten Bewegung."

FOR PAGE 84

Diskobolos Ludovisi: Paribeni, *Sculture V Sec.*, no. 9; good illustration in *EncArAn* 6, p. 575 fig. 665. I know the replica in Side through the kindness of Prof. Jale Inan, who will publish it in her forthcoming catalogue. Replica of the head in the Vatican (remote): Helbig⁴, no. 594 (Fuchs).

On the Cirò Apollo see infra, p. 122.

On the Apollo the Archer in Rome: S. Stucchi, "Statua di Apollo saettante dalle rovine del Tempio Sosiano," *BullCom* 75 (1953-55) 1-47; G. Hafner, *Ein Apollonkopf in Frankfurt* (Baden-Baden 1962); W. Fuchs, Helbig⁴, no. 1642. Good illustrations in Langlotz, *Magna Graecia*, pls. 115-17.

On the Perseus see Carpenter, *MAAR* 18 (1941) 18-25; on the head in Rome see most recently W. Fuchs in Helbig⁴, no. 1771: he also questions the identification as Perseus and suggests a possible attribution to Pheidias on the basis of the similarity with the Kassel Apollo, therefore implying a mid Fifth century date.

On Myron, besides the account in *EncArAn*, s.v., see P. E. Arias, *Mirone*; Quaderni per lo studio dell'Archeologia, no. 2 (Florence 1940), and V. Poulsen, "Myron. Ein stilkritischer Versuch," *ActaA* 11 (1940) 1-42.

FOR PAGE 85

For a recent study of the Diskobolos' position see V. Sümeghy, "Das Problem des myronischen Diskobol," *Atti VII Convegno Internazionale*, 1 (1958) 281-85, with illustrations of a living athlete and representations in vase painting. Cf. also Carpenter's perceptive comments in *Greek Sculpture*, pp. 82-85, in which he postulates a graphic prototype for the Diskobolos.

Athena and Marsyas. For a complete discussion of the problem see Carpenter, *MAAR* 18 (1941) 5-18; illustrations in Arias, *Mirone*. Carpenter's dating of the Marsyas has not found wide acceptance; cf., lately, W. Fuchs in Helbig⁴, no. 1065, pp. 764-67. The political implications of the group have been recently discussed by J.

Schlaf, "Hermeneutyka grupy Myrona 'Marsjasz i Atena,'" *Meander* 20:10 (1965) 371-82 with Latin summary on p. 399; a didactic element ("hybris will be punished") is also detected; by the same author, on the same subject, see also the philological and archaeological discussion, "Grupa Myrona: Marsjasz i Atena," *Meander* 19:5 (1964) 214-26 with Latin summary on p. 237. Pliny's list of Myron's works can be taken to be in alphabetical order if "satyrum . . . Minervam" are considered as a single item: but this argument has relative validity. J. Boardman has connected the erection of the group with the performance of Melanippides' Dithyramb "Marsyas": *JHS* 76 (1956) 18-20; I owe this reference to Prof. M. Robertson.

FOR PAGE 86
On Poulsen's theory about Myron's Erechtheus see *ActaA* 11.
J. Dörig, "Myrons Erechtheus," *Antike Plastik* 6 (1967) 21-27 and pls. 9-12.

FOR PAGE 87
J. Dörig, "Kalamis-Studien," *JdI* 80 (1965) 138-265; idem, "Der Dionysoskopf Heemskerck I fol. 412," *Antike Plastik* 6 (1967) 59-62 and pls. 36-37.
P. Orlandini, *Calamide. Bibliografia e sviluppo della questione dalle origini ai nostri giorni* (Bologna 1950); *Calamide; 1° Le Fonti, 2° Ricostruzione della personalità di Calamide attraverso le fonti, 3° Il problema della Sosandra* (Bologna 1950).

CHAPTER 7

Lingering Archaic and Lingering Severe

THE PREVIOUS chapter has pointed out that many masters started their careers in the archaic period proper but continued their activity well into the Severe phase, while other sculptors began working before 450 B.C. but continued to produce after the middle of the Fifth century. This situation is partly responsible for the survival of earlier traits into a more advanced period, but the problem of the "Lingering Archaic" and the "Lingering Severe" is of a more complex nature and depends on a variety of factors: personal inclination, "provincialism," religious conservatism, and perhaps also time lag.

Since admittedly traits of the Severe style already appear during the archaic period proper, what criterion should govern the dating of sculpture in which archaic and Severe elements mingle? Obviously it is not a question of numerical balance or even merely of preponderance. Unless historical events or other external factors are instrumental in determining the chronology of a given piece, the ultimate answer rests with the individual scholar and his stylistic judgment. It is therefore not surprising that the date of many such monuments is still controversial. It is also natural that most of them should belong to the sphere of funerary or religious art.

The most important work to show a mingling of archaic and Severe elements is the famous Seated Goddess in Berlin (Fig. 125). It was found in Tarentum in 1913 and two years later it reached Berlin via Paris. Some additional fragments of the throne were acquired through the same dealer as late as 1925. The exact location of its discovery is known, and no question therefore exists as to its provenience though the nationality of its maker is still in dispute. Equally uncertain is the nature of the statue, some scholars being inclined to believe it is a cult image, while others want it a representation of a heroized dead woman. This latter supposition stems from the observation that the area from feet to knees is weathered as if from prolonged exposure, such as would occur if the statue, rather than in a temple, had stood in the open, perhaps in a naiskos within a funerary temenos. On the other hand, votive terracottas of later date, which seem to reproduce the same image, support the theory of a cult purpose. They supply also important information about the attributes which the figure must once have held in her hands: a mesomphalic phiale and an oval object interpreted (perhaps erroneously?) as an alabastron. The objects, and the attested existence of a cult and sanctuary of Persephone in Tarentum, make it plausible to recognize that deity in the Berlin Goddess, though Hera, Aphrodite, and Demeter have also been suggested as possible identifications.

If the statue does represent a goddess, as seems to be the case, its importance becomes enormous. As testimony of ancient religious practices, it represents perhaps the earliest extant cult statue of proven identity.[1] As a work of art, its archaic traits can be explained not as provincialism, but as religious conservatism, and its departures from the norm appear all the more revolutionary. Though at first glance the goddess seems stately, immobile, and archaically frontal, many deviations can be discovered on close observation:

---

[1] Because of the votive terracottas which reproduce it. All other monuments usually classified as cult images can be, and have been, questioned: see, e.g. the large Hera head in Olympia (Lullies and Hirmer, pl. 10), which has been called a sphinx, part of a pedimental composition, etc.

her feet are not aligned, the left one protruding beyond the edge of the footstool; her right arm is held higher than the left, and in keeping with this position her left shoulder is lower and perhaps even longer than the right. The last touch of movement in the composition is completely obscured by the frontal view, and only visible from the sides: the tips of the goddess' shawl are draped over cushion and throne with a swinging curve as if windblown. This last touch must be an obvious concession to the artist's progressive style since it was mostly lost on the worshiper: the statue was definitely meant to be viewed from the front, as indicated by the presence of the massive support under the throne, invisible when hidden by the figure's legs, but quite apparent from the side.

Besides these willful, if discreet, attempts to break the archaic law of frontality (though frontality should have been a major requirement in a cult statue!), other traits suggest that the sculptor already knew the Severe style. The face of the goddess, for instance, despite its enigmatic smile, has the heavy proportions and solid jaw line of Severe works; and the hair, still with the old-fashioned locks over the breast and the frilly valances at the temples, nonetheless rises to a peak in the center of the triangular forehead and is gathered in a *sakkos* over the nape. The drapery too, for all its archaic patterns, adheres to ankles and footrest with doughy consistency.

The conservative elements are fairly obvious: the deity still wears chiton and himation, with the addition of a small mantilla over the shoulders; the drapery itself displays the same crinkly folds and decorative zigzag edges of an Acropolis kore, and adheres unnaturally to the protruding right breast. Also the position is archaic, with the impossible angularity of the bend at the waist and the consequent flat lap. Yet the master was so expert that he could blend these incongruous elements into coherent and pleasing unity. Other fusions have taken place within the composition: the great similarity of the statue to contemporary Magna Graecian terracottas betrays a coroplastic tradition, while carpentry is fully represented in the many articulations of the throne, with details that seem turned on a lathe. It is because of this mingling of techniques that the master should most plausibly be considered local: an Ionian, an Aeginetan, or a Euboean sculptor, as sometimes suggested, would have depended much less on these heterogeneous traditions, but a South Italian artist, conditioned by a country without good local marble, could not forget his training in clay and wood. The material of the Berlin deity is, of course, imported, presumably Parian marble. The statue has been dated around 480 by Blümel, while Langlotz, probably correctly, prefers a date around 460 B.C.

The Berlin Goddess has often been compared to the seated matron on the so-called Leukothea relief in the Villa Albani (Fig. 126), itself probably of South Italian origin. The nickname derives from the maternal implications of the scene, with the enthroned woman receiving a child from the hand of a standing maiden, while two more figures recede as if in vanishing perspective into the background.[2] Ino/Leukothea was known as the mother of Melikertes/Palaimon and as a nurse of Dionysos; the Albani relief, however, has no connection with this goddess, and the representation must have a human

---

[2] See R. Carpenter's comments in *AJA* 54 (1950) 327; he interprets the largest maiden as the oldest daughter, and the other two as "additional offspring in assorted sizes" whose alignment "threatens to start a perspective *regressio ad infinitum*; but this sudden vista into generative space is an accident: the girls do not grow smaller because they recede in distance from the eye, but because of the ordered intervals of their birthdays."

connotation. As a purely funerary stele its complexity has no known precedent,[3] but it is difficult to interpret it as a narrative or votive relief because of the indoor setting: the wool basket under the seat and the attire of the attendants, be they additional daughters or servants, who wear only the thin chiton.[4] It is, more probably, the funerary stele of a matron, identified and heroized as head of a large family. Lippold dates it still around 480, but surely it must be later (ca. 470?) as suggested by the short hairstyles of the maidens, their forceful profiles, the treatment of folds and drapery in general. The enthroned lady has long hair falling on her chest and shoulders, but figures with a special divine, or, as in this case, heroic connotation often display old-fashioned styles of hair and attire, and indeed the Albani woman wears chiton and himation. The coiffure becomes one more element of characterization and emphasizes the contrast with the "human" attendants.

A similar matron appears twice on the reliefs from the Harpy tomb in Xanthos, Lycia (Fig. 127). The monument is in non-Greek territory but, as for the buildings on the citadel, Ionian masters must have been called in to execute the sculptures. A high pillar served at the same time as a triumphal monument and the heroon-tomb of a Lycian family. The burials were placed within the hollowed top of the monolithic shaft and were surrounded by the reliefs, capped with a large stone and, perhaps, surmounted by a lion or a standing statue: a tradition attested by other similar monuments though perhaps not followed for the Harpy Tomb. The subject matter of the carvings remains enigmatic in details, but clear in general: several seated personages accompanied by attendants receive offerings from "worshipers," while sirens at the corners of two of the slabs carry away small puppet-like figures (Fig. 128), presumably the souls of the dead: a motif that has earned the tomb its erroneous nickname. Although many of the details, and perhaps the composition of the scenes as a whole, remain somewhat foreign to Greek taste, the individual figures can easily be paralleled within the sphere of Greek funerary art; and also the idea of the heroized dead is known to Greece, witness the series of Spartan funerary reliefs, the Leukothea relief already mentioned, and many other tomb monuments from Magna Graecia and Greece.

The style of the carving is definitely Greek, perhaps Milesian. Yet this time the conventions seem more coherently archaic and it is difficult to point to discrepant traits that might betray incipient Severe forms. Miss Richter and Pryce date the reliefs around 500 B.C. E. Akurgal lowers them to ca. 480, and Demargne, on somewhat vague historical grounds, brackets them 480-470, therefore within the Severe period though not in Severe style. Provincialism and time-lag are relative considerations if the artists indeed came from Asia Minor; more pertinent perhaps is the assumption of religious conservatism, but in that case individual renderings could still have pointed to a more advanced style. In a recent study, Himmelmann-Wildschütz has attempted a general chronology of Asia

---

[3] Although see the relief from Kalchedon with a funerary inscription datable ca. 550 B.C. or slightly earlier, representing a woman collapsing surrounded by attendants; *BSA* 50 (1955) 81-83, pl. 10a; Jeffery, *Local Scripts*, p. 366 and 371 no. 41.

For a possible "descendant" see the relief from Ikaria signed by a Parian sculptor, of which however only a very brief account and a detail have been published: *BCH* 80 (1956) 334 and fig. 13 on p. 333; dated ca. 470 B.C. Its subject is said to recall the Leukothea relief.

[4] The second in line also wears a diagonal himation, but since the dress of the farthest figure is completely smooth, we can assume that the artist was aiming at contrast in textures rather than at specific characterization.

Minor archaic sculpture and against this background he places the Harpy Tomb reliefs around 480 at the latest. It would, therefore, seem that we have here a case of true, rather than lingering, archaic.[5]

More definitely archaic, but for different reasons, are series of reliefs which resemble the Harpy Tomb in some of their scenes, yet were definitely manufactured during the Severe period: the so-called Locri Pinakes (Figs. 129-30). These terracotta plaques, in an area with limited supply of stone, take the place of marble reliefs and can be considered major, rather than minor, art. They were mold-made, with many individual modifications added at the last moment on the single plaque, or even on the matrix as variant of a specific type. The Lingering Archaic style of most of these works is therefore simply a technical necessity, since family trees of molds can be established, as for manuscripts, and despite changes the style of the descendants is still somewhat conditioned by that of the ancestor. Yet many of these pinakes were produced for the first time within the Severe period, as shown for instance by the shorter coiffures, the use of the peplos instead of the Ionic attire, the heavy features of some of the faces. These traits coexist with many archaisms, such as the long hair, the obsolete costume, the mannerism of pulling the skirt aside, and in such cases it is justified to speak of religious conservatism or perhaps even of provincialism. The *pinakes* were dedicated to Demeter and Kore, though many other divinities are also represented; the production seems to range from ca. 480 to ca. 450 B.C.; the style closely parallels that of the Leukothea relief, but Attic influence, as well as Ionic imagery, can be detected in some of the plaques.[6]

Definitely local, if not "provincial," should be considered a Thessalian grave stele in the archaic tradition (Fig. 131). It represents a draped youth to left, stiffly erect within the narrow confines of a pillar stele of the type common in archaic Attica. The material is old-fashioned limestone, while classical Thessalian monuments are made of marble; the relief is quite low, almost a silhouette applied against the background. The youth holds a long staff in his right hand and a fruit in his left; his shoulders are drawn back in an awkward position and foreshortening is poor. The heavy chin and short cap-like hair leave no doubt that the sculpture belongs within the Severe period, shortly before 450 B.C., but the general composition is archaic and strongly reminiscent of early Fifth century vase painting. In this particular instance, since the piece comes from a fairly isolated area of Greece, it is perhaps fair to accept "lingering archaism" rather than religious conservatism as a reason for the rendering.[7] Other Thessalian sculptures, both in relief and in the round, seem to perpetuate traits of the archaic style; among the stelai see, for instance, Biesantz' K 4, K 5, K 27 and K 55; in free-standing sculpture, particularly interesting is the head of a "kore" with archaic roundels of hair over the temples, narrow slanted eyes, and a faintly smiling mouth; yet the hair parted in the center of the tri-

[5] See however the comments supra, Ch. 4, App. 5, on the Nikai relief from Xanthos and its possible dependence on ceramic prototypes.

[6] See, e.g., the resemblance to Harmodios in one of the Dioscuri, Kidnaping of Kore, type 2-15 a; and the siren on a fragmentary pinax illustrated by G. Jacopi, "Un askos di bronzo configurato di Crotone," *ArchCl* 5 (1953) pl. 8. See also further comments infra, p. 120 n. 16.

[7] Contrast the survival of archaic *motifs* for symbolic purposes. H. Luschey, "Zur Wiederkehr archaischer Bildgedanken in der attischen Grabmalkunst des 4. Jhdt. v. Chr.," *Neue Beiträge zur klassischen Altertumswissenschaft*, Festschrift B. Schweitzer (Stuttgart, 1954), 243-55, pls. 55-56; see especially pp. 250-51.

angular forehead, the strong chin, and the general unity of the face support a dating within the Severe period, perhaps ca. 460.

If archaic traits continue in Thessaly beyond 480 B.C., so do the Severe beyond 450. Indeed Biesantz remarks that a streak of Severe style parallels a more classical current down into the Fourth century. Examples are most easily found among the gravestones. A stele of a woman holding a hare shows the typical profile pose with bent leg of the Girl with Doves in New York (Fig. 66) and the repetitious concentric catenaries of the Orchomenos stele by Alxenor of Naxos; yet the slight torsion in the position and the rendering of the curved kolpos support Biesantz's dating in the third quarter of the Fifth century. Contemporary or slightly later is the funerary relief of a woman with a child (Fig. 132); represented frontally with over-long apoptygma, she recalls the Dephi Charioteer (Fig. 47) in the regularity of her folds, and Angelitos' Athena (Fig. 39) in the awkward arrangement of the garment over the bent leg; but this latter is thrust laterally, with toes overhanging the border, while a certain motion is implied in the asymmetrical rendering of the kolpos, the figure's shoulders, and the direction of her breasts; in the large eyes, the upper eyelid overlaps the lower at the outer corner, a mannerism in vogue in the second half of the Fifth century.

Since this Lingering Severe occurs side by side with a more advanced style, it is impossible to assume that the isolation of the area prevented the adoption of new forms: deliberate choice can be the only answer. It is interesting to note that in Attic vase painting of the Severe period some masters continue to draw their figures with all the decorativeness of the archaic formulas, in a "manneristic" fashion, obviously from purely personal preference; the comparison is illuminating because these mannerists paint their human figures with the same mixture of elements noticed in the sculptural works previously examined: costumes remain archaic, but faces are oval, jawlines prominent, positions correctly foreshortened. The high quality and skill of the paintings, and their provenience from an attestedly progressive artistic center, make the chronology of the vases beyond dispute.[8]

Judgment is more difficult when the object comes from a little known, peripheral area, and when its aesthetic value is not first rate. This is the case of the two Sinope stelai (Figs. 133-34). They come from a town on the coast of the Black Sea, better known for its finds of Greek pottery than of Greek sculpture. The gravestones represent basically the same scene: a seated woman, with attendants,[9] within a framework which in the earlier and more elaborate of the two is definitely architectural, with Ionic columns and dentils. To the controversial field of funerary art these two reliefs have brought added fuel since they seem to imply that the architectural framing so well attested for Attic grave stelai of classical times already existed in Asiatic territory during the Severe period. Also, with

[8] See, for instance, the work by the Pan Painter, and the recent discussion by A.-B. Follmann, *Der Pan-Maler* (Bonn 1968), who dates the activity of the painter between 500-450 B.C. and comments on his position in the contemporary production of Attic vases and on archaistic traits in the art of the first half of the Fifth century in general (pp. 76-82). These archaizing traits are found especially in the minor arts. Cf. e.g. the bronze statuette of a dancing maenad, G. Niemeyer, "Attische Bronzestatuetten der spätarchaischen und frühklassischen Zeit," *Antike Plastik* 3, pl. 26 no. 6514 on p. 29, dated after the Persian invasion.

[9] Note the bird under the seat and compare with the same motif in the Banquet Relief from Thasos (Fig. 64). Is this an Ionic feature?

their intimate domestic atmosphere, they set the pattern for monuments like the famous Hegeso relief. Sinope was not an important artistic center; the logical assumption is that its funerary art reflected customs familiar elsewhere in Asia Minor, perhaps the mother town Miletus, of which we know so little in terms of Severe sculpture. This pioneering repertoire of Ionic funerary art is in contrast with the general assumption that no local tradition in figured gravestones existed in Asia Minor during the archaic period prior to the arrival of Attic influences around 500 B.C. when funerary monuments seem to have been discontinued in Attica proper. The evidence of the Sinope reliefs becomes thus all the more important, and suggests that in turn Ionic artists introduced the architectural framing and the intimate content into Athens when its funerary art was resumed.[10]

To support this theory it is crucial to establish that the Sinope stelai truly belong to the Severe period and not just to the Severe style. Akurgal dates the more elaborate of the two around 460 B.C., and the second, more modest and clearly derived from the first, between 460 and 450 B.C. Although apparently supported by the inscription on this latter, dated by Jeffery "ca. 450?," this chronology has been questioned by Biesantz, who considers both reliefs of Fourth century date, provincial and conservative rather than pioneering. Yet Biesantz's doubts seem somewhat unjustified: the Severe style on the Sinope stelai appears mixed not with later but with earlier traits, such as the meander border on the matron's garment on the larger relief, the large undetailed eyes, the fingers with the upcurving tips, the awkward foreshortening. The very elaboration of the earlier gravestone confirms a Severe date, since discrepancies would be more obvious, the more detailed the rendering. As for the relative importance of the Sinope stelai within the larger picture of Greek gravestones, it is perhaps best to assume that the typical Attic format of the classical period originated from a variety of sources, both local and foreign, and under different stimuli.[11]

Still within the realm of funerary art, another monument can claim affinities with the Severe style: the so-called Satrap's Sarcophagus from Sidon, dated ca. 430 B.C. It is one of four sculpted caskets from the Royal Nekropolis, obviously made by Greeks for non-Greeks within the Fifth and Fourth centuries B.C. They were found in a context open to many foreign influences: Egyptian, Persian, and of course Phoenician and Greek; in fact the interior of the Satrap's sarcophagus is anthropomorphic, while the exterior has a rectangular shape. The long sides illustrate the main occupations of an Oriental potentate, while the short sides repeat the common motif of the "funerary banquet" (Fig. 135) or are filled with attendants. The relief runs parallel to the background, against which the figures appear in clear *staccato*, almost as if applied separately. The drapery is treated simply, sedately, except on the charioteer where the "spinning skirt," so typical of Asiatic-

[10] This position has been disputed by M. Andronikos ("Epitymbia stēlē ex Thrakēs," *ArchEph* [1956] 199-215), who claims that the idea of an architectural framing came to the Attic funerary stelai from votive reliefs as a logical consequence of the enlargement in the format, in itself conditioned by the addition of auxiliary personages: a purely morphological problem; cf. especially p. 210. Andronikos bases his comments on a stele from Thrace now in Saloniki, dated ca. 460-450 B.C., also showing a seated lady attended by a maid and crowned by a pediment.

[11] L. Jeffery ("The inscribed gravestones of Attica," *BSA* 57 [1962] 150) discusses some archaic bases for unusually wide stelai and suggests that the type of the seated matron, perhaps with an attendant, was already accepted in Sixth century Athens.

Greek renderings, makes its appearance. On one of the short sides the veiled matron at the foot of the couch is a typical example of Severe style, easily comparable with the similarly garbed woman on the Ludovisi Throne. Yet the torsion of the figures and many other compositional details, as well as the exquisite moldings, confirm a chronology after the mid Fifth century.

Closer to the linearity and massiveness of the Severe style, yet further removed in date, are the so-called Phoenician sarcophagi (Fig. 136), many of which can be assigned to the first half of the Fourth century. A theory based on the origin of the marble would want them carved by a Parian school, but Egyptian influences are obvious, in some cases to the point of producing the typical "false beard." The lid is carved in the shape of a human figure reclining, not as if on a couch, but supine. Arms and hands are sometimes included, holding objects, but mostly the carving is limited to the head, with only masses and contours suggesting the rest of the body. The hair of many of these "portraits" is characteristically linear, whether arranged in short locks or in long strands festooned in and out of fillets. This rendering is not the only Severe trait: the faces are also massive (though tapering), with large eyes, pronounced lids, and heavy jaws. A stylistic and chronological sequence has been attempted, on somewhat tenuous grounds; yet if the individual dates can be questioned, the general period, well after the Severe phase, seems established.

The heads of these anthropoid sarcophagi can be considered portraits only in a very general sense, yet the Severe period seems to have already known portraiture in the modern sense of the word, as the art of making a realistic representation of a specific individual and not just of a type. Portraiture according to this definition seems not to have appealed to Greek artists at least until the late Fourth century b.c., if not later. Even the famous portrait of Perikles by Kresilas emphasized the peculiar shape of the politician's head, but presumably conformed more to the general *strategos* type than to a realistic portrait of an individual if we are to judge from the replicas which have come down to us. Kresilas, however, worked during the advanced Fifth century, when the classical style was at its peak and idealizing tendencies had already pervaded it. The Severe period, with its more realistic inclinations, its interest in emotions, its novel focus on characterization, might well have produced true portraits. One such example is the head of Themistokles from Ostia (Fig. 137).

The only preserved Roman copy identified as the Athenian general by its inscription, this herm has such striking physiognomic characteristics that many scholars have refused to accept it as Severe. Yet since Themistokles died around 460 b.c.,[12] a realistic portrait reproducing his features can only date from the Severe period, or it should be a "character portrait" made posthumously at an unspecified date. The Fourth and First centuries b.c., as well as the Third a.d., have been suggested as possible times for the creations of the Ostia herm, thus making it a typical "lingering Severe" monument. Yet this standing image shows a very consistent brand of Severe style, such as would be difficult to recreate at a much later date. Not only the general structure of the head, with its cubic geometry, but also the close adherence of the hair to the skull, the rendering of the locks over the nape, the few surviving curls with drilled centers in the beard, and the large bulbous eyes, are well in keeping with a Severe date. The Roman copyist who made the Ostia

[12] The actual date seems to oscillate between 462 and 459, though Linfert says "459 or later"; Themis- tokles was exiled from Athens around 470 b.c.

herm might have exaggerated the Michelangelo bar over the eyes,[13] but grooved fore-heads are already present in the Olympia sculptures and elsewhere,[14] and this linear rendering is fully compatible with the smooth modeling of the cheeks. Still questionable perhaps is the definition as a portrait, though the intent of portraiture is undeniable. Certainly the degree of characterization of this head is greater than what is found, for instance, in the Tyrannicides or in Severe herms, and the closely set eyes in their deep cavities convey an impression of intensity not found in standard types.

As a foil to the Themistokles let us consider some of the centaurs from the South metopes of the Parthenon. The most interesting, though also the least human, almost mask-like, is the head of the centaur in South metope 31 (Fig. 138). The hair is articulated with the same curved cut over the forehead, rising in two peaks above the outer corners of the eyes, almost as if the strong arching of the eyebrows had caused a corresponding motion into the hair. The centaur's locks are long, while Themistokles' are short, but the general outline of the cranium is the same, and also the inward turn of the strands in front of the ears. The Severe traits in the surviving Parthenon metopes have often been pointed out: some scholars have seen in them the style of Kritios and Nesiotes, others that of Myron; all have agreed that the metopes must be counted among the earliest of the Parthenon sculptures. Carpenter has revived a theory that would date the south metopes earlier than the Periklean temple, supposing them carved for a Kimonian prede-cessor and only re-employed in the present Parthenon; yet the latest work on the metopes, Brommer's catalogue raisonné, strongly discounts this possibility. The Severe traits are unmistakable and the similarity with Olympia remarkable;[15] compare, for instance, the head of the bearded man in metope S 16 with that of Herakles in the Olympian metopes of the Cretan Bull, the Keryneian Hind, the Amazon, and the Augeian Stables: they show the same hair calotte, with a roll faintly indicated over the nape, the same lined forehead, with the hair receding in the center, the same thick lids and prominent cheeks outlined by the swelling mass of the beard, the same mouth deep in the shadow of the moustache. Obviously the Olympia centauromachy must have greatly influenced the Athenian metopes: they reflect equal violence, equal pain (equally manifested by wrinkled brows and bared teeth), even similar poses. But the more striking affinity consists not in these external elements but in the technique: veins are indicated, hair is often (and for the last time in the Fifth century?) treated as a solid undetailed mass, and the drill is some-times used at the center of curls. The dates of the Periklean Parthenon are undisputed: it was begun in 447 and completed in 432 B.C.; by 438 the cult statue was inside the build-ing and therefore the roof must have been in place; the metopes should have been exe-cuted between 447 and 440/439. Are they a typical example of lingering Severe, easily explained by the Problem of Generations,[16] or are their stylistic traits so consistent as to

---

[13] Although cf. Parthenon Metope S. 1, the cen-taur; Brommer, *Metopen*, pls. 155-60.

[14] See, e.g. the seer of the East pediment, the bitten Lapith of the West, the fatigued Herakles of the Nemean lion metope, etc. A line also bisects the forehead of the athlete on the Nisyros stele.

[15] An interesting parallel can also be established with the head of Aristogeiton once in the Vatican Magazines and now in the Conservatori (supra, p.

81, n. 1, no. 4 in the list), and the head of the Centaur from South metope 5, Brommer, *Metopen*, pl. 180. The comparison becomes more evident if the two pieces are seen in the following illustrations: Aristogeiton head: *AthMitt* 71 (1956) Beil. 82; Centaur head: Schefold, *Meisterwerke*, p. 245, fig. 299.

[16] The so-called Problem of Generations stems from the fact that older and younger artists may be

force a revision of the accepted chronology? Since Carpenter's study is not yet in print, judgment should perhaps await publication of his evidence.

The last monument to be considered in this category brings up several important and problematic points. In order to evaluate them fully, a brief statement of the situation must be made.

A type of seated woman with head covered by the himation had long been known in Roman copies and identified as Penelope, the wife of Odysseus, through similar representations in the minor arts. Shortly before World War II, the excavation of Persepolis, the Persian capital destroyed by Alexander the Great in 330 B.C., brought to light a fragmentary statue, obviously a Greek original and obviously of the Penelope type. Since the statue was buried in the ruins, it could not have been seen by the copyists of Roman times; the question therefore arises: *what* were they copying? Is the Persepolis statue a "twin," or is it an original taken by the Persians and later replaced by the Greeks somewhere in Greek territory where it could be accessible for copying? Moreover, and most important, what are the dates of the various extant examples of the type, and the possible date of the prototype they copy? Is the Penelope from Persepolis a truly Severe original, or is it an example of lingering Severe created toward the end of the Fifth century?

The extant replicas include:

a) The headless statue from Persepolis (Fig. 139)
b) a statue in the Vatican, restored with an unrelated head (Fig. 140)
c) a relief in the Museo Chiaramonti, also headless
d) a headless statuette in the Conservatori
e) a head in Berlin
f) a head in Copenhagen, formerly in the Giustiniani collection (Fig. 104)
g) a battered head in the Terme[17]

The head type was identified on the basis of traces of the right hand, still visible in the Berlin copy, on which the head once rested, a pose which corresponded to that of the Penelope as given in the minor arts and in what was preserved of the sculptural replicas. These latter vary in quality and execution: both the Vatican (b) and the Conservatori (d) statues were probably made during the early imperial period, but while the former adheres closely to the type as known through the other replicas, the latter is a freer interpretation, with differences in the rendering of the folds and with the upper torso more strongly in profile. Of the other replicas, the Chiaramonti relief (c) has at times been considered a Greek original, and its marble seems possibly Boeotian. In the latest studies of these monuments the Vatican statuette (b) is said to copy a Greek original made around 460 B.C.; the Chiaramonti relief (c) could be a mid Fifth century Boeotian gravestone, or possibly a neo-Attic copy, in either case after a type of around 470-460 B.C.;[18] the Conservatori statuette (d) is labeled a free adaptation in post-Parthe-

---

working at the same time on the same building, so that both a conservative and a progressive style can appear side by side without implying chronological differences: see, e.g. the metopes of the Athenian Treasury in Delphi, perhaps the best exemplification of the problem (recently discussed by Harrison, *Agora* 11, 9-11).

[17] A fragment of another head is mentioned by Paribeni (*Sculture V Sec.*, p. 47 no. 78) as "Quondam Tabularium," no. 7 in his list of replicas.

[18] W. Fuchs (Helbig[4], no. 341) suggests that the prototype might even have been pictorial, in the new three-dimensional style associated with Polygnotos of Thasos.

nonian style, but because of the liberties taken by the copyist, not because of the date of the original; the head in the Terme (g) is considered a replica of an early Severe original, ca. 480-470 B.C.

As for the Persepolis statue, opinions vary: C. M. Olmstead, who published it, suggested that it was a Greek monument carried off by the Persians around 430 B.C., made shortly before that date, and replaced by the Greeks shortly afterwards with what became the prototype for the Roman copies. D. Ohly placed both original and postulated replacement around 465-455 B.C. Eckstein considered the statue in Persia one of two exemplars made around 460-450 B.C. and sent as a Spartan gift to the Persians, while the other remained in the Peloponnese where it was copied by the Romans. Langlotz at first thought that we had the Larisa by Telephanes of Phokaia, sent by the homonymous city to please the Persians; he later changed the identification to that of Aphrodite mourning for Adonis, but in either case he believed the Persepolis statue to have been made around 400 B.C. copying a 460 B.C. original. G. Neumann returned to the Severe date and to the claim of "originality." Also in discussions of the other replicas the Persepolis Penelope has been variously interpreted. Fuchs at first dated it to the late Fifth century, but later considered it carved around 440 B.C. at the latest, in imitation of a 460 B.C. original. Paribeni, acknowledging the difficulty of reconciling both the Roman copies and the Persepolis statue, was forced to postulate multiple originals as imitations and transformations of the type in different artistic circles; to him the style of the Persepolis statue seemed late Fifth/early Fourth century.

In summary, while the prototype of the replicas has been consistently dated within the Severe period (from 480-470 to 460-450), the Persepolis Penelope has been dated within the Severe period, the advanced Fifth century and even the beginning of the Fourth. As for its relation to the Roman copies, the possibilities are as follows:

a) two statues were made at once, one was sent to Persia, the other remained in Greece and was copied in later times.

b) The original statue was stolen by the Persians. The Greeks replaced it (after a studio model?), and the replacement was seen and copied in later times.

c) A statue was made and set up in Greece (where it was copied by the Romans). At some later time another replica was made and sent to Persia.

Both b) and c) imply that the Persepolis statue is different in date from the prototype of the Roman copies, but b) makes it earlier, c) later and thus this latter should be favored in view of the general agreement as to the Severe style of the Roman copies. It is, moreover, difficult to explain why the Greeks would replace a statue taken away by the Persians since an image of Penelope or other mythical personage does not carry the political and historical implications of the Tyrannicides. Yet is it possible to dissociate the style of the Persepolis statue from that of the "Roman" copies?

A remarkable correspondence of folds exists between the Persepolis statue (a) and both the Vatican statuette (b) and the Chiaramonti relief (c).[19] Moreover all three pieces

[19] It should, however, be stressed that the Chiaramonti relief and the Vatican statue are much closer to each other than to the Persepolis figure: could one have been copied from the other? This theory would eliminate one element from the total list, but the surprising fact remains that the similarity between the Persepolis monument and the Roman representations is closer than that usually found among replicas of the same original.

agree in dimensions, while the Conservatori statuette (d) is smaller in size. This last sculpture is useful in determining how "Severe" the drapery of the other three monuments is by comparison: notice, for instance, how the himation over the legs helps model the thighs by following their contours with its pronounced curves, while in a), b), and c) the folds cut straight across the lap and somewhat flatten the composition. In d) the kolpos of the chiton overlaps the mantle in a flurry of tiny ridges, and the individual folds are difficult to follow upward to their origin; in the other three the ridges are fewer, far more tubular, and the bend of the material at the waist creates a series of simplified swallowtails which can be easily isolated and followed. Finally notice the fold-by-fold correspondence of a) b) and c), especially the V-lines originating at the sleeve buttons, and the gathering between the breasts; in the Persepolis statue notice also how grooves end in large, flat ridges, quite similar to the rendering of the Olympia sculptures.[20]

The best comparison and contrast can be established with metope 32 on the North side of the Parthenon (Fig. 141), where the seated figure closely resembles the Penelope in general pose and attire though her legs are not crossed and her mantle falls over her left shoulder. The truly classical rendering of the thin chiton, the complete omission of pattern around the sleeve buttons, the great liveliness of folds in the right sleeve, where its edge touches the lap, and finally the strong contrast in texture between chiton and himation, highlight the equal consistency of both garments in the Persepolis statue, the uncomplicated rendering of the chiton, the stylization of its folds at the sleeves— all those elements that are in keeping with the Severe style. Yet the Parthenon metope itself has a fairly doughy treatment of the mantle folds, but in their complicated course these clearly betray a more advanced stylistic stage than the Penelope.[21]

The so-called Cat Stele in Athens at first glance seems to provide a parallel for the Persepolis drapery. But the cloth around the youth's legs creates sharp-edged folds, much more "metallic" in appearance than in the Parthenon metope, and in certain areas adheres closely to the body with ogival curves entirely missing in the Penelope.[22] The Cat Stele, with its prominent selvedge, appears stylistically later than the Parthenon metope, but this latter in turn seems later than the Penelope, either the Persepolis statue or the Roman versions. The replicas of the head, as preserved, support this position in the sequence; in particular, the one in Copenhagen strongly resembles the Omphalos Apollo in the rendering of the hair over the forehead, and has sometimes been attributed to the same master. A Severe date around 460-450 for the Penelope type seems, therefore, confirmed on both counts.

This conclusion does not explain the position of the Persepolis exemplar in relation to the Roman copies. It is perhaps safer to assume, with Paribeni and Richter, that multiple originals existed, of which one found its way to Persia. Historical events are either lack-

[20] Notice, for instance, the fold toward the left armpit, below the left breast, especially visible in *AJA* 54, pl. 8. Comparisons with the doughy material of Olympia are even better for the folds over the back of the Persepolis statue, but since probably the rear of the composition was not meant to be seen, the treatment of the drapery might have been simplified; contrast instead Langlotz (*JdI* 1961), who thinks that the copyist made the front in true

Severe style, after the original, but carved the back in a freer, later manner.

[21] Another good Parthenonian contrast is with the Artemis of the East frieze, slab 6, Lullies and Hirmer, pl. 157, detail (Fig. 142).

[22] This is not because of the difference between garment-over-flesh and garment-over-garment, since also in the Cat Stele a similar area appears at the point where the mantle overlaps.

ing or chronologically impossible to reconcile with the presence of a Greek statue in Persepolis. The identity of the type is perhaps also multiple since some later representations in the minor arts portray Elektra, and it is doubtful that the correct identification of the type would explain its presence at the Oriental capital since the statue was probably taken more for its extrinsic than for its intrinsic value: the throne on which it sat was decorated with precious inlays, and the sculpture was kept in the Treasury, where it was found, despoiled and abandoned in fragments by Alexander's soldiers. Most important for our knowledge of Greek techniques, however, would be to know whether sculptors, as early as the mid Fifth century B.C., could reproduce[23] pre-existing statues with such fidelity that the resemblance carries, even at second hand, through the Roman copies. Certainly even in the archaic period statues were often made in pair with minimal differences between the two: witness the famous twins Kleobis and Biton, two female figures from Cyrene, probably Leto and Artemis, and the two korai from Chios. It could be assumed, though it is not likely, that the Persepolis statue was originally part of a group of two almost identical figures, of which one was taken by the Persians for unknown reasons (greed?) and the other remained in Greek hands to be copied by the Romans.[24]

In other ways the Penelope may be connected with a group: given its Severe date, it is surprising to find the figure still wearing chiton and himation rather than the ubiquitous peplos. Is this a trait of "lingering archaic," or is it rather a means of differentiating the personage from another of slightly different status? What comes to mind, of course, is the group Demeter/Kore, which also in the great Eleusinian relief in Athens similarly distinguishes between mother and daughter.[25] Presumably because of the costume, and for its alleged dissimilarity to the Olympia sculptures, the Penelope has been termed East Greek or Ionic.[26] Yet the difference with the Olympia sculptures may be morpho-

[23] It seems impossible to speak of *copies* at such an early date. The concept of mechanical copying to obtain *exact* duplicates does not seem to arise until the late Second century B.C. Close reproductions could, however, occur as early as the Fifth century, as in the examples listed infra. See also F. Brommer, "Vorhellenistische Kopien und Wiederholungen von Statuen," *Studies Robinson* I (1959) 674-82 and his bibliography. The idea of the use of models and of a rudimentary pointing system has already been mentioned (supra, p. 19).

[24] At first consideration it would seem impossible that a group would be composed of identical statues *facing in the same direction*, since the Roman representations illustrate the same pose of the Persepolis piece. But Mr. James Wright, Ph.D. candidate at Bryn Mawr College, has pointed out to me that a funerary monument could have more than one mourning figure in identical, not simply reversed, pose. In Attica such monuments do not occur before the Fourth century (see, e.g., the two servant statues in Berlin, C. Blümel, *Die klassisch griechischen Skulpturen der staatlichen Museen zu Berlin* [1966] no. 45, figs. 62-69, last third of the Fourth century B.C.) and usually involve only mirror-images, but in

Asia Minor the practice, though not yet attested, might have started earlier and have been more complex. A funerary connotation seems to be implied in the type even if the identification as Penelope is correct, in that good brides were compared to that symbol of conjugal faithfulness: see for instance the epitaph discussed by W. Peek, "Die Penelope der Ionerinnen," *AthMitt* 80 (1965) 160-69, early Second century B.C., from Didyma.

[25] Obviously, however, if the costume was meant to differentiate two similar figures, the Romans could not have copied the other member of the group after the first one had been removed from the composition, otherwise we would have the peplophoros represented in the Italian replicas. We would have to assume that the statue removed to Persepolis was replaced by an identical reproduction to complete the group. This assumption might explain the necessity for reproducing the missing statue (since a group could not be left in a halved state) and would apply even if not two female personages, but perhaps Penelope and Odysseus were represented.

[26] If the Chiaramonti relief is truly a Theban gravestone of the Fifth century B.C., it is unlikely that it would have imitated an Asia Minor prototype,

logical rather than stylistic since the chiton, with its rich possibilities for pattern, looks intrinsically different from the peplos. We know too little about sculpture in Ionia at this time to differentiate safely between schools. Neither the seated lady of the Thasian Banquet Relief nor the Philis on a Thasian gravestone seems a pertinent comparison.

In conclusion, the "Penelope problem" has raised points of origin, chronology, imitation, or straightforward accurate copying in Greek classical times, this last point already suggested by the replacement of the Tyrannicides and perhaps confirming that models of some sort were already used in the Fifth century. Of the other monuments considered as showing Lingering Archaic or Lingering Severe traits, some have perhaps been wrongly questioned and are truly archaic or truly Severe: the Harpy Tomb, for instance, or the Sinope Stelai. Yet it is significant that most of these monuments come from peripheral areas and belong to the sphere of funerary art, where conservatism and perhaps even provincialism are to be expected. In all cases, the suggested dates were never more drastically removed than half a century from the traditional chronology. Monuments which fall under the category of intentional imitations or re-elaborations of the archaic or the Severe style in late Hellenistic or Roman times present such a different problem as to require separate discussion. On the other hand, the proximity in chronological limits being fairly close, it could be argued that all monuments considered above can be explained by the Problem of Generations. This may be the case, for instance, for the Parthenon metopes, as already pointed out; yet this explanation seems somehow too facile, and cases of authentic Lingering Archaic and Lingering Severe exist well into the Fourth century and not only in the provinces.

Among the pieces with debated chronology, the Themistokles from Ostia occupies a special position since its inclusion within the Severe period would credit that phase with the inception of portraiture, a genre which seems to have been abandoned or drastically idealized during the classical period. Here, as in many other cases, full certainty cannot be reached; but in terms of coherent style, as we have seen it through our initial examination of Severe Greek originals and copies, the Themistokles rightfully belongs within the Severe period.

---

though island sculptors were active in Boeotia, as for instance the Alxenor of Naxos who made the

Orchomenos stele, Lippold, *Handbuch*, pl. 38:1.

1. *So-called Prytaneion reliefs, Thasos*: Three slabs, now in the Louvre, found by E. Miller in 1864. The structure incorporating the sculptures was at first thought to be the Thasian Prytaneion. Further research in 1912-14 showed that it was instead a passageway formed by two parallel walls inscribed with lists of names: hence the name Passageway of the Theoroi. But it was still thought that the passage led to the Prytaneion. Only the excavations of 1954 showed that the arrangement led to an open area surrounded by porticoes and buildings, none of which could be interpreted as the Prytaneion. The nature of the passage is still controversial. It lies at the NE corner of the Thasian Agora. See *Guide de Thasos* (Paris 1968) 37-39, fig. 12 no. 4 "Le passage des Théores."

The reliefs are equally problematic. The largest slab shows: Apollo being crowned by Artemis, a shallow niche, and three Nymphs moving toward the niche and Apollo. The other two slabs were at first reconstructed on either side of a similar niche, but it is now recognized that they formed the short sides of a cavity probably containing an altar. Their position in the passageway is still uncertain. The two short reliefs represent Hermes accompanied by a goddess (Hekate?) and three Graces. Both the Apollo and the Charites slabs are inscribed with rules for offerings and the cult.

The reliefs were at first dated ca. 490-480, a date which was later lowered to 480-479 B.C. on epigraphical grounds. But nothing in the content of the inscriptions provides an absolute date, and epigraphists felt uneasy about the developed forms of the letters. G. Daux proposed that the epigraphical dating be set at ca. 475-450 and stressed that inscriptions and reliefs need not be contemporary; he would, however, accept a chronology ca. 485-470 for the sculpture. L. Jeffery, who favors a date around 465 for the inscriptions, mentions that P. Jacobstahl would support that chronology for the reliefs. They would, therefore, be a typical example of lingering archaic: only one of the Nymphs wears the peplos.

The most extensive *sculptural account* is by Picard, *Manuel* 2:1, pp. 88-92, figs. 41-43; see also J. Pouilloux, *Recherches sur l'Histoire et les Cultes de Thasos* I, Etudes Thasiennes 3 (Paris 1954) 340-41.

The summary of previous excavations and the result of the latest research appear in *BCH* 79 (1955) 353-59 (G. Roux); see especially p. 359 for an attempt at placing the Louvre reliefs.

The epigraphical discussion in G. Daux, "Thasiaka," *RA* 29-30 (1948) 244-48; and Jeffery, *Local Scripts* p. 302, no. 70 p. 308 and pl. 58.

A comparable relief, with two maidens advancing toward a square niche containing the bust of a goddess, comes also from the Island of Thasos and is at present in the J. Paul Getty Museum in Malibu, California (H. Stothart, *A Handbook of the Sculpture in the J. Paul Getty Museum* [Malibu 1965] 11, A55.S-7). Cf. Picard, *Manuel* 2:1, pp. 87-88 and fig. 40.

2. *Votive relief in Eleusis: Kore as Hydranos*. Recently mentioned and illustrated in G. Mylonas, *Eleusis and the Eleusinian Mysteries*, Princeton 1961, p. 194 and fig. 70 (paperback, 1969). It shows a matronly figure holding a bowl (which was inserted separately and is now missing) over the head of a naked youth. The female personage has been compared with the Corinth/Conservatori type (see supra, Ch. 5, App. 6), and this similarity must have influenced the date assigned to the relief. Anti, Buschor, and Lehmann-Hartleben have all considered it Severe, ca. 460. E. Simon has pointed out the scarcity of votive reliefs at that time, and other stylistic details of the woman's dress which presuppose the Parthenon ("Zum Bruchstück eines Weihreliefs in Eleusis" *AthMitt* 69/70 [1954-55] 45-48; see especially pp. 47-48 for the chronological discussion with previous bibliography). Miss Simon places the relief "in the other 'Severe' period of Greek art: the early Hellenistic." Mylonas dates it in the first half of the Fourth century.

3. *Apollo the Archer, from the temple of Apollo Sosianus in Rome*. This statue has already been mentioned several times. For general comments and bibliography see p. 74 and p. 91. Langlotz, Fuchs, and others tend to date the piece around 440-430 B.C., while Italian scholarship prefers a Severe date, ca. 460. Undoubtedly the heavy jawline of the Apollo's profile, the rather old-fashioned hairstyle, the simplified drapery,

APPENDIX FOR CHAPTER SEVEN

the purely silhouette pose and the Severe stance (cf. the Tyrannicides), would support the earlier chronology. But a certain refinement of face (frontally) and musculature, the rendering of the eyelids, and (presumably) the association with the Niobids in the Terme and Copenhagen, have induced other scholars to lower the date. It is also uncertain whether the Apollo statue came from a pediment, or from a group on a semicircular base. Nobody disputes, however, that it was part of a mythological representation (the Killing of the Niobids).

If the Apollo is truly to be associated with the extant Niobids, it is an undoubted case of Lingering Severe. The head in Frankfurt, which Hafner attributes to the same master, and to another semicircular group with Apollo and the Muses, is instead not related, and probably a forgery (see Jucker's review of Hafner's book in *MusHelv* 21 [1964] 191). No speculation has been made as to the Magna Graecian temple from which the Apollo would originate, but everyone agrees that the statue must be the product of a Tarentine or otherwise Western workshop.

FOR PAGE 93

Seated goddess in Berlin: B. Blümel, *Die archaisch griechischen Skulpturen der staatlichen Museen zu Berlin* (1963) no. 21, pp. 29-33, figs. 55-59; see also E. Langlotz, *Magna Graecia*, figs. 50-51, and notes on p. 266. On the circumstances of its discovery see E. Langlotz, *AA* 1957, cols. 359-60. For comparison with later terracottas, see Blümel, *op.cit.*, figs. 60-61. H. Herdejürgen, *Die thronende Göttin aus Tarent in Berlin* (Bayern 1968), unfortunately appeared too late to be consulted.

FOR PAGE 94

Leukothea relief: *BrBr*, 228; K. Friis Johansen, *The Attic Gravereliefs*, p. 143 and fig. on p. 142. Lippold, *Handbuch*, p. 94, pl. 26:4.

FOR PAGE 95

Harpy Tomb: *FdX* I, P. Demargne, *Les piliers funéraires* (Paris 1958), reviewed by G. M. A. Richter in *AJA* 63 (1959) 400-1. Interesting articles on the Harpy tomb by F. J. Tritsch, "False Doors on Tombs," *JHS* 63 (1943) 113-15, and especially "The Harpy Tomb at Xanthos," *JHS* 62 (1942) 39-50.
For parallels with Greek Funerary art see E. T. Wakeley, "The H. T. frieze—A New Interpretation," paper summary, *AJA* 70 (1966) 196. For Greek heroizing reliefs see supra p. 47, n. 3. Suggested chronology of the Harpy Tomb: Richter, *AJA* 63, *loc.cit.*; Pryce: F. N. Pryce, *Catalogue of Sculpture in the British Museum* I:1 (1928) 126; E. Akurgal, *Die Kunst Anatoliens* (Berlin 1961) 134-35. N. Himmelmann-Wildschütz: *IstMitt* 15 (1965) 24-42.

FOR PAGE 96

Locri Pinakes: An entire corpus of this very interesting material has not yet been published; preliminary accounts appear in P. Zancani Montuoro, "Note sui soggetti delle tabelle locresi," *AttiMGrecia* N.S. 1 (1954) 71-106 with earlier bibliography, and idem, "Il Corredo della Sposa," *ArchCl* 12 (1960) 37-50; for illustrations see Langlotz, *Magna Graecia*, pls. 71-75 and color pl. IX, with notes on p. 271. H. Prückner, *Die lokrischen Tonreliefs* (Mainz 1968), has appeared too late to be consulted.
Thessalian Grave Relief: H. Biesantz, "Ein archaisierendes Grabrelief strengen Stils aus Krannon," in *Festschrift F. Matz*, 1962, 56-65,

and idem, *Die thessalischen Grabreliefs*, 1965, no. K. 20, p. 14, pl. 10.
Thessalian head of kore: Biesantz, L 9, pl. 30, p. 29, from Atrax; see also comments on p. 122.

FOR PAGE 97

For Biesantz's remarks on the survival of the Severe style, see pp. 164 and especially p. 43 and n. 23.
Stele of woman holding hare: Biesantz, K 29, pl. 4, p. 18, probably from Mopsion.
Relief of woman with child: Biesantz, K 22, pl. 7, p. 15, from Larisa.
The most manneristic of Attic vase painters is the Pan Painter: see, e.g. Arias and Hirmer, pls. 160-65 and notes on pp. 346-48, or Boardman/Dörig/Fuchs/Hirmer, pl. 149.
Sinope stelai: The main study is by E. Akurgal, "Zwei Grabstelen vorklassischer Zeit aus Sinope," *BerlWinckPr* 111, 1955; see also, by same author, *Die Kunst Anatoliens*, pp. 269-73 figs. 237-38.
On Sinope see, e.g. J. Boardman, *The Greeks Overseas* (Penguin 1964) 266.

FOR PAGE 98

On the dating of the Sinope stelai: L. Jeffery, *Local Scripts*, p. 369 and p. 373 no. 73, pl. 72.
Biesantz: *Thessalischen Grabreliefs*, p. 62 and n. 72.
Satrap's Sarcophagus from Sidon: most recently, I. Kleemann, *Der Satrapen-Sarkophag aus Sidon* (Berlin 1958).

FOR PAGE 99

On Phoenician sarcophagi see, e.g. E. Kukahn, *Anthropoide Sarkophage in Beyrouth* (Berlin 1955); see also *EncArAn*, s.v. *Sarcofago*, Fenicia.
Themistokles from Ostia: A. Linfert, "Die Themistokles-Herme in Ostia," *Antike Plastik* 7 (1967) 87-94 pls. 39-46, where the prototype is considered Ionian, ca. 460 B.C. The article includes a comprehensive bibliography with an indication of the chronology favored by each author. Summaries of previous positions can be found also in G. M. A. Richter, *The Portraits of the Greeks* 1 (1965) 97-99 with figs. 405-8, and in H. Sichtermann, *Gymnasium* 71 (1964) 348-81. Comparisons with the Olympia sculptures and the Parthenon metopes can be found in Linfert; for an illuminating comparison with the head and neck of Aristogeiton, see L. Curtius, *RömMitt* 57 (1942) 78-91.

FOR PAGE 100
Parthenon Metopes: F. Brommer, *Die Metopen des Parthenon*, 1967. South Metope 31: pls. 233-34; South Metope 16: pls. 202-5. See also Brommer's discussion on the chronology of the metopes, pp. 174-75 with summary of opinions. Carpenter's theory was presented as a lecture for the Philadelphia chapter of the Archaeological Institute of America on Jan. 19, 1966, and is developed in a forthcoming Penguin book on the Parthenon.

FOR PAGE 101
Penelope: Vatican Statuette: W. Fuchs in Helbig⁴, no. 123; Chiaramonti relief: W. Fuchs in Helbig⁴, no. 341; headless statuette in the Conservatori: W. Fuchs in Helbig⁴, no. 1502; head in Berlin: K 165, C. Blümel, *Katalog*—but discussed without the evidence of the Persepolis replica and therefore not considered here among the recent studies; the same applies to the Copenhagen head, Ny Carlsberg inv. no. 1944, F. Poulsen, text to EA 4622-24 (1938) and *Catalogue of the Ny Carlsberg Glyptothek*, 1951, no. 407; battered head in the Terme: Paribeni, *Sculture V Sec.* no. 78.

FOR PAGE 102
Persepolis Penelope: C. M. Olmstead, "A Greek Lady from Persepolis," *AJA* 54 (1950) 10-18.
D. Ohly, "Dia Gynaikon," *Robert Boehringer, Eine Freundesgabe* (1957) 433-60.
F. Eckstein, "Aidos," *JdI* 74 (1959) 137-57.
E. Langlotz, "Die Larisa des Telephanes," *MusHelv* 8 (1951) 157-70; idem, "Zur Deutung der 'Penelope,'" *JdI* 76 (1961) 72-99.

G. Neumann, "Archäologische Gesellschaft zu Berlin, Sitzung am 8 Mai 1961," *AA* (1962), 852-56.
W. Fuchs, in Helbig⁴, no. 341, pp. 260-61: not the original from which the Roman copies were made; Helbig⁴, no. 1502 p. 318

FOR PAGE 103
Parthenon Metope North 32: F. Brommer, *Die Metopen*, pls. 135-36.
Cat Stele, Athens Nat. Mus. no. 715, Lullies & Hirmer, pl. 182, note on p. 82, where it is dated ca. 420.
G. M. A. Richter, *Ancient Italy* (1955) 48-49: a lucid summary of the situation; see her figs. 162-67 for echoes of the type in other forms of art.

FOR PAGE 104
Kleobis and Biton: Lullies and Hirmer, pls. 14-15 and notes on p. 56 (contrast, however, G. Kaschnitz-Weinberg, "Die ungleichen Zwillinge," *Studies Robinson* 1 [1953] 525-31).
Female figures from Cyrene: E. Paribeni, *Catalogo* nos. 8-9 pls. 12-15 pp. 10-12; *Korai* nos. 168-69 figs. 536-39.
Korai from Chios: J. Boardman, "Two Archaic Korai in Chios," *Antike Plastik* 1 (1962) 43-45 pls. 38-44; *Korai* nos. 37-38 figs. 122-28.
Eleusinian relief in Athens, Nat. Mus. 126, Lullies and Hirmer, pls. 172-73.

FOR PAGE 105
Philis' gravestone in the Louvre: *BrBr* 232a; Lippold, *Handbuch*, p. 116 and pl. 41:4.

CHAPTER 8

The Severe Style in Late Hellenistic and Roman Times:
Neo-Attic Reliefs and Akroliths

THE Chiaramonti relief of the Penelope type discussed in the previous chapter has been considered either a Greek original or a neo-Attic copy of a Severe work. It serves as a good introduction to the sphere of neo-Attic art.

The term neo-Attic was coined by H. Brunn in 1853 to define the production of artists, active from the First century B.C. to the Second century A.D., who specialized in the reproduction of earlier Greek works, and who signed their sculpture with the ethnic "Athenian." If, however, the neo-Attic current found its impulse in the classicizing tendencies of Second century B.C. Athens, it is also true that the practice of copying or imitating ancient works spread very rapidly, and that neither the monuments copied nor the artists who copied them were always from Athens. The term is here retained simply as a convenient label for all sculpture which not merely imitates but especially adapts creations of previous artistic periods so as to form coherent unified compositions, usually for decorative purposes. Though the name can apply also to statuary in the round, it is best known with reference to relief, and thus used hereafter.

Neo-Attic reliefs mainly select their repertoires from three phases of Greek art: the late archaic, the ripe Fifth century, and the second half of the Fourth century B.C. When elements from different periods are juxtaposed, usually a superficial stylistic unity is attained by modifying the prototypes to a common stylistic denominator. The prototype may be repeated fairly faithfully, so that different neo-Attic reliefs found in different geographical areas may agree not only in details but even in dimensions, or variations may be introduced by the individual copyist, such as the addition or removal of some item of clothing, or the omission of a satyr's tail. Similarly, the entire original composition may be reproduced, or individual figures alone, and these in turn may be combined with elements from other prototypes. Scale and context may also drastically change: for instance, the famous Fifth century maenads have been found reproduced as ornament for large round bases (which was probably the form of the original monument), as three-figured panels, as single-figured slabs and, in much smaller scale, as decoration for marble vases, candelabra, and altars.

Neo-Attic reliefs often copied relief prototypes, but in some cases statuary in the round was converted into two-dimensional compositions. If the Chiaramonti Penelope is truly neo-Attic, it provides a good example of this practice, since more or less contemporary copies in the round of the same type also exist. Another example is offered by the so-called Lanckoronski relief, now in Richmond, Virginia (Fig. 143). Once considered a Fifth century original, it was recognized by Fuchs as an eclectic neo-Attic creation because of its high projection and treatment of the background. Compared to the Mourning Athena (Fig. 69) indeed, the displacement of the main figure to one side, and the complicated spatial relationship implied by the position of arm, shield, and herm, reveal the later character of the work. Also the costume of the Athena, with the peculiar rendering of the overfold on the left hip and the short apoptygma over the kolpos, seems to be the interpretation of the late carver rather than a true replica of a Severe peplos.[1] Yet the flavor of the individual figures is in keeping with the Severe period, and Harrison has recently suggested that the herm portrayed in the Lanckoronski relief is an actual reflection, if not an authentic picture, of the Hermes Propylaios seen by Pausanias on the Acropolis. Similarly, it has been suggested that the Athena is inspired by Severe prototypes in the round, as attested by works in the minor arts like the Athena Elgin in New York. In comparison with the Severe statuette, the peplophoros in the relief shows different, more elongated proportions, and unquestionably a different type of garment; but the general pose with the owl is characteristic enough to warrant the comparison, and both helmet and hairstyle reinforce the general similarity. It is perhaps safe to assume that statuary in the round was combined and adapted by the neo-Attic artist of the relief.

But to what extent did neo-Attic artists adhere to their prototypes in composing their decorative works? The question requires an individual answer for each case, especially for the late Republican period when, after Sulla's sack of Athens in 86 B.C., many workshops moved from Athens to Rome, enlarged their repertoires to include Pergamene and South Italian models, and finally transferred their patrimony into Roman decorative art. The difficulties of evaluating this ambiguous material can be best exemplified by the terracotta plaques in Munich, excavated in 1778-1780 at Tor Paterna (Porcigliano) in the so-called Pliny's Villa.

These rectangular panels have been called either wall decoration or ceiling coffers, and are unanimously dated within the Augustan period, around the turn of the century. All authors also agree that they are moldmade, with individual retouches. Less agreement exists as to their fidelity to Severe prototypes. Beyen considers them typically Italian because of their distinctive enframing molding and excludes the possibility that even the matrix might have been imported, but he believes that each representation corresponds to a famous Severe monument of the Peloponnesian school. Furtwängler calls them free creations; Karouzos characterizes them as free copies of Severe originals; Stucchi attempts to provide a single prototype even for one type that Karouzos recognizes as a mixture of different archaic and Severe traits. Though the plaques, because of their material and purpose, are somewhat outside the scope of this work, their interest for an understanding of Roman classicizing practices is so great as to justify a detailed description.

Plaque 185 (Fig. 144) at first glance seems to confirm the theory that the panels reproduce specific statuary types of the Severe period since the bust of the divinity here shown appears a close replica of the God from the Sea. In fact Karouzos, though with commendable reservation, uses it to support his identification of the Artemision bronze

---

[1] Particularly significant in this respect is the over-elaboration of the skirt, complicated by too many folds of uneven width which are surprisingly repeated also on the kolpos. The awkward merging of two pleats over the area of the left leg (level with the lower tip of the staff) and the residual swallow-tail above the left ankle are also out of keeping with Severe drapery. Finally the lack of interest in balance, despite the pose with the advanced right foot, is all the more striking in that contemporary sculpture, both in the round and in relief, constantly exploits the significant outline of a bent knee. The Mourning Athena, which does not display this feature, nonetheless crosses her feet, thus at least suggesting a less static balance. The Demeter of the classical Eleusis relief (Lullies and Hirmer, pl. 172), which resembles the Lanckoronski Athena in the columnar over-all appearance, shows an ungainly bent leg, even at the expenses of anatomical coherence.

as Poseidon, since the trident added to the terracotta plaque leaves no doubt as to the identity of the figure there represented. The Greek scholar, however, adds a most penetrating analysis of the points in which the Roman portrayal differs from the truly Severe work, so that in effect only the very close similarity of the coiffure justifies the comparison. The most striking feature of the Roman version is the eye, in the narrow, elongated, heavy-lidded rendering which Karouzos calls Augustan. Another typical trait is the open mouth, and finally the complete absence of the ear, hidden by the "bangs." In the hair rendering too there are differences, especially the calligraphic and lively ending of the curls both in the beard and over the forehead, and the even thickness of the braids which do not taper, as would be natural, toward the end. If, however, the Artemision shipwreck occurred during the middle Hellenistic period, the Augustan coroplast could not have used the bronze statue as his direct model and must have been copying it at second or third hand, perhaps through some neo-Attic relief or sketch now lost.

Plaque 186 is more difficult to evaluate (Fig. 145). Karouzos suggests that the identification as Omphale precludes a true Fifth century prototype since the representation of that legend was not favored at the time. He stresses the similarity with the female face of plaque 187 (Fig. 146), and assumes that the Roman artist, needing another female personage to balance his series, has arbitrarily borrowed from a different figure, adding the lion's skin for identification. Against this opinion, Beyen believes that the plaque represents not Omphale but Herakles himself, admittedly beardless, and ventures a possible connection with a famous Herakles by Ageladas. Again, the "Roman" traits are most apparent in the rendering of the eye and the linear emphasis on the jaw; the treatment of the lion's mane is also impressionistic, with its alternation of purely engraved hairs and thicker locks.

Plaque 187 (Fig. 146) is the "Aspasia," and as such it has received fewer comments since the dependence upon the famous type is unmistakable. Orlandini uses it to support his identification of the Sosandra by Kalamis, but indeed it simply implies the popularity of the prototype, not its identity, since no qualifying attributes are apparent. In terms of style one may perhaps note that the proportions of the original have been considerably altered, especially in the distance between edge of mantle and eyebrows, so much greater in the statuary replicas, and in the concentration of the facial features toward the center of the face, as against the more even distribution in the large-scale works.

Plaque 188 shows the upper torso and head of a male figure (Fig. 147), presumably Apollo, with a complicated hairstyle: thick even braids encircle the skull, while long strands departing from the dome end over the forehead in several rows of snail curls, over the nape in a flaming chignon. The panel is restored at this point, but enough of the original is preserved to show the band tying the hair, so that only the termination of the chignon is missing. Karouzos sees it as a combination of Severe and archaic hairstyles and admits the difficulty of finding appropriate parallels in extant Fifth century works. Beyen insists that a famous prototype must be behind this plaque too, in support of his general theory that all panels reproduce important originals. He suggests that the terracotta portrays the Apollo Philesios by Kanachos, modified somewhat in hairstyle by the exuberance of the copyist and with the addition of a mantle not part of the original. Yet recent studies on the Philesios show that its hairstyle was characterized by long locks over the chest, a feature which the Roman copyist would not have omitted if he intended to identify his figure as Kanachos' work. A recent proposal by Stucchi would establish a correlation between the plaque and the marble statue of a Severe Apollo found in Rome, to which bronze locks were added at a later time, but the similarity would exist only with the arrangement over the forehead, not with the distinctive (and unnecessary) chignon at the back, and the parallel does not seem valid. The answer lies perhaps in accepting that the coroplast followed archaistic rather than Severe models for this particular image; the artists of the First century B.C. seem to have been somewhat confused in their understanding of earlier hairstyles, or at least to have enjoyed combining separate coiffures in new arrangements. The typical example is the Piombino Apollo, which displays two hairdos usually mutually exclusive: the loop and the chignon. But most closely pertinent in the case of the Munich plaque is the Elektra of the "Pasitelean" group in Naples (see infra, Ch. 9, p. 135), who combines the rolled hair of the Kritian Boy with the braids of the Poseidon and the chignon of the terracotta panel. In the Elektra a typically male hairstyle (the braids) has been combined with two other fashions (which may also belong to male coiffures), and it is logical to assume that the artist of the Munich terracotta either followed a similar procedure on his own, or was copying a classicistic prototype of the First century B.C. not known to us.

Plaque 189 is the last of the series (Fig. 148), and has been recomposed from two unrelated fragments. The lower part shows the aegis of Athena and the termination of loose curls similar to those of the Poseidon plaque, the upper part preserves the forehead fragment of a face that has been variously interpreted as male (Karouzos) or female (Beyen). The Apollo Pitti (Fig. 149), which Karouzos suggests as a possible inspiration for the hairstyle, has in effect a different coiffure, with long strands curled around a fillet although the mediocre marble in Florence flattens the spirals and fuses them together. Beyen compares the Berlin Penelope, but here too, to judge from the Copenhagen version, the similarity seems due to the flattening treatment of the copyist. Beyen moreover admits the difficulty of reconciling a Severe female head with braids. This difficulty disappears if the rendering of the plaque is taken to be a typical "Melonenfrisur," anachronistic of course in the Severe period but possible in an Augustan work as further example of the freedom with which classicizing artists adapted hairstyles. The braids would not be incompatible with a female figure of the same period—witness the Elektra—though difficult for the Severe.[2]

In summary, an analysis of the Munich plaques shows that only two surely followed specific prototypes (the Aspasia and the Artemision God) though with the stylistic modifications typical of the late First century B.C. Of the others, no certainty can be reached for the Herakles/Omphale, while the Apollo and the upper fragment of plaque 189 definitely seem to reflect the anachronistic creations of classicistic ateliers. It may well be that the Romans did not distinguish between true replicas of Severe works and the new types in Severe style created by "Roman" artists; or perhaps the appreciation for the style was greater than that for the period itself, and therefore a work with Severe features was as pleasing to the Roman customer as a genuine copy. Given the ornamental nature of the plaques, the decorative program might have required a specific number

---

[2] Female figures of the Fourth century wear braids; see, e.g. a girl from a funerary monument, Richter, *Catalogue of Greek Sculpture in the Metro-politan Museum*, no. 92, pl. 75 a-b, dated to the mid Fourth century. But this is in no case a common fashion.

of panels, too many to be filled only with truly Severe prototypes, and the coroplast might have felt free to improvise on his own to fulfill the requirements of the arrangement. Whatever the correct answer may be, the plaques demonstrate considerable Roman interest in the Severe style and allow sound speculations on the ways in which the style was reinterpreted in later periods. Indeed, a whole series of architectural terracottas, the so-called Campana reliefs, seems inspired by monuments of the Severe style, and individual panels have at times been used to reconstruct statuary prototypes now lost or incomplete.[3] Within the same Campana series a braided type of Zeus has been considered basically similar to the Poseidon of the Munich plaque; its importance lies in the fact that a stone example of the type also exists, in the Terme. Its material, Italian marble, and the considerable asymmetries in the rendering of the face suggest that it is a fragment from a neo-Attic relief with the typical high projection of such works; but in this case the Severe prototype might also have been two-dimensional, as shown by a low-relief once in Mittelschreiberhau dated ca. 470 B.C. (Fig. 150).

We may conclude that such decorative "Roman" works, both in marble and other media, incorporated within their repertoire genuine Severe originals, both in relief and in the round, as well as classicizing versions in Severe style, also presumably extant in both techniques. The difficulty lies in correctly assessing the nature of the work reproduced through the stylistic language of the Roman copyist.

A case in point is a fragmentary relief in the Rhode Island School of Design Museum (Fig. 151). It represents a seated man, leaning forward toward a now unrecognizable object, holding something in his left hand. Though the interpretation of the scene as a whole is unclear, the comparison with the so-called seated Philosopher type is striking, and several parallels can be established between the Rhode Island piece and other reliefs or even statuary in the round of Hellenistic date. The representation of the seated philosopher came into vogue during the Fourth century B.C. and was especially popular in the Hellenistic period; it was adapted for votive or even funerary reliefs and enjoyed wide diffusion. What is surprising is that the Rhode Island relief seems Severe in style: the flatness of the folds, the arrangement of the himation with its concentric curves which recall Alxenor's stele, the sinewy anatomy, the almost archaic upturned fingertips, the over-all simplicity of the composition, suggest a date around 460 B.C. We should perhaps assume that its maker recast a Hellenistic prototype into a Severe mold, and indeed Dontas has suggested that the relief is a classicizing work of the First century B.C. If this assumption is correct, "Roman" ateliers not only must have copied truly Severe works but must even have translated later compositions into Severe style.

Conversely, of course, the opposite may be true, especially when several replicas of the same type exist and show variations in rendering and style. The most difficult monument to evaluate, in this respect, is perhaps the famous relief of the Three Graces, the Charites, supposed to be by the sculptor Sokrates from Boeotia. The representation is mentioned by Pausanias twice: once in his account of the Athenian Acropolis, together with the Hermes Propylaios (1.22.8), and once in his discourse on the Charites in general (9.35.3 and 7). In both instances, he mentions that the work was by Sokrates the son of

[3] See infra, Ch. 9, p. 135, for a discussion of the Theseus/Charioteer in the Conservatori, and Ch. 8, App. 9.

Sophroniskos, the famous philosopher (who lived 469-399 B.C.). The monument has been identified as a relief, surviving only in later copies of which the most complete is in the Chiaramonti Museum in the Vatican (Fig. 153); but since the figures appear to be in the Severe style of ca. 480-470 B.C., the authorship given by Pausanias has been discounted because of its chronological impossibility, and the suggestion has been made that the Charites were by a Boeotian Sokrates, otherwise known as a sculptor for having collaborated with his compatriot Aristomedes in making a statue commissioned by Pindar (Paus. 5.27.8).

Harrison has recently suggested that the Hermes of the Acropolis should also be considered by the same Sokrates, or at least as early classical in date, in refutation of the widespread belief that the Hermes Propylaios mentioned by Pausanias was by Alkamenes. Indeed the epithet Propylaios is appropriate to any guardian divinity and cannot be reserved exclusively for the protector of the entrance to the Acropolis, even less for the famous Herm made by Alkamenes, which may not have stood there at all. With this clarification the picture seems to have become even more coherent: Sokrates is an attested Boeotian sculptor of the Severe period since he worked for Pindar; the Charites and the Hermes Propylaios on the Acropolis were by him, and later Athenians misunderstood the homonymy and believed them to be by the famous philosopher, who was also supposed to have attempted sculpting. As a result, the Charites became popular and were often copied in neo-Attic ateliers, not because of their aesthetic value but because of the anecdotical connection with the famous Sokrates. Perhaps for the same reason the tightly knit composition was also faithfully reproduced without interpolations or adaptation of its individual figures into other contexts, as is so often the case with the neo-Attic repertoire. Since most of the extant replicas come from Athens, the original must have stood there, and an appropriate position inside the Periklean Propylaia has been suggested, within a sort of niche where the SW wing joins the main body of the gateway; a comparable position on the opposite side must have been occupied by the Hermes, as indicated by the cuttings on the floor. Both the Hermes and the Graces, if made during the Severe period, must have stood in the earlier entrance to the Acropolis but they were not scrapped with the earlier building, presumably because of their sacred character; they were, so to say, re-employed in the Mnesiklean building in appropriate positions.

This very logical picture rests, however, almost exclusively on the assumption that the style of the Charites relief truly reflects a Severe protoype. Should a date around 470 for the original be questioned, the entire argument would be shaken. With this question in mind, let us examine the Chiaramonti relief.

This plaque, found in 1769 near the Lateran in Rome, has usually been considered the most faithful, though uninspired, reproduction of the original. The other replicas listed by Fuchs are incomplete or somewhat alter the character of the representation, as we shall see below. The Three Graces are represented holding hands and supposedly dancing. This interpretation is confirmed by the poses of the individual figures, three-quarters, almost frontal, and profile respectively, though Feubel has attempted to show that the convention of representing the central Grace in a frontal pose goes back to archaic prototypes. A tradition of Charites reliefs is attested from the early Sixth century on;

the closest in time and spirit to the type under discussion[4] is a late archaic fragmentary slab in Berlin with the heads of two female figures in high relief. The marked projection of the Chiaramonti Graces would therefore seem part of the tradition, and not a modification of the copyist in keeping with neo-Attic practices.

The leader of the three wears a peplos with apoptygma and kolpos; this latter is remarkably long, suggesting a low girding. Though this fashion occurs in the wearing of the chiton,[5] it is not common in Severe peploi; the closest rendering appears in the second half of the Fifth century, in the matronly figures of the Parthenon East frieze. More surprising for the Severe period is the short mantle which the Charis holds aside with her right hand; the gesture itself is common, a survival of the archaic fashion exemplified by the late Acropolis korai; but whenever it is found in a peplophoros, the skirt of the peplos is held, not an additional garment. It is also difficult to understand how the mantle adheres to the left arm, since the artist of the relief has not made clear the distinction between the overgarment and the sleeve-like arrangement of the peplos.[6] The hairstyle of this Charis, with the long strands loose over the nape, recalls the Propylaia kore, Akr. 688 (Fig. 46), who also has a similar shawl-like mantle, though differently worn. On the basis of this parallel one should date this figure to the very early Severe period, shortly

[4] Chronologically closer are the Graces of the Thasian "Prytaneion" in the Louvre (Schwarzenberg, pl. 2) and the three maidens of the Harpy tomb (Schwarzenberg, pl. 3), dated ca. 479 and 500/480 respectively. But the Thasian Charites form *pendants* to the Nymphs (see Lippold, *Handbuch* pl. 40:1) and therefore do not follow an independent typology. Moreover, the basic difference consists in the "offering motif," which requires a processional composition with figures facing the receiver, as contrasted with the "dancing motif," which presupposes no other personage as the ultimate goal of the motion. From this point of view, the Chiaramonti Charites are closer to the dancers of the relief from the Acropolis (Schwarzenberger, pl. 5; Schrader, pl. 178, no. 430, Akr. 702), whose identification however remains controversial. For further information on the Thasian "Prytaneion" reliefs see Ch. 7, App. 1.

[5] For examples, in vase painting see for instance the work by Makron (e.g. the interior of the cup Louvre G 147, Boardman/Dörig/Fuchs/Hirmer, fig. 137 on p. 265; or the cup in Berlin no. 2290, Richter, *Sculpture and Sculptors*, fig. 287). Indeed Poulsen (SS, p. 134) in speaking of the Charis' attire calls it "sehr chitonähnlich" and can only refer to vase painting for comparison (Beazley, *Vases in America*, p. 64, fig. 40 = Brit. Mus. E 161, Hydria attributed to the Syriskos Painter; Beazley, ARV², p. 262 no. 41; *CVA*, Great Britain 7, pl. 71:1).

E. Harrison has suggested to me that the long kolpos may simply mean that an adult-sized dress is being worn by a short person or a child. However, none of the Severe examples I can find shows the kolpos quite so low, almost at mid thigh. On the contrary, Severe instances of an unusually long *overfold* do exist in statuary; see, e.g. a statuette in the Barracco collection (von Steuben in Helbig⁴, no. 1866, *JdI EH* 15, pl. 59a) or the Artemis in the Villa Albani (*BrBr* 606).

[6] The himation is to be understood as thrown over the left shoulder and coming down as low as the edge of the apoptygma since one of its weights is indicated at the end of the vertical fold. At first glance this arrangement is so close to the box-pleat originating from the right breast and belonging to the peplos, that one can easily misunderstand the mantle folds as being also part of the overfold. The illustration in Beazley, *Vases in America* (see supra, n. 5) helps to visualize the fashion. The difficulty over the arm remains, however, even when this point is clarified. Moreover, the artist has not made clear the separation between himation and peplos on the proper right side, so that a superficial examination suggests that the peplos, not the himation, is being held aside. Yet this is impossible, since the mantle is not symmetrically thrown over both shoulders, as in the above-mentioned vase painting. Color probably once might have helped differentiate between the two garments, but certainly the sculptural rendering is vague. Replica (i), is, however, unmistakable in this respect though an adaptation rather than a true copy (Fig. 154). Could this unlikely holding of the himation be actually an adaptation of the classical rendering in which the three dancers (Nymphs or Charites) hold *one another* by their mantles? Cf. Fuchs, *Vorbilder* pls. 3-5.

after 480, yet the treatment of her skirt, with folds between and along the legs and drapery adhering to the thighs, is closer in fashion either to archaic (cf., e.g., Fig. 2) or to classical (cf., e.g., Fig. 66) than to the tenets of the Severe style, which would prefer a fairly uniform fluting of the cloth.

The second Charis wears the fully developed peplos of the period around 470-460, which however lies flat on her high bosom, without the animation at the neckline already common in the Olympia sculptures. The shelf-like arrangement of curls over her forehead is difficult to date. It appears in late archaic figures, for instance in the terracotta Athena from Olympia or the Fleeing Maiden in Eleusis (Fig. 156), and is exemplified in vase painting, but during the Severe period it appears only early and not with the tightly packed snails of the Chiaramonti relief. This latter form is closer to the hairstyle of Hermes, for instance the so-called Hermes of Alkamenes, where it represents an archaizing feature; it is, it seems, more typical of male than of female fashions, and it does not occur again on a woman until the Artemisia from Halikarnassos.[7]

Finally, the third Charis. Her profile pose, with the long line going from right breast to left ankle, is awkward and surprising for a period which already had considerable experience with foreshortening. But more surprising is her attire: she wears the Ionic costume with chiton and himation, not however in the fashion of the Severe period, so as to be completely enveloped in her cloak, nor even in the classical manner, with the mantle looped lower, below the waist, revealing a great deal of the chiton. Her arrangement is closer to Fourth century renderings,[8] as shown for instance in votive or record

---

[7] The Boeotian stele of Polyxena in Berlin (dated ca. 420 B.C.; C. Blümel, *Die klassisch griechischen Skulpturen der staatlichen Museen zu Berlin* [Berlin 1966] no. 6, pp. 17-18, fig. 12 = K 26) is often quoted as an indication of survival of such fashions, but her hairstyle, as described in the Catalogue, is quite different, with a diadem and an unfinished area in the center of the locks, over the forehead, on which vertical lines can still be distinguished (hair waves?). Admittedly, the heavy concentration of the hair over the forehead is similar to that of our Charis, but the argument can also be used to prove that the Charis belongs to the end of the Fifth century, rather than vice versa.

Another monument usually mentioned as a possible comparison, the Kriophoros Barracco (von Steuben, in Helbig⁴, no. 1865, illustrated in *EncArAn* 4, p. 4, fig. 5, s.v Hermes), is generally supposed to reproduce a work of around 470 B.C., but to me its prototype seems fully archaistic, perhaps First century B.C. (as also suggested by Dörig, *JdI* 80 [1965] 222-23). As a parallel to the Charis, moreover, the Kriophoros is not valid, whatever his correct dating, because it is a male figure.

[8] Admittedly this fashion is known in the late archaic and Severe periods through vase painting. See, e.g. Arias and Hirmer, pl. 127 (the Kleophrades Painter, ca. 480 or shortly after); pl. 144 (Douris, ca. 490); pl. 172 and color pl. XXXVI (Lyandros Painter,

ca. 460). It is also frequently used for male figures, but again only in painting, to my knowledge. The motif extends also to terracottas, as for instance the two examples of a votive relief from the Athenian Acropolis, showing a seated woman (Athena?) with chiton, himation, and a low stephane over a projecting shelf of curls, who thus considerably resembles the Charites relief (*JHS* 17 [1897] 310-11 fig. 2 and pl. VII:2; reg. no. 1337 and 1338). In actual statuary, this particular arrangement of the mantle occurs on a Severe bronze statuette in the Fogg Museum, Cambridge, Mass.: the so-called Watkins Aphrodite. G. Hanfmann ("An Early Classical Aphrodite," *AJA* 66 [1962] 281-84, pls. 73-74) has dated it ca. 450 B.C., and has pointed out the connection with a group of heads assembled by Schuchhardt (see supra, p. 65, n. 11) which Hanfmann calls "the Budapest group" from the location of one replica. The Fogg statuette however wears *only* the himation, and its draping therefore leaves her right breast bare. It might be suggested that the unusual fashion was introduced exclusively to reveal her breast, as a characterization of Aphrodite ("the partial nudity is still attributive, hieratic," Hanfmann, p. 284), and therefore is peculiar to her alone.

A comparable statuette from Thessaly (Biesantz, *Thessalischen Grabreliefs*, pl. 61, L 105, pp. 34-35) has been dated to the third quarter of the Fifth cen-

reliefs; indeed Laurenzi, in publishing a replica of this third Charis in Kos, did not recognize it as part of the famous composition and dated it to the Fourth century. Only the schematization and simplification of the folds gives the drapery a Severe look.[9] It is obvious that the variations in attires and coiffures, like the variations in the poses, were introduced to differentiate and identify three related and similar individuals, but the chronological range implied by the selection seems too wide to fall within the Severe period. In summary, a close analysis of the Chiaramonti relief suggests that it has definite Severe style traits, but that it contains many discrepancies arguing against a Severe period prototype.

The other replicas do little either to refute or support this contention. Of those listed by Fuchs, the Giustiniani relief (once Stroganoff, Fuchs' b) is quite similar to the Chiaramonti, and both date probably from the Late Republican period. Fuchs suggests that the harshness of their rendering should be tempered by comparison with the two early neo-Attic replicas from the Acropolis (c and d). These are highly fragmentary and headless, but seem to repeat basically the same scheme of the Chiaramonti relief; the hat-like curls of the second Charis are also repeated in a head in the Vatican Magazines (e) which Fuchs dates within the Flavian period as an example of pictorial style, together with a fragment of the third Grace in the Antiquario Comunale del Celio (f). More significant are perhaps his items g-i, since they reproduce different versions. Unfortunately the two relief plaques in the Peiraeus (h) are still unpublished; Fuchs calls them late Hadrianic adaptations, and there is no doubt that an adaptation (perhaps of the late Second century A.D., according to the same scholar) is the relief in a private collection in Rome (i) which increases the space between the figures and arbitrarily mixes stylistic traits of different periods (Fig. 154). The most important relief remains the fragment from the South Slope of the Acropolis (Fuchs' g) which retains the entire, though headless, second Charis (Fig. 155). Fuchs places it in a separate category of its own ("Umstilisierung"); and though agreeing with Feubel in seeing Third century B.C. traits in its style, judges the relief itself neo-Attic and therefore later. Poulsen, however, believes that this fragment comes closer to the original than any of the other replicas and supports the Attic character of the prototype; what is usually termed Boeotian in the other exemplars, he suggests, is simply the imprint of the copyist. But this Acropolis Charis is definitely later in style than the Severe period, and the sculptor has even added a chiton sleeve under the peplos, in a fashion which seems typical of the Fourth century. Should

---

tury, and seems obviously derivative, since her hairstyle is different and a chiton has been added under the mantle, yet the pose with the bird and the overall appearance are strikingly similar. Perhaps the variation in clothing was meant to differentiate the worshiper from the goddess. By the end of the Fifth century the fashion seems to have entirely lost its characterizing connotation and to have been used for a variety of personages and divinities: see, e.g. the stele of Krito and Timarista (Lullies and Hirmer, pl. 185). Here, however, as in all other examples, the mantle tip falling behind the left shoulder is clearly indicated, while in the replicas of the Charites this detail is omitted.

[9] As a final point, notice the quasi-transparent treatment of the drapery: an approach suggestive of a date at least as late as 450-440 B.C. It has been often said that the relief contains archaizing traits, perhaps because of religious conservatism, and this fact is indisputable. I maintain, however, that the Severe traits also should be considered part of the same "archaizing" tendency, rather than an expression of contemporary style. Indeed the type could almost be classified as Magna Graecian provincial "Lingering Severe," were it not for the fact that as many as five of the eleven extant replicas come from Athens and its harbor. (Of the remaining six, one was found in Kos, the others presumably all in Rome.)

this be considered an arbitrary addition of the neo-Attic master or a closer reflection of the prototype? Is it possible that later copyists, in the late Republican period, super-imposed a Severe veneer on a work that dated in fact from a different artistic phase?[10] Or are the makers of variants g-i responsible for "modernizing" their Severe prototype?[11]

The answer seems to depend on the authorship of the original model. Sokrates the sculptor belonged to the Severe period since he worked for Pindar; is this not sufficient evidence to confirm the early chronology of the prototype? On second scrutiny one finds that it is not. Sokrates is not an uncommon name, and indeed an homonymous painter of the Fourth century is mentioned by Pliny, who even admits that some identified this painter with the sculptor (*NH* 35.137 and 36.32).[12] Another Sokrates is known through an inscription to have dedicated a relief to the Nymphs (often confused with the Charites) around 350 B.C. This confusion with names is, however, inadequate basis for lowering the date of the Charites relief to the Fourth century. Much more serious is the objection that Pausanias, in describing the Acropolis Charites, speaks of *Agalmata* in the plural (9.35.7); though the singular form could be used to mean a relief, the plural, even to imply a three-figured composition, seems unusual and inappropriate.[13] In no way can we prove that Pausanias saw a relief rather than a group in the round. Indeed, the cutting on the Propylaia floor is for a large rectangular base, more suitable for a three-dimensional monument than for a relief.[14] The possibilities therefore are as follows:

[10] The case of the so-called Perseus has already been discussed supra, p. 84; the stylistic discrepancies between the replica in the British Museum and that in Rome may be attributed to a conscious "severizing" of the artist who made the head in Rome. The Esquiline Venus and the Spinario, discussed infra pp. 132-33, have been defined "translations into pseudo-Severe style of late classical and Hellenistic works" (Fuchs in *EncArAn* s.v. Neo-Atticismo); similar comments on the Tralles-Cherchel Karyatids (Ch. 9, App. 6) have been made by Buschor (Buschor and Hamann, p. 31, under the heading "Zum Kopieenwesen").

[11] A case in point may be the peplophoros in Argos, J. Marcadé, "Sculptures Argiennes," *BCH* 81 (1957) no. 9, pp. 433-35, fig. 17. See in particular n. 5, where the author suggests that the folds of the skirt may have been "modernized." The statue is published as a copy of a mid Fifth century prototype, perhaps with modifications in the head and the position of the right arm.

Note that, in at least one of the two replicas in the Peiraeus, a chiton sleeve was again added under the peplos, this time to the first Charis.

[12] In the second passage Pliny mentions the sculptor as the maker of the Charites on the Acropolis but this statement also can be questioned if Pliny, aware of the chronological discrepancy in assigning the neo-Attic Graces to the Fourth century painter, corrected his statement on the same principle followed by the modern scholars who dispute Pausanias' attribution to the philosopher.

[13] This objection has already been raised by

E. Petersen, *JdI* 23 (1908), 16-17, together with other points which Arndt attempts to refute in his text to *BrBr* 654r.

[14] Schwarzenberg, p. 18 n. 42, states that the cutting in the Propylaia indicates a slab 125 cm. long, while the Chiaramonti relief is 187 cm. in length. His statement is, however, based on the erroneous dimensions given in Amelung's catalogue and repeated in Helbig⁴ no. 351. The text to *BrBr* 654r gives the length as 0.87, and Fuchs (*Vorbilder* p. 63 n. 15) as 0.82-85. These measurements are undoubtedly correct since the relief figures are under life size, and would not be incompatible with the cutting in the Propylaia, allowing for a projecting base. Schwarzenberg also suggests (pp. 16-17) that since two replicas of the type were found in or near the Propylaia, they must have formed a pair, and that such *pendants* in architectural contexts do not occur before the second half of the First century B.C. Perhaps one relief was made as counterpart for the other after the Sullan sack, and both adorned the entrance to a newly erected sanctuary: hence they cannot be identified with the single monument mentioned by Pausanias within the Propylaia. The same scholar points out the initial lack of differentiation among Charites, Nymphs, and Seasons, and quotes M. Ervin ("The Sanctuary of Aglauros," *Archeion Pontou* 22 [1958] 129-66; see especially p. 160), who believes that the worship of the Charites as such was introduced into Athens probably during the second half of the Third century B.C., or at least did not find separate sculptural expression until then.

1) the original was a group of three figures in the round created during the Severe period. The neo-Attic artists copied them and partly misunderstood them; they therefore altered certain details, like the hairstyle of the second Charis which was translated into archaistic terms, or the gesture of the first for which a mantle was arbitrarily provided instead of the peplos skirt. The author of the original group might be Sokrates the Boeotian, and Pausanias refers to his work, though believing that it is by the philosopher.

2) The original was a group of three figures in the round created during the late Fifth or the Fourth century B.C. in an archaizing vein. This archaistic flavor is reflected in the Chiaramonti relief and perhaps enhanced by the conversion into two-dimensional terms. This late date would explain why the original monument could find its place in the Periklean Propylaia, since it would be either contemporary or later than the construction of the building.[15]

3) The original was also a relief, and had no connection with the monument seen by Pausanias on the Acropolis (and therefore no connection with Sokrates, either the philosopher or the sculptor). In this case we have again the same variety of possibilities:

    a) the original belonged to the Severe period and was modernized by the sculptors of replicas g-i

    b) the original was truly classical, but "Severized" by the sculptors of replicas a-f

    c) the original was archaizing, though made during the classical period

    d) the original was a purely late Hellenistic or neo-Attic invention.

Of all these possibilities, 1 and 3a-b should be discarded on the basis of fashions: alterations can involve the adding or removal of folds, but not the way of wearing a peplos or a mantle.[16] Possibilities 2 and 3c seem the most plausible, while 3d appears stylistically somewhat less probable. In any case the alleged exact correspondence of all

The cutting in the Propylaia (*H*) could easily have accommodated a long and narrow base supporting three figures side by side. Stevens (*Hesperia* 5 [1936] 446) points out that the pavement of the niche "was dressed down to its final surface," as contrasted with the protective layer left all over the building, and that "the care with which these surfaces (of the two niches) were cut indicates that the monuments were put in place at, or about, the time the Propylaea was built." It is indeed unlikely that such a prominent position was left empty until Sullan times.

[15] The authorship of Sokrates the Philosopher in this case might even be defended. It is indeed supported by M. Bieber in Thieme-Becker, s.v. Sokrates II, as distinguished from Sokrates I, the Boeotian sculptor. The Philosopher was undoubtedly the son of a sculptor; though he did not continue in the family tradition, he might still have known how to carve, and his lack of touch with the profession might explain, according to Bieber, the "retarded" style of the Chiaramonti relief. She does not state, however, whether the original Sokratean work was two- or three-dimensional. Another explanation for its conservative style may lie in Sokrates' explicit admiration for adherence to tradition in art; see Plato, *Laws* 2, 656 d-e. Other ancient sources besides

Pausanias credit the philosopher with making statues of the Charites; pertinent passages are discussed by O. Benndorf, *AZ* 27 (1869) 55-62.

[16] In support of an early Severe date for the prototype, either in the round or in relief, one could perhaps quote Fuchs' theory (*RömMitt* 63 [1956] 102-21) that one of the metopes in Temple E at Selinus imitated the Charites relief. However, the two heads on which the entire hypothesis rests do not correspond so closely to the neo-Attic version on the Chiaramonti relief: notice especially the entirely different arrangement of the curls in the second "Charis," notably in profile, Fuchs pls. 49:2 and 52. Langlotz (*Magna Graecia*, p. 281) discounts the theory because of stylistic discrepancies between the heads and the lack of any fragment of the bodies. The Locri pinakes mentioned by Fuchs as corroborating evidence (Quagliati, *Ausonia* 3 [1908] 217-21 figs. 65-69 and Schwarzenberg, pl. 2 b), though comparable in some respects, show a contamination between the "dancing" and the "offering" motif, and are probably more closely related to the latter than to the former, as shown by the complete absorption of the Graces either in the seated figure toward whom they move, or in themselves (central Grace turning back toward companion).

replicas to the original can be questioned, because of the obvious variations in some of them, thus further undermining the anecdotical connection with Sokrates (see supra, p. 115). Yet, if the appeal of this attribution did not exist, why was the type popular? The neo-Attic repertoire supposedly did not favor the Severe period. When Fuchs mentions a stronger preference for Severe prototypes in late republican ateliers, he bases this statement mostly on the presumed fidelity of the Charites reliefs (a) and (b), stressing at the same time the eclectic nature of many contemporary creations (p. 173). If, however, we accept a classical date for the prototype of the Chiaramonti Charites, its apparent isolation disappears. Furthermore, our picture of Roman taste remains somewhat distorted if we confine our examinations to the neo-Attic production. The purely decorative and local Italian output, represented for instance by the terracotta plaques in Munich, attests to a greater interest in the Severe style, and the same is confirmed by a study of contemporary statuary in the round.

One more point should be made in connection with the Charites relief. In discussing the second Grace, her hairstyle was defined as more typically male and closer to archaistic than to archaic. Yet a contemporary parallel on a female head is seemingly provided by the coiffure of the so-called Ludovisi Goddess in the Terme (Fig. 157). This colossal piece was once part of an akrolithic statue, a figure whose body was of a cheaper material than the exposed extremities carved out of marble. The reason for the technique is usually economic in areas where stone is scarce; the over life-size of many of these akroliths is also a factor, since a body in wood or terracotta to be covered with drapery could be made much faster than a colossal torso in marble. The practice is well attested for the Severe period through literary sources (even the famous Pheidias made an Athena in this technique for Plataia) and probably goes back to archaic times; it seems to be especially suitable for cult statues and presumably had its roots in the chryselephantine technique, which also must have provided bodies of less precious materials. In Sicily and Magna Graecia akroliths must have been especially popular because of the local scarcity of stone, and an akrolithic technique of sort can be recognized in the metopes of Selinus Temple E, where female heads and limbs were carved in marble and inserted on the limestone bodies.

The Ludovisi Goddess was found in Rome, in the area of the gardens of Sallust which yielded the stumbling Niobid and the Ludovisi Throne also now in the Terme. It is obvious, therefore, that the site contained several pieces of probable Magna Graecian origin and undoubted Fifth century date. Yet the Ludovisi head strikes a peculiar note and its chronology could be questioned. It must be kept in mind that the present state of the piece is far from its original appearance: aside from the loss of the body, the obvious restorations and the lack of color, the cheeks seem to have been smoothed down, since they completely lack the patination and weathered surface of forehead and neck. The bronze additions are also lost: earrings, extra locks over the forehead, two masses of strands originating behind the ears and framing the neck, perhaps even a veil over the head. Paribeni dates the sculpture between 490 and 480 B.C.; Langlotz after the victory of Himera in 480 B.C. But is the head truly Severe?

Obviously the cult purpose of the image must be responsible for some of its "retarded" stylistic features. The frequent comparison with the Kritian Boy and the Delphi Charioteer stresses instead the Severe traits. The striking difference between the heavy structure of cranium and face and the superficial linearity of the hair mass (especially where it spills over the fillet in the back) have been ascribed to typical Magna Graecian tendencies, and indeed parallels can be found, for instance with the Agrigentum Ephebe. Yet contrast the Ludovisi Goddess and the Seated Demeter from Tarentum in Berlin and the differences will be immediately apparent. It is not only a question of different hands or schools: it is a question of conception. The long chin, small mouth, over-large eyes, low forehead, which would have been rendered even lower by the bronze curls,[17] the abstraction of contours in face and cranium, the lack of indentation around the fillet, are all disturbing features which can only be approximated but not exactly paralleled in other pieces, whether in stone or terracotta. Particularly important seems to be the rendering of the hair strands over the nape; though a veil might have covered that part of the coiffure, other pieces exist in which the same contrast between plastic curls and linear strands prevails: yet they belong to a much later period, the First century B.C.[18] Could a similar date be suggested for the Ludovisi Head?

A comparable doubt has been advanced recently for another akrolithic head, the so-called Cirò Apollo in the Reggio Museum (Fig. 158). This controversial piece was found, together with a pair of marble feet and a fragmentary left hand, in the ruins of the temple of Apollo in ancient Krimisa. Variously dated during the Severe or the classical phase, down to ca. 440-430 B.C., the head has been called Hadrianic by Schuchhardt because of its "cold" quality, the linearity of its Venus' rings in the neck, the mouth with its peculiar sweetness, the shape of the eyes, and the modeling of the orbital muscle: a stilted style in strong contrast with the naturalism of the related feet. The German scholar's criticism, however, also rests heavily on the bronze wig which supposedly covered the bald head of the Apollo and on the restoration of the entire statue suggested by Orsi and De Franciscis. A new reconstruction has now been proposed, on convincing grounds. The position of feet and ankles makes it impossible to visualize the statue as standing, and the fragmentary hand cannot be holding a phiale. As a seated Apollo playing the cithara, the fragments find instead a good parallel in the Vatican Citharode, which supposedly copies an akrolithic original of the Severe period (Fig. 152). The Vatican Apollo has the same hairstyle as the Mantua Apollo type (Fig. 180)—a coiffure very popular with creations of the classicistic period, and indeed the Citharode in Rome should also be considered classicizing rather than a *bona fide* copy. We have, however, no way of knowing what hairstyle the Cirò Apollo sported, since the bronze wig found in its vicinity could not fit the head[19] and the attachment holes on the marble cranium are not distinctive enough to allow a reconstruction of the original coiffure.

[17] The addition of bronze curls is not in itself proof positive of a Greek date, since examples of this practice exist also in Roman times: cf., e.g. the Apollo Sosianus, or the Apollo Citharode in the Vatican, especially the detailed photograph in *AttiM-Grecia* N.S. 2 (1958) pl. 21:1.

[18] See, e.g. the Piombino Apollo, the so-called Diana Nemorensis in the Terme, and other examples mentioned in B. S. Ridgway, "The Bronze Apollo from Piombino in the Louvre," *Antike Plastik* 7 (1967) especially p. 61 and ns. 122 and 123.

[19] The wig is too narrow for the head, and could never have been worn by it; its considerable estimated weight (ca. 13 kg.) makes it also dangerous for an akrolithic statue. One theory advocates that the wig was originally made for the Apollo and then discarded, though kept in the temple, when it was found that its dimensions did not fit the head; another and more plausible theory suggests that the wig is an independent offering, not necessarily to be connected with the cult image. The cranium of the Apollo shows slight concentric waves, and it is possible that it was once covered with gold foil; under a complete wig the plastic rendering of the cranium would be totally unnecessary.

The Vatican statuette is not sufficient in itself to prove the Severe date of the Cirò Akrolith since the former either could be, or could have been inspired by, a contemporary classicistic creation. On the other hand, the two might be only vaguely connected typologically and therefore remain independent of each other. More cogent seems the fact, pointed out to me by C. W. Carpenter, that the Temple at Krimisa, built during the Archaic period and remodeled in the Fifth century and again in the Third, was presumably destroyed during the Second century B.C. Since the akrolithic fragments were found within the ruins of the temple, they should not post-date its destruction. Despite its peculiar qualities and a certain lack of aesthetic appeal in its present condition, probably the Cirò Apollo truly belongs to the late Severe period. In contrast with it, the Ludovisi Goddess appears not simply earlier but quite different, and the acceptance of the Apollo as a genuine Severe work might reinforce the case for a later date of the female head.[20] It should, however, be stressed that in dealing with works somewhat removed from the main stream of Greek art not only because of their origin but also because of their purpose and technique, the difficulties of dating multiply and complete assurance is impossible. The same uncertainty exists in evaluating statuary of the classicizing current, to decide whether individual statues are merely copies of earlier monuments or new contemporary creations.

In summary, an examination of neo-Attic reliefs has suggested something of the range to be found in these works. The Chiaramonti Penelope exemplifies how accurately a Severe prototype in the round could be reproduced. The Lanckoronski relief shows the eclectic character of some neo-Attic creations which utilized Severe sculptures in arbitrary combination with later forms and cast them into Hellenistic spatial frames. The Munich terracotta plaques prove not only the stylistic changes which may occur in reproducing a Severe original in the round, but the freedom with which genuine Fifth century statuary was used together with contemporary creations. The Terme fragment with the head of Zeus suggests the transformations that may occur even if a two- and not a three-dimensional prototype is being copied, specifically the increase in the height of the relief; along the same lines the seated philosopher type at Providence indicates the "Severizing" of a later motif. Finally, the entire series of the Charites reliefs illustrates the problem of evaluating the nature of the model, since in this case the original might well have belonged to the classical rather than to the Severe period.

The akroliths briefly examined in this connection present a similar difficulty, not because of copyist's alterations but because of their peculiar nature and partly also because of their "provincial" origin. Next to the Cirò Apollo, and also among other akroliths in Rome, the Ludovisi Goddess stands out more perhaps for her sculpted hair than for other dissimilarities. Yet in comparison with other works of attested Severe date, it cannot be denied that these stone "appendages" have a character of their own which should be taken into account in any study of the Severe style.

---

[20] Fuchs (*RömMitt* 65 [1958] 4) believes, however, in the strict connection of all the major Fifth century akrolithic pieces in Rome and the Cirò Apollo.

APPENDIX 8

1. *Herm-heads from the Odeion of Agrippa stage front, Athens*: Harrison, *Agora* 11 (1965) nos. 219-20, pl. 59. Though these female heads were carved in relief against a plaque, the type is known also in the round and is receiving renewed attention in recent studies. The list of replicas given by L. Budde & R. V. Nicholls (*Catalogue of the Fitzwilliam Museum, Cambridge* [1964] 20-22, nos. 40-41; see also Harrison, *loc.cit.*, n. 91) is considerably lengthened by E. Berger (*AntK* 11 [1968] 73-77 and especially n. 97 on p. 75; *ibid.*, p. 124), who announces a dissertation on this topic being prepared by Ch. Landwehr. The type has been considered a classicistic creation of the First century B.C., as well as a true copy of a mid Fifth century prototype, adapted by Neo-Attic ateliers to a variety of decorative purposes. It is also still debated whether the head belonged originally to a sphinx, or whether the fusion with an animal body was effected in eclectic times. Harrison believes in a purely human origin, Nicholls and Berger support the theory of a sphinx-prototype, perhaps in a group with Oedipus. G. Lippold ("Der Plaste Sotades," *MJb* 3/4 [1952/53] 85-95.) has even suggested that the Roman copyists enlarged and translated in stone a metal rhyton of ca. 460 B.C. This is a theory which opens up interesting possibilities on the relationship of minor arts to classicizing works. It is interesting to note the ease with which Neo-Attic ateliers transposed a type in the round into a relief, a herm, or a table support. On this practice see also comments infra, p. 132-33 and App. 2-3.

2. *Achilles and Telephos Relief, Naples*: From Herculaneum. The relief clearly falls into two halves: the left one shows a standing hero and a woman seated on a rock, the right half—the Telephos scene proper—represents Achilles bending over the elderly, seated Telephos and scraping the point of his spear with his sword. The relief was mentioned as a clear case of Neo-Attic juxtaposition of unrelated scenes (Th. Kraus, *MdI* 5 [1952] 147 and n. 27; pl. 7:2) and Fuchs concurs (*Vorbilder*, p. 138 and n. 96). The Telephos scene is, however, interpreted as an echo of a famous painting by Parrhasios which included also Agamemnon and Odysseus (Pliny, *NH* 35, 67; see *EncArAn* s.v. Telefo, p.

670 fig. 789, E. Paribeni; cf. also G. Hafner, *Geschichte der griechischen Kunst* [Zürich 1961] 258 and fig. 264) and which, therefore, should be in the style of the Fourth century B.C. But the strong anatomy of the figures, the curly locks of Achilles, with drilled centers, the marked curve of his jawline, and the stylized, almost archaistic folds of his mantle, seem more in keeping with Severe style. Since the emotional content of the scene would be unusual in the Severe period, the relief should perhaps be considered a classicistic creation or adaptation of a painting from the early Fifth century. Cf. for instance the cup by the Sosias Painter in Berlin, with Achilles bandaging Patroklos (Boardman/Dörig/Fuchs/Hirmer, fig. 139 opp. p. 294). For a comparable suggestion see E. G. Pemberton, *AJA* 70 (1966) 378, who, however, identifies the scene as Orestes and Aigisthos.

3. *Relief with Apollo and a Bird in Turin*: It seems to have been the revetment plaque for one side of a statue base. Its most extensive description and analysis is by H. Schrader (*ÖJh* 16 [1913] 22-28 with previous bibliography and fig. 14), but it has since received scarce attention. I can find only a brief mention in Ch. Picard, *Manuel* 2:1, p. 40 n. 1; and in Ch. Karouzos' article on the Melian disc (*JHS* 71 [1951] 110, n. 62). Schrader correctly interpreted the relief as a classicistic adaptation of the early Imperial period, presumably after a Severe monument in the round comparable to the Athena Elgin. It is interesting to note the juxtaposition of a Severe figure and a Hellenistic altar. The high projection of the relief is typical of Neo-Attic works. The relief is not mentioned by Fuchs, nor can I find it included in Lippold's *Handbuch*.

4. *Relief from Tralles, Aydin Museum*: published by H. P. Laubscher (*Ist Mitt* 16 [1966] 115-29, pl. 17) as a copy of an Attic votive relief dated ca. 420 B.C. or slightly later. The female divinity undoubtedly copies late Fifth century prototypes, but the god, with his braided hair, seems to hark back to Severe times. Rather than a unified composition faithfully reproduced in neo-Attic times, the relief would seem to me a First century B.C. creation obtained through the juxtaposition of two classical types of slightly different date.

5. *The Broomhall Throne*: Most extensive anal-

ysis by C. Seltman, *JHS* 67 (1947) 22-27; good photographic reproductions in G. Hafner, *Geschichte der griechischen Kunst*, p. 138 fig. 126 (Tyrannicides) and p. 153 fig. 139. The Throne was probably carved around 290 B.C. It is decorated with a scene in relief on each side: side a) shows the Tyrannicide group; side b) a Greek, probably Theseus, striking a fallen Amazon, probably Antiope. Seltman has suggested that the Tyrannicides reproduced on the throne are the original group by Antenor, but the idea has not met with general approval. Whether the earlier or the later monument, however, it is interesting to see that adaptation in relief of free-standing statuary of earlier date was already practiced in the Hellenistic period. Hafner suggests that the Theseus/Antiope relief is also after a statuary group as part of a series on the deeds of Theseus. For a discussion exclusively in relation to the Tyrannicides see S. Brunnsåker, *Tyrant-Slayers*, p. 107 and pp. 115-16.

AKROLITHS

6. *Goddess Head in the Vatican*: This piece has been recently discussed by G. Hafner ("Der Kultbildkopf einer Göttin im Vatikan," *JdI* 81 [1966] 186-205), who conveniently summarizes previous arguments and bibliography. The head has traditionally been identified as Athena, and the holes on the bold cranium and nape have been interpreted as fastenings for a metal or a wooden helmet, or, more rarely, for hair. Hafner advances the ingenious theory that the head represents Juno Sospita as she was venerated at her sanctuary in Lanuvium, with the characteristic attribute of the goatskin on her head which hid all but the goddess' face. He also should like to restore the missing parts in terracotta, and supports his theory with a fragment of a goat's hoof in that material, from Lanuvium, which he believes did not belong to a terracotta statue. Hafner dates the Vatican head in the early Fifth century, as traditional, and assigns it to a Greek artist of Magna Graecian origin who came to work in the vicinity of Rome. He attributes the strange appearance of the head, so difficult to parallel stylistically, to the fact that a Greek artist was trying to reproduce a non-Greek divinity with definite local iconographic connotations. Though Hafner's identification may not meet with general agreement, his refutation of a reconstruction with a helmet is most convincing,

and therefore the old Athena identification should be dismissed.

7. *Akrolithic Head from Sant'Omobono*: Helbig[4], no. 1653 (W. Fuchs) with previous bibliography. The head was probably used in Roman times for a cult purpose different from its original destination. It has been suggested that it represented the Goddess Ops, but it is difficult to determine the head's identity in Greek times. The hair was made of a different material, presumably stucco, but the eyes, contrary to general akrolithic practice, were not inset. It is uncertain whether the lower part of the face has been subject to some reworking in Roman times, but it is difficult to believe that all the modeling of the face is to be attributed to these hypothetical retouches. Fuchs has repeatedly stressed the similarity between the "Ops" and the Cirò Apollo, and has further emphasized the close relationship between the Apollo and the other akroliths in Rome ("Ops," Ludovisi Goddess, Vatican Goddess; see *RömMitt* 65 [1958] 3-4), but I find a great difference between the cold, unmodeled features of the Apollo and the plastic appearance of the "Ops." Indeed this head is so different from the other akroliths (which, more or less, repeat the abstract character of the Apollo) that I wonder whether it should be considered a cult statue or even an akrolith. Its style is, however, related to Magna Graecian works like the Selinus metopes, the head in Hannover, and the Barracco head fragment published by Fuchs (*RömMitt, loc.cit.*; Helbig[4], no. 1882—identified as Orpheus), and its date is correctly given as ca. 450-440. Its brand of "Severe style" is however not as strong as that of the Cirò Apollo or even the Apollo Sosianus (see supra, Ch. 7, App. 3), and the Ops would not have been included in this Appendix, were it not for its constant association with the other "Severe" akroliths in modern scholarship.

8. *Akrolithic Head of Apollo from Cyrene*: Paribeni, *Catalogo* no. 29, pl. 35, p. 24. One of several heads from Cyrene which might be akrolithic and Severe; the "Apollo" is certainly the lastest among them. Notice the pronounced turn of the head and compare with Sicilian sculpture.

TERRACOTTA

9. *Campana Reliefs*: The basic difference between them and the Neo-Attic reliefs consists in the fact that the former are in terracotta, while

the latter are of marble. They are called after the Marchese Giampietro Campana who began collecting these architectural terracottas in the early 19th century. They were meant as decoration for buildings, depending on a long tradition of Etruscan and South Italian revetments but based on a "classical" repertoire. They date from about the middle of the First century B.C. to the Second century after Christ. The most recent study is A. H. Borbein, *Campanareliefs, Typologische und stilkritische Untersuchungen, Röm-Mitt. Ergänzungsheft* 14, 1968.

BIBLIOGRAPHY 8

FOR PAGE 110

The subject of Neo-Attic art has been recently treated by W. Fuchs in *Die Vorbilder der neuattischen Reliefs*, *JdI EH* no. 20, 1959, and in *EncArAn* s.v. Neo-Atticismo. Of interest are also the comments by G. M. A. Richter in *Three Critical Periods* (Oxford 1951) 51-52, *Ancient Italy* (Ann Arbor, 1955) 40-41, and her review of Fuchs' *Vorbilder* in *JRS* 49 (1959) 175-76. For another important review of the same work see also Th. Kraus, *Gnomon* 32 (1960) 463-68.

On the correspondence of Neo-Attic reliefs from various origins see, e.g. Richter, *Three Critical Periods*, p. 50: the Maenad reliefs in New York and Madrid.

For variations introduced by individual copyists, see e.g. the so-called *tympanistria*, the maenad with the tympanon, usually shown with her mantle wrapped around her left arm (e.g. the relief from Ptolemais, G. Caputo, *Lo Scultore del grande bassorilievo con la Danza delle Menadi in Tolemaide di Cirenaica*, Rome 1948, pl. 12 fig. 23), and the version of the same figure in the Villa Albani (G. Rizzo, *Thiasos*, Rome 1934, fig. 7) where the mantle has been omitted, but the left arm is still enveloped in cloth. For the omission of a satyr's tail, see e.g. the Neo-Attic vase fragment in the Rhode Island School of Design Museum, inv. no. 26.270, B. S. Ridgway, *Catalogue*, MS 28, with examples there cited.

On the Fifth century Maenads see the list of replicas in Fuchs, *Vorbilder*, pp. 73-91, and the comments by Carpenter in *Greek Sculpture*, pp. 156-59. Fuch's conclusions differ from Carpenter's in the number of figures attributed to the original monument.

Lanckoronski relief: most recently illustrated and discussed by E. Harrison, *Agora* 11, p. 135 and pl. 65 c-d. Fuchs, *Vorbilder*, p. 173 no. 23—considered late Republican.

FOR PAGE 111

Athena Elgin—once on loan to the British Museum, London, and purchased by the Metropolitan Museum in New York in 1950. Its main publication is by O. Neugebauer, *Die Antike* 11 (1935) 39-48; see also G. M. A. Richter, *Handbook of the Greek Collection*, Metropolitan Museum of Art, 1953, pp. 81-82 and pl. 61. A related statue is published by D. K. Hill in the *Catalogue of Classical Bronze Sculpture in the Walters Art Gallery in Baltimore*, no. 185, but the helmet and dress are different; see also *Master Bronzes* (Cambridge, Mass., 1967) no. 92 p. 96 for further bibliography and comments on the date.

A recent article by Maria H. Groothand, "The Owl on Athena's hand," *BABesch* 43 (1968) 35-51, suggests that the owl was traditionally associated with Athena at the time of Pheidias, and that probably the Promachos held the bird in her hand. This iconography changed later, when a Nike replaced the owl on the Parthenos' hand, as a result of a different conception of Athens' position and importance. The Lanckoronski relief and the Athena Elgin are included in the discussion of monuments in the earlier iconographic tradition.

Porcigliano plaques, once in Munich (probably destroyed during World War II): on the actual find see C. Pietrangeli, *Scavi e Scoperte di antichità* (Rome 1958) 128 no. 25 and n. 6; see also Ch. Karouzos, *Deltion* 13 (1930), 95-101 figs. 34-38: a most extensive discussion of the types portrayed. See further Beyen and Vollgraff, pp. 47-50, and, more recently, Orlandini, *Calamide* 2 (1950) 25-26 and S. Stucchi, *BullCom* 75 (1953-55) 42-44. Furtwängler's opinion appears in his *Beschreibung der Glyptothek* (Munich 1900) 74 and nos. 62-66.

FOR PAGE 112

On the date of the Artemision wreck see supra, p. 63 n. 5. For the theory of a neo-Attic relief or sketch as prototype for the plaque, see Beyen and Vollgraff, p. 50; also Karouzos, p. 100.

For a recent study on the Apollo Philesios see E. Simon, "Beobachtungen zum Apollon Philesios des Kanachos," *Charites* (Bonn 1957) 38-46; also E. Bielefeld, "Statue des Apollon. Rom, Museo Antiquario Forense" *Antike Plastik* 8 (1968) 13-17.

FOR PAGE 113

Stucchi, *op.cit.*; for a more extensive bibliography on the Apollo in Rome see supra p. 107.

On the Piombino Apollo's hairstyle see B. S. Ridgway, "The Bronze Apollo from Piombino in the Louvre," *Antike Plastik* 7 (1967) 43-75 and especially pp. 47, 55-57, 61-62.

For details of the Elektra's coiffure, see M.

Borda, *La Scuola di Pasitele* (Bari 1953) figs. 7-9.

Pitti Apollo: EA 208-9.

FOR PAGE 114

Stone example of Campana type: Paribeni, *Sculture V Sec.*, no. 119, p. 66, compared to Campana Terracotta from Castelgandolfo, von Rhoden-Winnefeld, *Antiken Terrakotten*, pl. 94.

Relief once in Mittelschreiberhau: EA 3906; Schefold, *Meisterwerke*, p. 238, fig. 292, and p. 81, now in a private collection in Genf and dated by Schefold after 450 B.C.

Rhode Island Relief: Inv. no. 57.171, B. S. Ridgway, *Catalogue*, MS 27, said to be from Tegea.

On the Seated-philosopher type see G. Dontas, *Eikones kathemenon pnevmatikon anthropon*, Athens 1960; the RISD relief is discussed on pp. 91-92 and illustrated on pl. 36 B; for comparison see the relief in Budapest, Richter, *Portraits of the Greeks* 2, fig. 1679, and other illustrations in Dontas; see also a funerary relief from Rhodes in *To Ergon* 1958, p. 175 fig. 182.

On the Charites reliefs see Fuchs, *Vorbilder*, pp. 59-63, with previous bibliography; to his list on p. 60 should be added one more fragment with the third Charis, from Kos, pointed out by Harrison *Agora* 11, p. 122 n. 112, and illustrated by Laurenzi, *ASAtene* N.S. 17-18 (1955-56) 147 no. 218.

Another recent treatment of the subject, by Fuchs, in Helbig⁴, no. 351 (the Chiaramonti relief).

The most recent account on the cult of the Charites in Athens is by E. Schwarzenberg, *Die Grazien*, Bonn 1966, pp. 14-19; see also F. W. Hamdorf, *Griechische Kultpersonifikationen der vorhellenistischen Zeit* (Mainz 1964) 45-46 and 103-4.

FOR PAGE 115

For Harrison's suggestion see *Agora* 11, pp. 122-24 and p. 135.

On the tradition of Sokrates the Philosopher as sculptor, see the comments in Pollitt, *Sources*, p. 87, and infra.

On the possible location of the Charites relief within the Propylaia see G. P. Stevens, "The Periclean Entrance Court of the Akropolis of Athens," *Hesperia* 5 (1936) 446-47, fig. 2, position H.

On the archaic origin of the typology of the

Charites see R. Feubel, *Die attischen Nymphenreliefs und ihre Vorbilder* (1935) 15-18.

FOR PAGE 116

Fragmentary slab in Berlin: C. Blümel, *Die archaisch griechischen Skulpturen der staatlichen Museen zu Berlin*, 1963, no. 9 p. 18 figs. 25-26, dated ca. 510 B.C.

For the Parthenon Peplophoroi, see e.g. Lullies and Hirmer, pl. 159, Parthenon East frieze, slab in the Louvre.

For peplophoroi holding the peplos skirt see, e.g. the Locri Pinax, Langlotz, *Magna Graecia*, color pl. IX, or a bronze statuette, also from Locri, pl. 92 right. For many mirror supports in this pose see also Poulsen, SS, pl. 1 and figs. 11-16.

Propylaia Kore, Akr. 688, Schrader, pls. 30-32.

FOR PAGE 117

Terracotta Athena from Olympia: E. Kunze, "Terrakottaplastik," *Olympiabericht* VI (1958) 169-94, pls. 66-70, dated ca. 480 B.C.

For the so-called Fleeing Girl from Eleusis, see supra, Ch. 2, App. 1, p. 26 (dated before 480 B.C. because destroyed by the Persians).

For examples in vase painting, see e.g. the Berlin Painter's krater in Tarquinia, with Europa and the bull, dated ca. 490 B.C. Arias and Hirmer, pl. 154 and color pl. XXXV. "Hermes of Alkamenes": Richter, *Sculpture and Sculptors*, fig. 628.

Artemisia from Halikarnassos: Richter, *Sculpture and Sculptors*, fig. 313.

For Severe figures enveloped in their mantles, cf. e.g. the so-called Sosandra, supra, pp. 65-68. For the classical manner of wearing the himation over the chiton, see e.g. the Kore of the Eleusis Relief, Lullies and Hirmer, pl. 172.

For Fourth century examples of this fashion see *votive*: The so-called Gandy Deering relief from Rhamnous in the British Museum, B. Ashmole, "Torch Racing at Rhamnus," *AJA* 66 (1962) 233-34 pl. 59:3 goddess to extreme left; the work is dated to the late Fourth c.

record reliefs: H. K. Süsserott, *Griechische Plastik des 4. Jhdt v. Chr.* (Frankfurt am Main 1938) pl. 3 no. 2, Athenian record relief dated 375/374: the figure of Athena (= Lippold, *Handbuch*, pl. 88:2).

funerary reliefs: Attic marble Lekythos in Munich, Lullies & Hirmer, pl. 204, dated by comparison with the above-mentioned record relief.

FOR PAGE 118

Laurenzi: *ASAtene* N.S. 17-18 (1955-56) 147 no. 218.

Giustiniani relief: illustrated in *BrBr*, text to 654 r, fig. 1; the heads are not pertinent.

Fragment c in Athens, EA 732.

Fragment d in Athens, *AZ* 27 (1869) pl. 22:3.

Head in Vatican Magazine: Kaschnitz-Weinberg, *Mag.Vat.*, no. 2 pl. 8.

Fragment f in Antiquario Comunale: *BdA* 36 (1951) 110, fig. 6.

Slab in Rome, private collection, (i): *BdA* 36 (1951) 109, fig. 5.

Fragment from South slope of Acropolis (g), Fuchs, pl. 12a; discussed by Fuchs on p. 61; by Poulsen, SS, on p. 134. For the addition of a chiton sleeve under the peplos as a Fourth century trait, see Harrison's comments on archaistic dresses, *Agora* 11, p. 53 and n. 29.

FOR PAGE 119

Sokrates' dedication to the Nymphs: IG II², 4592 = Athens, Nat. Mus. 2351.

FOR PAGE 121

Ludovisi Goddess: *BrBr* 223; Langlotz, *Magna Graecia*, pls. 62-63; Paribeni, *Sculture V Sec.*, no. 1, p. 11, figs. 1a-b.

FOR PAGE 122

Agrigento Kouros: Richter, *Kouroi²*, no. 182, figs. 547-49; see also Amelung's comparison of the top of the two heads in *JdI* 35 (1920) 57 fig. 4.

Cirò Apollo: W.-H. Schuchhardt, "Zum Akrolithkopf von Cirò," *AJA* 66 (1962) 317-18 with previous bibliography; Langlotz, *Magna Graecia*, pls. 118-19. The new reconstruction is by C. Turano, "L'Acrolito di Cirò," *Klearchos* 23-24 (1964) 61-72.

Vatican Citharode: lately W. Fuchs in Helbig⁴, no. 135, with previous bibliography. Some authors (Amelung, *VatKat* 2, p. 592 no. 395; K. A. Pfeiff, *Apollon*, p. 160, n. 280) question the pertinence of the head, and Pfeiff and Lippold (*Handbuch*, p. 132 n. 2) tend to date it later than the Severe period, though still within the Fifth century.

FOR PAGE 123

C. W. Carpenter has discussed orally with me the possible dating of the Cirò Apollo as part of her research on akrolithic sculpture, which is, however, still unpublished. The date for the temple's destruction is deduced from P. Orsi's rather vague statements in "Templum Apollinis Alaei," *AttiMGrecia* (1932) 7-182; see pp. 174-79 where the complete absence of Roman coins is stressed. Recent excavations have brought back to light the foundations of the temple first exposed in 1928 but later covered by soil. However, no new element was added to the present state of our knowledge. See G. Foti's account in *Santuari di Magna Grecia*, Atti del Quarto Convegno di Studi sulla Magna Grecia, Taranto-Reggio Calabria, 11-16 October 1964 (Naples 1965), pp. 145-46.

CHAPTER 9

The Severe Style in Late Hellenistic and Roman Times:
Sculpture in the Round

Lingering Severe, as a stylistic phenomenon, seems to have lasted into the early Fourth century B.C., but not much later. Of earlier periods, it was the archaic style, with all its potential for decoration and its implication of a venerable nature, which appealed to the more sophisticated taste of the late Fourth century and the early Hellenistic period. A return to the sober simplicity of the Severe style occurred only in the First century B.C. when taste, having become entirely jaded rather than simply sophisticated, required new approaches and combinations.

From a certain point of view, however, even the florid baroque of the middle Hellenistic phase had something in common with the Severe period because it aimed at the same expressionism, the same lively action, the same characterization which had interested the sculptors of the early Fifth century. The differences lie of course in the vastly superior technique of Hellenistic sculptors, who had complete control over their material, be it bronze or marble, and who knew, so to speak, all the tricks of the trade. We therefore find in advanced Hellenistic times the same emphasis on contours which had characterized Severe works, for instance the interest in pyramidal compositions, or the attempt to flatten a truly three-dimensional pose into a two-dimensional scheme intelligible and significant only from a single point of view. We also find the emotionalism, the expression of violence, the interest in age range, and even that trait which was so well represented in the Aeginetan and the Olympia sculptures—the psychological demand on the spectator for participation in the telling of a story.

More significant, however, is the occurrence of actual renderings, which go beyond a mere sharing of aim or content. When this intentional imitation of Severe style takes place, the result is usually so puzzling that no complete agreement exists among archaeologists as to the correct evaluation of the material. A case in point is the famous Athena with the crossed aegis from Pergamon (Figs. 159-60), which was considered by Bulle a Hellenistic version of the statue made by Myron in a group with Herakles and Zeus for Samos, a Myronian label which has proved most difficult to shake. It is true that the Attalids ordered many replicas of Fifth century originals which were more or less adapted to Hellenistic tastes, such as the obvious reproduction of the Athena Parthenos for the Pergamene Library. But the "Myronian" Athena is so elaborate in style that it can hardly be brought back to a Severe prototype and should be considered a Second century creation along classicizing lines: the complicated drapery and the backward lean of the pose are totally foreign to the Severe period. Only the head tends to support the attribution, so much so that Kalkmann could doubt its pertinence to the body. It is interesting to see, however, how close the Hellenistic sculptor could come to the Severe rendering in the shape of the heavy-lidded eyes, the mouth, and the heavy chin.

Another member of the Samian group reconstructed by Bulle has found more credibility as a true replica of a Myronian work: the Herakles known from three statuettes, in Boston (Figs. 161-62), Oxford, and Madrid; yet it too has been doubted, and at least the Roman version in Boston, with the pictorial touches in the rendering of the lion skin and the spring water near the tree-trunk, surely points to a Hellenistic date at the earliest.

More difficult to evaluate is the Drunken Old Woman preserved in the two copies in Munich and the Conservatori. Pliny (*NH* 36. 32) tells us that Myron made an *anus ebria*, but on the basis of the extant replicas it has been assumed that the sculptor cited is not the famous Fifth century master but an homonymous artist of the Second century B.C., whose name appears in an inscription from Delos. Only Carpenter, and before him Waldhauer, have argued that the compact composition and the peculiar behavior of the drapery where it touches the ground speak in favor of a mid Fifth century date and have, therefore, tried to ascribe the original to the great Myron. Carpenter believes that the extreme realism of the old woman's face has been increased by copyist and modern restorer; Waldhauer even defends its plausibility within the Fifth century B.C. A further possibility could be that a late Hellenistic or "Roman" master decided to combine a Severe type of statue with a purely Hellenistic head (and a Hellenistic bottle) in what is usually defined as a pastiche. Yet the mannerism of the slipped strap over the emaciated right shoulder of the Old Hag is such a ferocious take-off on the "Aphrodite" of the Parthenon East pediment that one wonders whether the entire statue should not rather be interpreted as an intentional caricature of Fifth century motifs, or perhaps as a Hellenistic hyperbole of the Myronian prototype.

It is admittedly difficult to reconcile such a genre subject as a drunken woman with the spirit of the Severe period. Terracottas, which undoubtedly portrayed genre even in the Fifth century, are not in the same class with the major arts, and sculpture of that time, though interested in old age, usually depicted it within a narrative or mythological context. It is, however, possible that Pliny's *anus ebria* referred to an actual myth, as his mention of Pythagoras' limping man probably refers to his Philoktetes. In any case, even scholars who reject the Myronian attribution recognize the "certain mannerism" in the collapse of the drapery over the base. If the date of the prototype truly falls within the late Second century B.C., the treatment of the Drunken Woman's garment would attest even at that early date, to a revival of interest not only in the spirit but also in the formulas of the Severe style.

There is no question that the Severe style must have exercised considerable appeal in Roman quarters during the First century B.C. and First A.D. The influence is obvious even in contemporary Roman portraits of late Republican or Augustan times when several ladies sport coiffures imitating the rolled-up hair of the Kritian Boy or other Severe prototypes. Among the booty carried off to Rome from Greece and other Greek centers, many Severe works are mentioned by the literary sources; and others have actually been found there, such as the famous Ludovisi "throne," the Apollo "Sosianus," the Esquiline stele, the Leukothea relief and even the puzzling akroliths. It is not surprising that the demand for such works increased to the point that artists no longer simply copied famous Severe monuments but also imitated them in what was not plagiarism but a true compliment to ancient excellence and perhaps finally even forged them, to obtain a higher price on the antiquarian market. With such wealth of material, motivations, and influences, the production of this period is one of the most difficult to evaluate, and a great deal of disagreement exists among scholars.

The simplest category is perhaps that of the pastiches. By this term is meant a work which juxtaposes *abruptly* elements of different styles, not in an eclectic fusion but in discordant contrast. The most obvious case of this procedure is the so-called Spinario in Rome, a bronze statue of a boy extracting a thorn from his foot (Fig. 164). Carpenter demonstrated how a head meant for an upright position had been joined to a bent neck and torso. Moreover, the complexity of the bodily pose and the genre quality of the subject spoke against an early date, while the head seemed in pure Severe style. Terracottas and statuettes have provided the missing links: the subject probably originated with a purely Hellenistic head (as shown by the marble Spinario Castellani in the British Museum), presumably in the Third century B.C. The motif became popular enough even to be caricatured and modified in terracottas of the late Second century B.C. with grotesque facial features. When this change also was no longer sufficient for the jaded taste of the First century, the final step was taken of making a Severe head fit the Hellenistic body in a composition attractive for its peculiar character and its high artistic quality.

That the joining of head to body was not a purely mechanical operation is proved by the fact that the imprint of a later style is visible also in the former, though basically a copy of a Severe prototype: notice, for instance, the small ringlets above the outer corners of the eyes, at the point where the hair divides to gather in a knot or to hang free along the cheeks. These small locks are missing in another replica of the head type, this time in marble, in the Conservatori, which, through its straight neck, shows its original appurtenance to an upright statue.[1] Comparisons have been rightly made with the Triptolemos of the Great Eleusinian relief and the Eros Soranzo in Leningrad (Fig. 163); yet a note of caution could perhaps be introduced at this point. Is the Eros Soranzo a genuine copy of a Severe original? Its rather surprised expression, the abrupt turn of its head in strong contrast with the frontal position of the torso, in itself out of keeping with the "Attic" stance, the unusual rendering of the hair over the forehead, seem strange in a truly Severe statue. Unfortunately the head is preserved only in the Hermitage replica, and the torsos in Sparta and Oxford provide no further clues, but the possibility of a First century dating should at least be considered.[2] Disagreement also exists over the replicas of the Spinario head, among which the head on the bronze and that in marble in the Conservatori Museo Nuovo are also suspect as being classicistic. Could they have been adapted in the round after a two-dimensional prototype like the Triptolemos of the

[1] This statement is made by Carpenter (*MAAR* 18, pp. 36-37), who refutes the technical arguments advanced by Mustilli (*Museo Mussolini* [Rome 1939] 144-45 no. 9, pl. 89 figs. 332-35) to prove the inclination of the head. The question was re-opened by Richter (*Ancient Italy*, pp. 50-51 and n. 97) on the basis of an experiment with plastelline to show the similar angle between head and neck in both the Conservatori and the bronze Spinario heads. Hence the Conservatori head, she claims, was also made for a bent position and belonged to another "Spinario" composition. Fuchs (Helbig,⁴ no. 1785), though quoting Richter in his bibliography, does not seem to accept her conclusions and returns to the theory of the upright position, more consonant with the Severe period.

Richter distinguishes different prototypes among the various replicas thought to reproduce the Spinario. She supports a date of ca. 460 B.C. for the original of the Conservatori bronze, which provided the inspiration for all subsequent adaptations. However, even the existence of exact replicas of the Spinario "pastiche" would not necessarily imply an earlier date for the prototype, since classicizing creations were copied as much as Greek originals (see infra, Stephanos' athlete).

[2] M. Robertson suggests to me that the upturned look of the Eros may imply that he was in a group with a larger figure (Aphrodite?) and that such a group can be more easily conceived in "Pasitelean" than in Fifth century terms.

Eleusinian relief?[3] Conversely, the newly created bronze Spinario was adapted in a relief of the Hadrianic period representing the sleeping Endymion.[4]

Another famous statue usually considered a pastiche is the so-called Esquiline Venus (Figs. 165-66). Obviously the question is still controversial if as late as 1955 an authority like G. M. A. Richter could support the theory that the statue is truly a replica of a 460 B.C. original. Yet even the torso of the same type in the Louvre is not sufficient corroboration for a Severe prototype, since classicistic works were also copied and adapted in later Roman times.[5] Carpenter has suggested that the artist of the Esquiline Venus had placed a genuine Severe female head on a Severe male youthful upper torso (with added breasts), in turn joined to a lower female body of Hellenistic origin (the Aphrodite of Cyrene type) in a pastiche of surprising appeal. The more widely accepted theory is that a Hellenistic body in its entirety was joined to a Severe head, while a third and perhaps more tenable possibility is that the entire statue was created not with exact copying but with only vague reference to specific prototypes; so that while the style is generally Severe, the conception and individual details betray a later origin. Indeed the statue of a nude woman in the Fifth century would be fairly revolutionary (pace Richter and Charbonneaux) and the slightly tiptoe position of the Esquiline Venus, with legs narrowly compressed in a *Pudicitia* pose, is hardly conceivable even in a period as experimental as the Severe. The head, with its peculiar eye form, recalls the terracotta plaques in Munich, and, except for the length of the strands in the strange nape knot, resembles male rather than female features.

It should be admitted that it is difficult to establish the difference between a pastiche and an eclectic classicistic creation. Perhaps the term pastiche is safely employed only when a Roman portrait head is used in conjunction with a Severe body, as for instance in the "Aspasia" type. When two different prototypes are used to form a different statue, but are organically fused together and recast, as it were, in the artist's personal language, the definition becomes more difficult. A case in point is what can be justly called "Müller's peplophoros," (Fig. 167), since Valentin Müller was the scholar who acutely analyzed the stylistic discrepancies of the statue. The sculptor obviously rendered a Severe peplophoros (Fig. 168), the so-called Candia type, in the style of the Fourth century B.C., as indicated by the denser folds of the skirt, the deviation of the pleat over the projecting foot, the arrangement of the kolpos; with the result that one cannot justifiably call the statue a pastiche, or simply an eclectic work, but perhaps should more correctly define it as a "modernization" of a Severe type.

[3] Fuchs (Helbig[4], no. 1785) suggests a Severe Eros or Triptolemos as prototype, but obviously as a statue in the round which in turn might have been echoed in the great Eleusinian relief. An interesting head in Basel, perhaps from a herm, seems closest to a Severe prototype: E. Berger, *AntK* 11:1 (1968) 71-73. Berger, who is restudying the type, does not exclude the possibility that the Severe original might also have been a *genre* subject, but he too seems to consider the Conservatori marble head a classicistic "Umbildung" after the bronze Spinario.

[4] Von Steuben in Helbig[4], no. 1331. For the comparison with the Spinario see Orlandini, *ArchCl* 4 (1952) 257-58, pl. 59:1; Richter (*Ancient Italy*, p. 51 n. 98) disagrees with the comparison on the basis of modeling and proportions, but these could have been altered to suit a youth rather than a child, as required by the subject.

[5] Indeed the two locks still visible on the torso's neck and missing in the Esquiline statue, as well as the different shape of the support, point to such an adaptation. Other discrepancies between the two works mentioned by Charbonneaux are, however, attributed to reworking or flaws in the marble.

More eclectic in character is the Athena statuette from Leptis Magna now in Istanbul (Fig. 169). Generally considered an Ionic or nesiotic work of the last quarter of the Fifth century, it has also been called an eclectic classicistic creation. The large head looks Severe[6] and forms a striking contrast with the body covered by the flimsy, lively drapery of the late Fifth century. But the relatively high belt, the elongated proportions, the unusual stance with shoulders thrown back, which has suggested that the Athena was leaning on a spear, are more typically Hellenistic traits and can hardly be imputed to Ionic ornamental calligraphy or to provincialism, as Berger obviously senses, though he still supports the early dating.

Similar discrepancies, though more organically fused, appear in the famous bronze dancers from Herculaneum (Figs. 170-71), which Lippold can still consider bona fide copies of Severe originals. A detailed analysis by L. Forti points out the mannerisms, incongruences, and irrationalities of the statues, which, however, given their decorative function in the garden of a wealthy Roman, are very effective pieces of "Roman" art. In a similar category should be included the large terracotta Nikai in "Severe" peploi recently found near the Athenian Acropolis. These, because of clay and workmanship, undoubtedly belong to Roman times and only recall Severe prototypes: one more confirmation of the popularity of this style in the commercial arts.

A more problematic piece—eclectic, pastiche, genuine copy, new classicistic creation?—is the so-called Charioteer in the Conservatori (Figs. 172-73). Its relationship to the Omphalos Apollo is indisputable, and several scholars have attributed it to the same master, or at least to his workshop. But as Homann-Wedeking first pointed out, its similarity to that famous statue is so pronounced as to lead to the suspicion that it intentionally reproduces it, with minor changes in the rendering of the bangs, the loose hair over the nape, and the way in which the braids are tied above the forehead. Von Steuben and Zanker, after proving the lock-by-lock correspondence of the hair over the dome, believe this difference in the braids (and especially the abruptness with which the braid on the left merges with the fillet) to be a misunderstanding of the classicistic artist. This position might now have to be revised in view of the recently found head in Corinth (Fig. 75), where a similar cord unites the braids, though without knot in the center. Obviously variations in hairstyles may go back to different local fashions, and the artist of the Charioteer may have fused together two different prototypes; even the "monotonous" bangs could be a somewhat more advanced rendering of the type of curls seen in the Corinth head. The presence of a genuine Severe parallel does not, however, necessarily rehabilitate the Conservatori statue as a true copy of an original Severe bronze. The irrational, abrupt ending of the braid still remains to be explained, and probably as a mistake; Homann-Wedeking's accusation, that the sculptor betrays his knowledge of more naturalistic anatomy, should also be seriously considered.

The correct interpretation of the statue is also in dispute. The "charioteer" label is obviously untenable, especially because of the struts on the right leg, which would have been completely exposed had the figure been mounting a chariot. The statue must have been set up so as to be seen from a specific point of view, as suggested by the peculiar contour of the face, with its pronounced distortion of the left jaw; a comparable distortion

[6] This is particularly true of the profile view, with the overly large eyes, the prominent jawline, and the heavy chin: see Ferri, *BdA* 27 (1933) 71 fig. 3.

exists in the torso. Hafner has suggested that we have Theseus fighting with the Marathon bull, a group which Pausanias saw in bronze on the Athenian Acropolis. Paribeni supported an interpretation as Theseus lifting the rock that concealed his father's sword, though he admitted that this composition did not satisfactorily account for the struts. Guerrini argued for Theseus kidnaping Antiope. A hero is indicated by the hairstyle, too long to represent a mere mortal after the archaic period; but even the mythological connotation does not necessarily imply a Fifth century prototype since Roman decorative art delighted in reconstructing such events, whether or not copied after genuine monuments in the round. As examples see the Campana plaque in the British Museum used by Paribeni to explain the position of the Conservatori "Charioteer" or a related panel in the Louvre with Perseus killing the monster. Even the fact that other replicas of the "Charioteer" exist is not in itself proof against a classicistic origin, as already mentioned for previous examples. It could be argued that in all previous cases the correct assessment of the work was in dispute (as, for instance, the Spinario and the Esquiline Venus), but little doubt seems to remain in the case of Stephanos' athlete.

The type derives its name from a statue in the Villa Albani signed "Stephanos pupil of Pasiteles" (Fig. 174). Stephanos, and his better known master, Pasiteles, lived in the First century B.C., and literary sources specifically tell us of the great interest Pasiteles took in masterpieces of earlier times. Richter has credited him with the invention of the pointing system for exact copying, and would consider Stephanos' work a true reflection of his teacher's influence. According to her, the youth in the Villa Albani is "consistently in the style of about 460 B.C." and also Lippold considers it a genuine copy of a Severe statue. But a growing consensus among scholars would place Stephanos' youth among the "Severizing" creations of the late Republican/early Augustan period, and this theory is supported by the stylistic peculiarities of the statue, hardly in keeping with the Severe period. Notice, for instance, the elongated proportions of the body, emphasized by the strange backward leaning pose, or the awkward attachment of arms to torso. The head of the type is known in two versions, differentiated by the hairstyle over the forehead; and it has been suggested that not the Albani, but the head in the Lateran, of which other replicas also survive, was the original form invented by the master.

Borda and Fuchs believe that the Athlete was created as a kind of sample figure (like the Canon/Doryphoros of Polykleitos?) which could be used in a variety of combinations, since it appears with other figures, often themselves of more openly eclectic nature. The most obvious example is the group in Naples, the "Orestes and Elektra" (Fig. 175), where the female personage obviously combines late Fifth century drapery with bodily proportions and forms comparable to those of the youth and with a complicated hairstyle derived from three different Severe coiffures mostly reserved for men. Indeed a comparable hair arrangement appears on a male personage, again in combination with "Stephanos' Athlete," in a group in the Louvre which has been called "Mercury and Vulcan" or "Orestes and Pylades," neither appellation probably correct. With the exception of the crossed legs, "Pylades" imitates the Naples Elektra also in the general pose, and should be equally considered a classicistic creation; fortunately in both companion figures in Naples and Paris either the drapery or the position belong to a later stylistic phase than the Severe and therefore there can be no question as to their eclectic character. The "athlete" with them may be considered more consistent in his Severe style, but the very fact that he is found in combination with such classicistic creations should confirm what has repeatedly been suggested on purely stylistic grounds.

The entire question of the Pasitelean school has recently been discussed by Borda and need not be amplified here since many of these "Pasitelean" creations derive their inspiration from styles later than the Severe; two points should, however, be emphasized: the funerary quality of some of these groups,[7] and the irrational or unprecedented hair-styles of the statues.[8] The first point supports the contention that the Tralles youth can be an eclectic creation of Roman times (Fig. 114), with a definite Severe body, despite the fact that it was meant as a funerary monument. The second point gives one of the few clues for identifying such later works.

It is impossible to mention here all the statues that either are, or at least have been suspected on good grounds to be, eclectic creations of late Hellenistic or Roman times. A thorough study of the classicistic production has not yet been carried out, though important contributions have been made in individual publications. The pioneering work remains the article by Rumpf, "Der Idolino," *Critica d'Arte* 4 (1939), 17-27, which discusses also statues in style other than Severe. An important list has been compiled by Buschor in his book on Olympia, where he specifically emphasizes that herms tend to "Severize." Comments on single sculptures can be found in all recent museum catalogues and in various articles mentioned below in the bibliography. It seems more important here to point to a few pieces and the problems they present, in order to gain some general guide-line for the evaluation of similar works. The hairstyle will be used as a major criterion for judgment.

As already mentioned, the Severe period, with its emphasis on bronze work and its love for linear renderings, favored complicated coiffures looping in and out of fillets in various combinations. But some arrangements cannot be exactly paralleled in any Severe original, while they are found so consistently in conjunction with ornamental Roman bronzes and marbles as to justify some doubt about the Fifth century origin of the coiffure. A typical example is the hairstyle of the so-called Mantua Apollo type (Fig. 180), already mentioned in connection with the Apollo Citharode in the Vatican (p. 122) (Fig. 152). From the end of the archaic period and the beginning of the Severe we have several instances of hair rolled around a fillet, as for instance in the Kritian Boy from the Acropolis, or the Agrigento youth, and even some of the Olympia figures, though there the details were left to paint. In actual bronzes the rendering appears more convincing, such as in the head of a youth from the Athenian Acropolis (Fig. 178), the Selinus/Castelvetrano Ephebe (Fig. 93), or the Acropolis jumper; but in none of these cases does the roll appear in conjunction with long spiral locks over the chest or shoulders. In the Mantua Apollo type, of which a bronze replica has been found in Pompeii, the hair parts in the center of the forehead, is twisted around a fillet, and ends in spiraling curls on either side of the neck. Clearest in the Pompeii replica, a further refinement is introduced in that one long curl stems from the forehead, the other from the nape, strands.[9] This elaborate

---

[7] For instance, the so-called Ildefonso group in Madrid (*BrBr* 308; Borda, fig. 15 and pp. 70-74), with the obvious symbolism of the extinguished torch, and the Orestes and Elektra in the Terme, signed by Menelaos (*BrBr* 309; Borda, fig. 19 and pp. 94-101) with a funerary stele behind the figures.

[8] See for instance the so-called Runner in the Vatican (*BrBr* 521) and comments on her hairstyle by Borda (pp. 87-88) and Ridgway ("Piombino Apollo," *Antike Plastik* 7, p. 60).

[9] Notice the detail in the photographs of the various replicas published by Congdon, *AJA* 67

coiffure has been closely analyzed by C. Saletti, who finds in its specific rendering confirmation for considering the Apollo an eclectic creation of the First century B.C. Many scholars, however, still support a date around 460 B.C. for the prototype which they attribute to the Argive school.

It is difficult to decide which opinion is closer to the truth: in stance, bodily proportions, and general appearance,[10] the type fits well within the Severe period, without any of the discrepancies so obvious in Stephanos' Athlete. Nonetheless the coiffure is somewhat disturbing, though close approximations exist in several other variants. The most interesting because definitely classical is the coiffure of the Kassel Apollo type (Fig. 176), most generally assigned to the early Pheidias. The traces of the Severe style are still visible in the heavy face, the fairly large eyes, and especially the drilled centers of the short curls massed over the forehead.[11] The braided arrangement itself is somewhat old-fashioned, though still in use for elderly figures well into the Fifth century, and the master of the Kassel statue has complicated it by establishing different layers of locks, braids, and fillet. There is no clear point of origin for the corkscrew locks behind the ears, but presumably they form part of the long hair over the nape, which has otherwise been braided.[12] In the Mantua type, however, whether originating from the front or the rear, the long strands are conceived as part of the rolled-up hair, in an arrangement which would be difficult to duplicate in reality.

A predilection for such twisting strands appears in many "Pasitelean" works, such as the Elektra in Naples, the Lateran-type head of the Stephanos' Athlete, and the so-called Pylades in the Louvre. In these cases, however, the locks, not long enough to continue down to the chest, stop at the temples in a whisker-like arrangement. Undoubtedly a

(1963) pl. 3:2 and 4, pl. 4:8, pl. 5:12, pl. 6:20. The only other statues which closely imitate this hairstyle are the Apollo Citharode in the Vatican (see supra, p. 122 and bibliography), where the locks emerging from the front roll were added separately in metal (the nape locks are restored), and the Apollo Pitti (Fig. 149) which varies slightly the basic pattern by increasing the number of long locks. Both works have been said to reflect Severe prototypes, but they may also be classicistic creations or adaptations.

[10] Saletti (pp. 252-54) believes, however, that the anatomical treatment is closer to Praxitelean works than to Severe monuments, and emphasizes the lack of digitations on the flanks and the soft muscular transitions.

[11] Although this detail may be part of the copyist's technique, the shape of the curls would lend itself to such treatment.

[12] This same combination of nape braids and long escaping lock clearly appears on coins of Leontini (C. M. Kraay and M. Hirmer, Greek Coins, 1966, pl. 6:18 R and 19 R, ca. 479 B.C.) which have been quoted in support of an early chronology for the hairstyle of the Mantua type (Saletti, p. 256; Congdon, p. 12 and pl. 5:15-16: the variety with the roll and the long lock = Kraay and Hirmer, pls. 7-8,

ca. 460-450 B.C.). But a most emphatic distinction should be made between escaping curls and strands which are definitely part of the coiffure. There is a basic difference, moreover, between locks stemming from the long hair at the nape and those forming part of the forehead hair. The former appear since the early archaic period, in conjunction with a fluent coiffure over the shoulders from which they branch off to fall over the chest, while the latter seem a classicizing contribution. All archaic and Severe examples of long locks quoted by Mrs. Congdon either form part of the main back mass or are "stragglers" from the nape roll, in which case they are usually single strands of little volume and definitely not a major element of the coiffure. Since they mostly appear on numismatic or pictorial representations, one wonders whether the artist introduced them to make clear that the personage involved had long hair, though twisted up in a roll. The detail might have been unclear in small-scale depictions, yet was important as characterization for a hero or a god. All the later examples in Mrs. Congdon's work (such as the late Hellenistic Spartan coin of pl. 5:17 or the Hadrianic tondo of pl. 6:21) support rather than undermine the late dating of the Mantua type hairstyle.

137

similar rendering must have been current in Severe times, as shown by the bronze athlete in Mt. Holyoke or head 1949 in the National Museum in Athens; it has even been suggested that these coiffures are of South Italian origin, which might explain their survival in the Pasitelean school, directed by a Magna Graecian master.[13] It is, however, logical to suppose that the classicistic masters exaggerated such renderings, or at least created new hairstyles based on a contamination of different prototypes.

A possible Hellenistic influence could also exist: some female coiffures, of which perhaps the earliest statuary example is the Eirene of Kephisodotos (Fig. 177), emphasize soft waves over the forehead and long spiral locks alongside the neck. The type and its evolution can best be followed in numismatic representations, which suggest a development from waves to roll and then to related curls, as in the Mantua Apollo. In general the type seems to begin ca. 400-336 B.C.; it continues 336-280 B.C. and most closely resembles the Apollo's hairstyle around 230 B.C., though it is attested as late as at least 100 B.C. The best development is traceable in the coinage of Smyrna, where both the head of Tyche and that of Apollo show parallel changes in coiffures, and where the evolution of the rendering clearly excludes the possibility that a Severe prototype is being imitated.[14]

On the other hand, the Mantua Apollo could be interpreted as a classicistic cross between the Kassel type and the Kritian Youth. In this connection it is interesting to note a bronze statuette once in the Winckelmann-Institut of the University of Berlin, where the Kassel type has been reproduced with a corresponding variant in the hair over the forehead, which seems rolled around a fillet; similarly a head in the Terme retains echoes of the Kassel, the Pitti and the Mantua types, and should be considered a classicistic adaptation. Particularly characteristic of this late version is the wide space over the forehead between the two first diverging convolutions of the hair around the fillet, so that a considerable length of the ribbon is revealed. The hair combed forward from the dome often forms a sort of *mandorla* above the fillet, then divides into two festoon-like waves below it, prior to twisting: this roundness of outlines seems typically "Pasitelean," as for instance in a head near the so-called Elektra type (Fig. 179). If this distinction is valid, the Mantua Apollo and the head in the Terme should be considered together. It is also worth noting that heads with this type of coiffure were used by the "Pasiteleans" for both male and female figures, as indicated by the similarity between the Elektra and the Pylades, and by the fact that some of these heads, found in isolation, have been differently interpreted.[15]

[13] This suggestion is made by Saletti, pp. 256-57, on the basis of coins and of a terracotta head from Tarentum (Saletti, fig. 72 c; Bulle, *BerlWinckPr*, p. 99), whose locks however fall *before* the ears, and, though longer, still remain within the area of the face without reaching the line of the shoulders. As for the numismatic depictions, they compare too closely with Attic vase painting to circumscribe the practice to Magna Graecia, and fall rather in the category of "stragglers" than of "hairstyles," as specified above. The rolled-up coiffure itself has been attributed to Magna Graecia by Amelung (*RömMitt* 40 [1925] 183-87), but again its examples come from too wide a geographical area to justify the assumption.

[14] D. B. Thompson (*Hesperia* 8 [1939] 304-7), in publishing a terracotta mold with a sphinx head from the Athenian Agora, assumes that the hairstyle of the Mantua Apollo is already somewhat old-fashioned for mortals around 400 B.C. But her head is shown frontally, and the long locks may be part of the nape hair, rather than of the forehead roll. Also, 400 B.C. may be the date of the inception, rather than of the end, of the style.

It is also important to remember the frequency of rolls and shoulder locks in Roman late Republican and Augustan coiffures: see the examples mentioned in the Bibliography to p. 131.

[15] See, e.g., the head in the Terme (Paribeni, *Sculture V. Sec.* no. 12) which was once thought

A case in point is that of the Lychnouchos Ephebe from Via dell'Abbondanza in Pompeii (Figs. 181-84), in itself a very controversial piece. Before its discovery in 1925, the head type, known through other replicas, was considered female and compared to the Athena Lemnia by Pheidias. The obviously male character of the Pompeii Ephebe came as a surprise and produced a revision of opinions as to the correct interpretation of the head; yet in recent years scholars have again asserted its feminine quality, attributing to the bronze Ephebe an eclectic origin which made use of a male body and a female head.[16] In support of this position come a replica of the head in Copenhagen, with pierced ears, and a herm in Annecy with female drapery. Yet it is not impossible that the same head was used ambivalently, without a definite character. Is this supposition sufficient to postulate a classicistic origin also for the head? The Ephebe from Via dell'Abbondanza falls within that category of decorative bronzes so difficult to assess. Rumpf considered it a late creation, and this opinion has been generally followed. Von Steuben, by suggesting that the original inclination of the head type was toward the left, as against the right turn of the Ephebe, implies a pastiche with mechanical adaptations, like the Spinario. On the other hand, another replica of the head in the Terme, as well as the Annecy example, come from herms which require strict frontality. It is therefore difficult to determine the exact position of the original from the head replicas.

Also the body of the Pompeii Ephebe has been found in a variety of versions, usually in bronze, and presumably all dating from the Augustan period; but the respective heads vary in style, from the "Polykleitan" head of the Idolino in Florence to the "Pheidian" head of the Volubilis Youth in Munich. Yet Richter believes that "many variations of a given type are due, not to the Roman copyist, but to slightly varied Greek originals"; she finds no inherent discrepancy between heads and bodies since all heads, though not stylistically the same, seem at least to fall within the Fifth century. One difficulty would seem, however, to resist this line of reasoning since in the Pompeii Ephebe the head is too early in style for the Polykleitan stance of the body, and in this instance at least one should postulate an eclectic origin for the entire statue. A good case could also be made for the Idolino and the other pieces, which however are not of immediate concern here since not influenced by the Severe style. Their importance to the argument lies in the variety of directions taken by the "Roman" artists to which they attest.[17]

---

female, and the discussion on the head in the Chiaramonti Museum mentioned by Schuchhardt in *Festschrift Weickert*, pp. 63-66.

The predilection for the coiffure is not limited to the "Pasiteleans." See, e.g., the herm in the Fitzwilliam Museum, Cambridge, England, which L. Budde and R. Nicholls (*Catalogue*, 1964, no. 103, pl. 34, pp. 65-66) describe as a classicistic creation of the Second century A.D. after a mid Fifth century prototype.

[16] For another instance of this procedure see the Apollo Ince-Blundell (Ashmole, *Catalogue*, no. 15), most recently discussed by Ch. Hofkes-Brukker, *BABesch* 42 (1967) 28-30, where a "Severizing" body has been joined to a female head close to that

of Paionios' Nike. The Roman practice of changing heads to statues is lamented by Pliny, *NH* 35.4. See also other references in Daremberg-Saglio, *Dictionnaire* 4, cols. 1483-84, nos. 8, 9, 16. Cf. Langlotz, *JdI* 61-62 (1946-47) 100.

[17] Another instance of this Roman eclecticism in ornamental works is expertly discussed and described by F. Chamoux, "Le Dionysos de Sakha," *BCH* 74 (1950) 70-81. The bronze statue compares well with the Pompeian *lampadephoroi*, and probably served the same purpose. Its coiffure recalls the Mantua Apollo. Chamoux dates the work between the last quarter of the First century B.C. and the end of the Augustan period.

Even accepting the eclectic nature of the Pompeii Ephebe and the ambivalence in gender of his head type, one is not bound to agree that the head type too is a classicistic creation. Indeed, in this case, the hairstyle appears coherent, though too calligraphic, linear, and with little volume even in the bronze rendering. What the original Severe appearance might have been is pointed out by Langlotz in his comparison with the so-called Orpheus head type, of which the best known representative is the basalt replica in Munich (Figs. 185-86). This head, once suggested as copy of the citharode Orpheus made by Dionysios for Mikythos' dedication at Olympia (Paus. 5.26.3), has also been attributed to a female body on the basis of parallels in the minor arts. The type was obviously favored by Roman copyists because of the decorative possibilities inherent in the ductus of the strands, and in some versions it is difficult to evaluate how far the imprint of classicism has removed the finished product from the classical prototype. The basalt head in Munich, for instance, repeats the mandorla effect above the fillet, but fills it with one short strand which does not continue below the ribbon: a rather improbable though attractive rendering which finds approximate comparison in purely Roman works.[18] Similarly, adaptors of the Pompeii Ephebe's head felt free to add long, flat locks alongside the neck in the herm versions of the type. A summary adaptation of the Orpheus head also appears in conjunction with a seated figure ascribed by Poulsen to the "Thorvaldenszeit des Altertums" together with the Spinario: the bronze Orpheus statuette in Leningrad.[19] Finally, it should be admitted that the Munich head looks too youthful for a representation of Orpheus, and that its delicate features and melancholic expression seem not so much feminine as non-Severe. The face is also noticeably assymmetrical, as characteristic of classicistic works.[20]

One last approach of classicistic art, though not limited to the First century B.C., is the adoption of a Severe hairstyle in conjunction with a more advanced type of face, or with a Severe face to which a different psychological content has been added. Seldom can this procedure be pinpointed with actual physical details. One obvious and well discussed example is the classicistic version of the Kassel Apollo in the Palazzo Vecchio, Florence, dating from Hadrianic times. The whole expression of the stern face has been made more "romantic" by parting the lips more pronouncedly; the forehead is taller because the contour of the locks has been rounded, and the entire hair hugs the cranium more closely; also the proportions of upper to lower face have been altered.

A comparable contrast can be seen between the head of a youth in Hannover, possibly a Greek original of Magna Graecian provenience, and another in Vienna which only

[18] For an example of a basic forehead pattern complicated by the addition of inner locks see the portrait of Julia Victorina on an altar in the Louvre dating from the Augustan period (TEL III, pl. 288; detail photograph in J. Charbonneaux, *La Sculpture Grecque et Romaine au Musée du Louvre* [1963] 158).

[19] G. Dontas (*Eikones*, p. 78) dates the Hermitage statuette to the First century B.C. and considers it a typical example of a Hellenistic body joined to a Severe head.

[20] This trait is pointed out by T. Dohrn in his discussion of classicistic works ("Neues zu den Lychnouchoi," *Festschrift A. Rumpf* [1952] 59-75), but seems to be also an undoubted feature of Severe originals. In support of a classicizing origin may also be the fact that the "Orpheus" head type was used for purely eclectic and classicizing female statues of unquestionably Roman date: see, e.g. EA 2209-2210 and 3535-3536. Langlotz considers the hairstyle, with the bob at the back, typically feminine, but the statuary type to which he attributes the prototype, the so-called Angerona, is known only through a Renaissance recast and other mediocre copies (*JdI* 61-62 [1946-47] 95-111).

the distinctive hairstyle suggests as a copy of the same prototype. As final examples we can mention a coiffure closely comparable to that of the Orpheus or the Pompeii Ephebe, but with forehead curls recalling the Kassel Apollo: its best version appears on the eclectic youth in Leptis Magna, but other replicas exist, all with slightly different facial features, some of them undoubtedly Severe. Once again we are led to wonder whether this hairstyle is an invention of the classicistic artist, only remotely based on Severe prototypes.[21]

As repeatedly pointed out, all these types are highly controversial, and complete agreement seems impossible at the present state of our knowledge. A significant parallel can, however, be established with cases where the portrait quality of the face leaves no doubt as to the correct chronology. One instance is the "classicizing" head of Hadrian from Ostia (Fig. 187), where the hair rendering strongly recalls the Apollo from the West pediment at Olympia (Fig. 73); even among portraits of the same emperor, well known for his philhellenism, this particular head stands out for its unusual brand of Severe style. Another instance is the portrait of Antinoos of the so-called Mondragone type, of which, besides the name-piece in the Louvre, two other replicas exist in Berlin (Figs. 188-89). Here an Apollo coiffure has been superimposed on a personalized face, with rather surprisingly coherent results. The emphasis on linearity in the strands, the "canopy" motif in the center of the forehead, the looping in and out of the fillet, strongly recall Severe hairstyles, without immediate correspondence with a specific prototype.[22] E. Schmidt has suggested that after the death of Hadrian's favorite in 130 A.D. a strong classicizing impulse was imparted to the representational arts in general by the need to portray the deified youth in the guise of the Greek gods; this theory is supported by the many depictions of the young Bithynian as a Greek deity, but also conversely by the influence of Antinoan portraits on sculpture in general, whether portraits or divine representations. This Severe influence in Antinoos' portraits is not limited to statuary in the round and to individual details such as the hairstyle: it appears strongly also in relief works where the awkward foreshortening, the partly frontal, partly profile pose of Severe stelai are intentionally imitated.

As portraits of Antinoos continued to be made even after the death of Hadrian, so the classicistic current continued beyond Antonine times. We have already mentioned that at least one scholar considers the Themistokles from Ostia a creation of the Third century A.D., another Third century head has been suggested as forerunner of Constantinian portraits for its "Severe" style, and more examples could be adduced. It is, however, impossible in this study to trace systematically all instances of Severe style in imperial art, and this pursuit should be left to a more competent connoisseur of Roman sculpture. It suffices here to point out this Roman penchant to achieve a better understanding of statues which are reputed to be Roman copies of Greek originals.

[21] For another example of stylistic differences between coiffures and faces see the female "archaistic" head in Vienna, ÖJh 46 (1961-63) 39-42 no. 11 figs. 21-22, with many points of resemblance to the coiffures under discussion.

[22] For another interesting example of "Severe" traits in coiffures, see the Antinoos bust in the Vati-

can (Clairmont, no. 47, pl. 6) with spiral locks, and the comments by K. Lehmann-Hartleben, *Die Antike* 5 (1929) 103-6, on antiquarian tendencies in Hadrianic times.

For Hadrianic classicizing creations aside from Antinoos' portraiture, see also App. 11-13.

A review of late Hellenistic and Roman sculpture therefore seems to yield the following results.

Mannerisms and traits of Severe style appear in Hellenistic sculpture as early as the Second century B.C. They can be limited to a specific rendering of drapery, or can involve the creation of an entire statue in classicizing terms. This approximate rendering of Severe stops with the advent of mechanical copying, when Severe prototypes can be accurately reproduced, but with this final technical achievement no limit can be put to the freedom of the sculptor. He can repeat exactly a Severe original, or he can partially change it and even transform it into a hip-herm, as was startlingly done for a motion statue like the Ludovisi Diskobolos. He can alter the facial features and infuse in them a new expression, he can combine different prototypes in a single statue, either by abrupt juxtaposition or by harmonic fusion, he can modernize a Severe model or "Severize" a later work. He can use a head type for male and female figures at will, introduce arbitrary additions of curls, superimpose a Severe coiffure on a classical head or even on a Roman portrait. There is no safe criterion to evaluate the share of the copyist in this production: this sober realization inescapably is reached whenever several replicas of the same *attested* Greek type are examined and compared. The variations and simplifications possible within the limits of recognition are endless.

On the other hand, a few traits seem characteristic of eclectic or classicistic creations. The most important is the elaboration and often the incongruence of hairstyles. When several different coiffures seem to be combined in one, without regard for male or female fashions, the likelihood is that the statue is a late creation. Discrepancies in style between head and body should also be significant, and sometimes even an anecdotical subject matter, usually in contrast with the more orthodox mythological and athletic repertoire of Severe sculpture. Finally, the decorative or utilitarian function of some statues may, though not necessarily, imply "Roman" invention or adaptation.

But the most relevant criterion, the one which in ultimate analysis will determine the verdict, is that undefinable "spirit" which only long familiarity with the monuments helps to capture and recognize. When all available external evidence has failed to produce an absolute date, stylistic judgment alone can supply suggestions; and since all such judgments are based on individual degrees of "sculptural eye," they are bound to be subjective. Ancient sculpture, after all, was not regulated by scientific criteria, and the study of sculpture cannot claim to be an exact science. It is because of this subjectivity of judgment that opinions can be so discordant and monuments so controversial; but *subjective* is not always the equivalent of *erroneous*, and style is objective enough, even if elusive at times. It is only on the strength of this conviction that the study of ancient sculpture is at all possible.

APPENDIX 9

1. *Nikokleia, Priestess of Demeter, from Knidos*: Lullies & Hirmer, pl. 246; comments on p. 99. A trend toward block-like compositions reappears during the Third century B.C. This statue in the British Museum is dated ca. 230 on the basis of the letter forms of the dedication. Though the differentiation between chiton and himation is typically Hellenistic, and the face of the priestess shows all the characterization of the time, the heaviness of the over-all contours, the almost complete disregard for the body beneath the drapery, the tent-like arrangement of the mantle, recall the Goddess Corinth/Mocenigo (Ch. 5, App. 5) or, more remotely, the Aspasia/Sosandra. Toward the end of the Third century, and during part of the Second, female figures were portrayed with wide-spreading skirts and straight outlines which almost turned their bodies into abstractions. Examples are e.g. the Nikeso from Priene, the "Praxitelean" Arezzo Athena (Schuchhardt, *Epochen*, figs. 98, 96 and comments on pp. 120-22), or some of the statues from Magnesia and Pergamon (Bieber, *Sculpture of the Hellenistic Age*[2], figs. 515, 520). From this point of view these statues could be called Severe, though the sophisticated treatment of their drapery leaves no doubt as to their Hellenistic affiliations. Hairstyles also recall Severe coiffures. Compare for instance the head of a Muse from Miletus (Bieber, fig. 506) with the Neo-Attic sphinx-head type mentioned in Ch. 8, App. 1, or, in general, with the Candia type (Ch. 5, App. 8). A more interesting comparison along the same lines, though not strictly within the Severe chronological limits, is the head "by Agorakritos" in Basel and its Antonine counterpart from Velia, recently discussed by E. Berger (*AntK* 11:1 [1968] 78-81, pls. 20:3-4 and 21; cf. supra, Ch. 5 n. 13). The short spiral curl in front of each ear is so typical of the period of the Pergamon Altar that one wonders whether the Velia head has been "Hellenisticized," or rather the Basel head has been classicized.

2. *Bronze bust of Priapos ("Dionysos") in Naples*: This work from Herculaneum was at first identified as Dionysos/Platon or as a priest of the Eleusinian Mysteries. It was also variously dated between the Severe and the classical periods. It was finally recognized that it belonged to the classicizing current of the late Hel-

lenistic period, and now the correct identification as Priapos, proposed by L. Curtius, has confirmed the date ("Zum 'Dionysos' aus Herculanum," *ArchEph* [1953-54] 230-34). It is interesting to note the Severe elements present in the bronze: the limited volume of the hair strands over the dome, the looping of the long locks over the temples, even the peculiar "tongue" in the beard, which recalls the Poseidon from Kreusis/Livadhostro or the bronze head of a warrior from the Athenian Acropolis (cf. Ch. 3, App. 9, and Boardman/Dörig/Fuchs/Hirmer, fig. 168). These traits are considerably softened or modified in a stucco head which might go back to the same prototype: Helbig[4], no. 1688 (von Steuben). On the hairstyle see Forti, *Danzatrici di Ercolano*, pp. 36-37 and n. 46.

3. *The Vatican Runner*: On this statue see also Ch. 9 n. 8 with bibliography. Add Helbig[4], no. 558 (Fuchs). Some authors still consider the statue a genuine copy of a Severe bronze original representing a runner in the women's race at Olympia, in honor of Hera. Yet the "Severe" impression is given solely by the unarticulated body, so lacking in femininity. The face, with its rather pointed oval and the strangely shaped eyes (notice the wide shelf formed by the upper lid) is certainly not typically Severe, and the coiffure, as noted by several, is unparalleled. Also unusual is the wide and high girdle, for which I know no parallel even outside the Severe period proper. A growing consensus places the Runner among "Pasitelean" creations.

4. *Head Alba in Madrid*: EA 1784-85. The most recent mention with bibliography appears in W.-H. Schuchhardt, "Weiblicher Kopf in Brescia," *RömMitt* 70 (1963) 5 n. 3, B 2. This female head was defined by C. Waldstein (*JHS* 5 [1884] 171-73, pl. 45) a classicizing creation after the Athena of the Atlas metope at Olympia. Recent studies tend to consider it a bona fide copy of a mid Fifth century prototype, like the head in Brescia discussed by Schuchhardt (*op.cit.*). The similarity with the Olympia metope head is not so strong as inescapably to imply imitation, but the possibility cannot be excluded, and the Alba head should perhaps be reconsidered in the light of our present knowledge on the date of the Olympia "Replacement Figures."

143

5. *The Hope Peplophoros in Baltimore* (the head is ancient but not pertinent): B. S. Ridgway, "Two Peplophoroi in the United States," *Hesperia* 38 (1969) 213-22. E. Paribeni, *ASAtene* N.S. 8-10 (1946-48) 103-5 fig. 1, mentioned the Hope peplophoros as a parallel to a female torso from Piazza Barberini in Rome, which he considered copy of an early Severe original. He attributed both works to the same artistic center, presumably in Magna Graecia, the Hope peplophoros being one or two decades later than the Barberini torso. But the peculiar treatment of the Hope statue's skirt undisturbed by the advanced left leg, the totally flat overfold adhering to the rounded abdomen, the peculiar belt-like kolpos, and especially a certain mannerism in the gesture of the lifted skirt, suggest that the statue is a classicistic creation of the First century B.C. The Barberini peplophoros published by Paribeni, with its linear catenaries and patternized folds, should also be considered classicistic.

6. *The Tralles/Cherchel Karyatids*: M. Schede, *Meisterwerke* (Berlin 1928) pl. 28. This type, known in the two above-mentioned replicas, is generally recognized as archaistic, but the strange smoothness of the himation, which recalls leather, its unusual arrangement, and the treatment of the chiton skirt, have prompted different dates for the prototype. Lippold (*Handbuch*, p. 244) believes in an original created around 370-330; P. Leveque (*BCH* 77 [1953] p. 108) goes as high as 470-460 B.C. Unquestionably, however, the Karyatids are a classicizing creation of the First century B.C.-A.D., mixing archaic with Severe traits. Two (Hadrianic ?) replicas of the head-type in the Athens National Museum have prompted H. P. Laubscher (*IstMitt* 16 [1966] 128-29 pls. 24-25; see also p. 126 n. 56 with bibliography) to suggest that the prototype was created not in Tralles but in Athens, in Neo-Attic workshops, not earlier than the late Hellenistic period, through a mixture of archaistic and Hellenistic elements. This theory can be maintained even if "Severizing" rather than archaistic elements are involved.

7. *Head of Athlete, Boston MFA*: Caskey, *Catalogue*, p. 131 n. 63; P. Arias, *Mirone* (1940) 21-22 pl. 11:41. The head is peculiar not only for its marked asymmetries, especially noticeable in the rendering of the mouth, but also for its surprising depth of features. The profile view in particular shows how deeply the eyes have been carved, so that almost a break is formed in the face at eye-level, with the forehead projecting like a shelf. The hairstyle, despite its apparent similarity to the Chatsworth Apollo, is also unusual. The head has been compared with the Perseus Rome/London and likewise attributed to Myron; but it should be considered a classicistic creation of the First century B.C.

8. *Nike in the Conservatori Museum, Rome*: *BrBr* 263, recently Helbig⁴, no. 1509. This statue is considered by several authors an original of Magna Graecian origin, but Stuart Jones (*Catalogue*, p. 222 no. 16) and Lippold (*Handbuch*, p. 134 n. 6) have suggested that it might be an archaistic adaptation of an earlier original. To the observations already made by Stuart Jones (the peculiar way in which the drapery surrounds the feet, the peculiar 45 degree angle of the wings) I would also add the strange effect of the apoptygma folds, which seem to correspond to those of the skirt, giving a definite impression of "drapery through drapery." Indeed the vertical pleats below the catenary produced by the breasts have no justification, unless one assumes that they echo the rippling of the garment underneath. The lack of concern for the body (the legs are thoroughly concealed), the oval contour of the upper torso with an unbroken line from shoulders through arms down to the curving edge of the apoptygma, and finally the peculiar elongation of the figure, seem somewhat incompatible with the style of the early Fifth century, even if the statue was an akroterion and therefore meant for a high setting.

9. *"Replicas" of the Herculaneum Dancers*: No true replicas exist for many of the Herculaneum figures. Only Dancer no. 4 (Forti, pp. 31-38) seems close to a marble statue of much better quality in the Gardner Museum, Boston (see Forti, p. 31 n. 40 with bibliography). Because of its greater artistic value, the Gardner statue has been considered closer to the Severe prototype from which the Roman maker of the Dancer may have derived his inspiration. I wonder, however, whether the motif of lifting the apoptygma over the shoulder can be considered truly Severe or should rather be classed as a manneristic adaptation of a Fifth century gesture. We know that the overfold could be lifted around the head for protection (cf. the Niobid

in Copenhagen, *BrBr* 712-14) but even this is an unusual gesture. Much more common is the lifting of a separate veil or mantle, as in the Sterope of the Olympia pediment or the Iris of the Parthenon East gable. Also the Cherchell Demeter and the Hestia Giustiniani have a separate garment as head cover. Could the Severe gesture of lifting a veil have been misunderstood by the classicizing masters, or at least have been transformed into a more elaborate motif? Another statue, with the gesture completed and her head covered, has also been compared by Bulle (text to EA 806-7, Rome, Orto Botanico) with the Herculaneum Dancer and may belong to the same stylistic phase. It is interesting to compare, for instance, how the motif of pulling the skirt aside, so typical of archaic korai, has also been transformed into pure mannerism in classicizing creations (Hope peplophoros, Herculaneum Dancer no. 2); the Conservatori Nike (supra no. 8) lifting the front edge of her overfold may be repeating with both hands the gesture of the Zeus from the Olympia pediment, or turn into an empty pose the motif of a woman gathering objects in her apoptygma (cf., e.g., some of the terracottas from Magna Graecia, Poulsen, SS, figs. 55-59). It cannot be denied, however, that the gesture of the Copenhagen Niobid, generally considered an original of ca. 440-430 B.C., is remarkably awkward with its harsh horizontal accent breaking the composition. The motifs of the lifted apoptygma and of the "niche garment" deserve more detailed study.

10. *Bust of a man in Madrid*: A. García y Bellido, *Esculturas Romanas de España y Portugal* (Madrid 1949) 58-59 no. 46 pl. 40; *AJA* 52 (1948) 262 pl. 28a. This bust is a remarkable example of Roman portraiture combined with Greek Severe forms. The individualized face of a man of late Flavian/early Trajanic times is adorned with a coiffure strongly reminiscent of that of the Kassel Apollo, especially in the pattern of locks over the forehead.

11. *Statue of a youth in Madrid*: H. Sichtermann, "Zu einer Knabenstatue im Prado," *Mitt-Madrid* 1 (1960) 155-63, with previous bibliography. The statue has usually been considered a copy of a Severe or a classical work (of the time of Polykleitos, or even of Euphranor). Poulsen (*SS*, p. 126) and Borda (*Scuola di Pasitele*, p. 90) recognized it as archaistic, or Severizing, but Lippold (*Handbuch* p. 104 n. 10) still considered it a diluted copy of a Severe original. Sichtermann establishes convincing parallels with Hadrianic sculpture, and especially with the portraiture of Antinoos—a comparison which had already been made by K. Lehmann-Hartleben (*Die Antike* 5 [1929] 105) who, however, did not carry it to its ultimate conclusion. Notice in particular the hairstyle with the corkscrew locks and the mannerism of the left hand resting with its back against the hip, as in the Hestia Giustiniani.

12. *Female head in Göttingen*: a late-Hadrianic or Antonine creation after Fifth century prototypes, probably representing Ceres, Terra, or Tellus. An interesting article by H.-J. Kruse ("Ein Marmorkopf der Göttinger archäologischen Sammlung," *AA* [1967] 568-72) includes a good discussion of classicizing hairstyles after Severe originals (see especially pp. 571-72 and n. 10).

13. *Meter Doria-Pamphili*: P. Noelke, "Zum Kopf der 'Meter' Doria-Pamphili," *BonnJhb* 167 (1967) 38-57, discusses Roman classicizing creations, centering around the head of the Doria-Pamphili statue but also listing many other examples, with chronological distinctions within Roman times and comments on hairstyles.

14. *Bronze statuette of Athena from Tamasi, Hungary*: at first glance the statuette appears archaic, since it wears chiton and himation; but the latter is treated almost like a peplos overfold and a curious "skirt" shows under the paryphe of the chiton. The face, moreover, appears classical. The piece is published as an Antonine creation of the mid Second century mixing traits of different stylistic periods, and having for its earliest prototype the Athena from the Aphaia temple. *Archäologische Funde in Ungarn*, ed. E. B. Thomas (Budapest 1956) 234-35.

FOR PAGE 130

For the two-dimensionality of the late Hellenistic period see comments and bibliography in B. S. Ridgway, "The date of the so-called Lysippean Jason," *AJA* 68 (1964) 113-28.

Pergamon Athena: Bulle's reconstruction of the Myronian group for Samos appears in *Festschrift P. Arndt* (1952) 62-86 and especially 63-78. The classicizing origin was upheld most recently by W. Fuchs, *EncArAn*, s.v. Neo-Atticismo; E. Berger, *AntK* 10 (1967) 85 no. 6, still considers it a copy of a ca. 430 B.C. original. Kalkmann's doubts on the appurtenance of the head are expressed in *BerlWinckPr* 53 (1893) 66.

Herakles: for a revindication of the Myronian attribution see G. Hafner, "Zwei Meisterwerke der Vorklassik," *AA* 1952, cols. 91-93 and n. 32 with previous bibliography at n. 33; a small torso in Göttingen may belong to the same type; G. Fuchs (*AA* 1967, pp. 407-14 figs. 9-12) claims that the prototype must also have been of statuette scale, but that, since the head type appears also in late Hellenistic terracottas (Caskey, *Boston Catalogue*, 134-35; gilded, "therefore after bronze original?"), the original could not have been a classicizing creation. E. Buschor, "Gruppe des Myron," *AthMitt* 68 (1953) 51-62, publishes a base that may have supported the Myronian group. He accepts the Pergamon Athena but rejects the Boston Herakles because of its ponderation, suggesting instead a colossal statue from Cherchel (Beil. 9a). He dates the whole group shortly after 439 B.C., during the period of Athenian supremacy (442-439 B.C.), and sees in the subject of the monument clear indication that interest in Athena is supplanting interest in Hera.

FOR PAGE 131

Drunken Old Woman: Carpenter, *Greek Sculpture*, p. 134; O. Waldhauer, *AJA* 50 (1946) 241-46. The "certain mannerism" in the drapery is mentioned by von Steuben in Helbig⁴, no. 1253. On late Republican and Augustan coiffures imitating Severe prototypes see the comments in M. Borda, *La scuola di Pasitele* (Bari 1953) 50 and illustrations in O. Vessberg, *Studien zur Kunstgeschichte der römischen Republik* (Lund 1941), pls. 38:2-3 and 40:1; see also TEL III, pls. 276-77.

For Severe works found in Rome see, e.g. R. Lullies and J. Le Brun, *Griechische Bildwerke in Rom* (Munich 1955).

For a picture of the general period see the excellent book by G. Becatti, *Arte e Gusto negli Scrittori Latini* (Florence 1951); see also G. M. A. Richter, *Three Critical Periods* (Oxford 1951) Ch. 3, and *Ancient Italy* (Ann Arbor, Mich. 1955) Ch. 3. For classicizing tendencies in Rome see F. Schachermeyr, *Die frühe Klassik der Griechen* (Berlin 1966) 290-92. For Roman "forgeries" of ancient works see B. S. Ridgway, "The Piombino Apollo in the Louvre," *Antike Plastik* 7 (1967) 43-75 and especially 62.

FOR PAGE 132

Spinario: Carpenter, *MAAR* 18 (1941) 35-41. W. Fuchs in Helbig⁴, no. 1448; also, idem, *Der Dornauszieher*, Opus Nobile 8 (Bremen 1958), with excellent illustrations, reviewed by P. Clement in *Gnomon* 33 (1961) 824-25. For the marble copy in Florence see Mansuelli, *Uffizi*, 1, no. 119.

Eros Soranzo: O. Waldhauer, *Ermitage Catalogue*, Vol. 2 no. 85 pls. 1-2; Poulsen, *SS*, p. 33 n. 16; Lippold, *Handbuch*, p. 130 n. 10; G. Hafner, *Geschichte der griechischen Kunst* (Zürich 1961) 194-95 figs. 190-91, where the statue is considered Agon rather than Eros.

FOR PAGE 133

Esquiline Venus: most recently, K. Parlasca in Helbig⁴, no. 1484 pp. 304-5 with bibliography. Richter's opinion in *Ancient Italy*, pp. 51-52.

Torso in the Louvre: J. Charbonneaux, *MonPiot* 39 (1943) 35-48: an interesting review of the problem with decision in favor of a Severe date for the prototype.

Carpenter, *MAAR* 18 (1941) 30-35.

Aspasia/Sosandra body with Roman portrait head: Berlin Museum, C. Blümel, *Kat.* 4 (Berlin 1931) pls. 53-54, K 167.

Müller's peplophoros: V. Müller, *JdI* 47 (1932) 139-56; see also von Steuben in Helbig⁴, no. 1390. The head, a Roman portrait, was added by the restorer as well as the attributes which turn the statue into an Hygieia.

FOR PAGE 134

Athena from Leptis Magna: Mendel, *Catalogue* 2, no. 32; the classicistic theory stems from S. Ferri, *BdA* 27 (1933) 68-74, in a most perceptive article, where the Severe character of the

Athena's head and its resemblance to the head Vogüé from Aegina in the Louvre are particularly stressed. E. Berger, *AntK* 10 (1967) 85 no. 14, dates the statue "410/400?"; see also p. 87.

Herculaneum dancers: Lippold, *Handbuch*, p. 133. L. Forti, *Le Danzatrici di Ercolano* (Naples 1959); by the same author also "L'Orante di Ercolano," *RendAccArchLett e Belle Arti* (Naples 1959).

Terracotta Nikai from the Athenian Acropolis: Y. Miliadis, *A Concise Guide to the Akropolis Museum* (Athens 1965) 34 nos. 6476-6476 A. Illustration in *AJA* 61 (1957) pl. 83:1.

Conservatori Charioteer: The most recent discussion is by H. von Steuben and P. Zanker in *AA* (1966) 68-75 with previous bibliography and other statues considered classicizing imitations of the Omphalos Apollo illustrated in figs. 15-17. For an attribution to a follower of the Omphalos Apollo Master see W. Fuchs in Helbig⁴, no. 1505. Homann-Wedeking's theory in *RömMitt* 55 (1940) 214-16.

Head in Corinth: see supra Ch. 5 p. 59 and bibliography p. 74.

FOR PAGE 135

Hafner's reconstruction in *Geschichte der griechischen Kunst* (Zürich 1961) 148-51 figs. 133-34 (reconstructed drawing).

E. Paribeni, *BullCom* 74 (1951-52) 13-18 pl. 1. L. Guerrini, *ArchCl* 11 (1959) 171-78 pls. 41-44. Panel in the Louvre with Perseus and the monster: most recently discussed by K. M. Phillips, Jr., *AJA* 72 (1968) pl. 14 fig. 42 and p. 13; the plaque is heavily restored and therefore no conclusions can be drawn from the Severe hairstyle of the head, entirely modern: I owe this information to the kindness of Andrew Oliver, Jr., of the Metropolitan Museum of Art.

For other replicas of the Charioteer, see the head in the Vatican, von Steuben and Zanker, *op.cit.*, figs. 11-14 and discussed by W. Fuchs in Helbig⁴, no. 300. Here, however, the shape of the cranium varies.

On Pasiteles, see Borda, *La Scuola*, Ch. 1; Richter, *Three Critical Periods*, pp. 41 and 44; *Ancient Italy*, pp. 115-16, for an interpretation of the ancient sources: Pliny, *NH* 33. 156; 35. 156; and 36. 39-40.

Stephanos Athlete: *BrBr* 301; Lippold, *Handbuch*, p. 129. The most extensive discussion in Borda, *La Scuola*, Chs. 2-4. See also the account by P. Moreno in *EncArAn*, s.v. Stephanos. For

the suggestion that the "original" head was of the Lateran type, see Borda, p. 34. The suggestion is accepted by Fuchs in Helbig, *Führer*, no. 1089; he there repeats Borda's theory (p. 31) that the Athlete was used as a sort of "canon." Orestes and Elektra in Naples: *BrBr* 306, Borda, figs. 7-9.

Mercury and Vulcan in the Louvre: *BrBr* 307, Borda, fig. 14. See also a replica of the Pylades/Vulcan head in the Terme, and Paribeni's ambivalent comments, *Sculture V Sec.*, no. 18.

FOR PAGE 136

Olympia sculptures with hair rolls: see, e.g. the second seer, fig. L, of the East Pediment, or the Peirithoos of the West.

Bronze head from Athenian Acropolis: Boardman/Dörig/Fuchs/Hirmer, pl. 182 (NM 6590) Acropolis Jumper: Athens Nat. Mus. 6445, Niemeyer, *Antike Plastik* 3, pp. 24-25 and pls. 17-19, 33 b-c.

Mantua Apollo: the type was so named by Poulsen, after the marble replica of the type in Mantua, SS, pp. 126-27, no. 6 (Mantua statue: no. 2 in the list of replicas). The most important copy is the bronze replica from Pompeii, C. Saletti, "L'Apollo Citaredo di Pompei," *ArtAntMod* (1960) 248-62, with summary of previous opinions; for an analysis of the hairstyle see especially his pp. 255-57. The Severe date has recently been advocated by L. O. Keene Congdon in connection with a brass replica in the Fogg Museum, Cambridge, Mass.: *AJA* 67 (1963) 7-13; see especially pp. 11-12 for a summary of previous opinions, though the possibility that the statuary type is "classicistic" is not even mentioned.

FOR PAGE 137

Kassel Apollo: The most complete publication of all the replicas in Evamaria Schmidt, *Antike Plastik* 5 (1966). For examples of braided hair in the Fifth century see supra, p. 65 n. 11.

FOR PAGE 138

Mt. Holyoke athlete: see supra, p. 18 n. 8. The main publication is by C. Galt, *AJA* 33 (1929) 41-52, with some interesting parallels; the most recent reference and illustration in *Master Bronzes* (Cambridge, Mass., 1967), no. 83 with bibliography.

Head Athens N.M. 1949, cf. supra, p. 35 and bibliography.

FOR PAGE 138
For details of the Eirene's hair see EA 840-43. On the coinage of Smyrna see J. E. Milne, "The autonomous Coinage of Smyrna," *NumChr* 5th Series, Vol. 3 (1923) 1-46 and especially pp. 20-24, Period VI 230-220 B.C., nos. 40-51, pl. 2. For numismatic representations in general see B. V. Head, *A guide to the principal coins of the Greeks* (London 1932) 42 no. 50 (Stymphalus, Arcadia) no. 53 (Chersonesus) = ca. 400-336 B.C.; p. 55 no. 20 (Messenia) = 336-280 B.C.; p. 70 no. 3 (Kyzikos) and especially p. 72 no. 15 (Smyrna, Tyche) no. 16 (Smyrna, Apollo) = 190-100 B.C. I owe these numismatic references to the kindness of the American Numismatic Society in New York.
Statuette of the Kassel type once in Berlin University: illustrated by E. Schmidt, *Antike Plastik* 5, fig. 9.
Head in the Terme: Paribeni, *Sculture V Sec.*, no. 15.

FOR PAGE 138
Head near the Elektra type: Borda, p. 53 fig. 11 and p. 54; EA 1456; Amelung, *RömMitt* 40 (1925) 185 fig. 2.

FOR PAGE 139
Ephebe from Via dell'Abbondanza: Richter, *Ancient Italy*, fig. 177; W. Amelung, "Bronzener Ephebe aus Pompei," *JdI* 42 (1927) 137-51, with many detailed photographs. A replica of the head type in the Museo Barracco is openly termed female: von Steuben, in Helbig⁴, no. 1880. See also Paribeni's comments in *Sculture V Sec.*, no. 40.
Head in Copenhagen: EA 4472-73.
Rumpf's opinion appears in his fundamental article cited on p. 136.

FOR PAGE 139
The various versions of the Ephebe's body are illustrated side by side in Richter, *Ancient Italy*, figs. 176-79. See her comments on p. 51.

FOR PAGE 140
Langlotz's comparison with the Orpheus head type: Langlotz, "Orpheus," *ArchEph* (1937:2) 604-7, see especially his pl. 1 figs. 3-4. For the identification as Orpheus see J. Sieveking, *AA* 1926, cols. 334-41.
Head in Munich: *BrBr* 698 and illustrations in the text. For the attribution to a female body see Langlotz, "Bemerkungen zu einem Basaltkopf in München," *JdI* 61-62 (1946-47) 95-111.

FOR PAGE 140
Bronze Orpheus statuette in Leningrad: Poulsen, SS, p. 33 n. 17; Lippold, *Handbuch*, pl. 33:1; text to *BrBr* 698.
Kassel Apollo replica in Florence, E. Schmidt, *Antike Plastik* 5, pls. 25-27, 48a, 49a, pp. 22-25; see also p. 24 n. 134 for a bibliography on "classicism" as an artistic phenomenon.
Heads in Hannover and Vienna: W. Amelung, "Archaischer Jünglingskopf in Hannover," *JdI* 35 (1920) 49-59 pls. 4-5; this instance of classicizing practices, and the following one (Leptis Magna Youth) were pointed out by von Steuben and Zanker, *AA* 1966, pp. 73-74 n. 7, as examples of stylistic differences between coiffures and faces.
For an interesting "cross" between the Hannover and the Via dell'Abbondanza head types see *BdA* 26 (1932) 282-84 no. 1 figs. 1a-b.

FOR PAGE 141
Leptis Magna Youth: *AA* 1962, p. 446 fig. 16; illustrated with other replicas by W. Amelung, "Von Meister des Omphalos Apollo," *Festschrift P. Arndt* (Munich 1925) 87-95. Cf. Helbig⁴, no. 2085 (von Steuben).

FOR PAGE 141
Head of Hadrian from Ostia: *Scavi di Ostia* 5, R. Calza, I Ritratti (Rome 1964) pl. 68 no. 117 pp. 73-74 with bibliography; cf. also *EncArAn* s.v. Adriano, Vol. 1, p. 85 fig. 131; G. Becatti, *The Art of Ancient Greece and Rome* (New York 1967) 338, fig. 315.
Antinoos Mondragone: Ch. Clairmont, *Die Bildnisse des Antinous* (Neuchâtel 1966) 57-58 nos. 58-60, pls. 33-34, comments on p. 36.
E. Schmidt: *Antike Plastik* 5, p. 25 n. 142.
Antinoos reliefs: Clairmont, pls. 7-8 (Banca Nazionale, Rome); pl. 20 (Villa Albani, Rome): Antinoos/Silvanus and A/Vertumnus.
Portraits of Antinoos made after Hadrian's death: *AA* 1966, p. 259 fig. 3, head of Antinoos from Tarentum.
Themistokles from Ostia considered Third century A.D.: H. Weber, *Gnomon* 27 (1955) 445-46.

FOR PAGE 141
Third century portrait in Rome: G. von Kaschnitz Weinberg, *Ausgewählte Schriften* (Berlin 1965), Vol. 2, pl. 37:1; cf. B. M. Felletti Maj, *I Ritratti*, Museo Nazionale Romano, no. 273, dated ca. 230 A.D. See also the comments by Langlotz, *JdI* 61-62 (1946-47) 95 and n. 2.

INDEX

I gratefully acknowledge the generous help of Dr. Katherine Coleman (Mrs. John E. Coleman) in the preparation of this index.

149

PLATES

1. Aegina, West Pediment, Athena (Munich Glyptothek)

2. Delphi, Athenian Treasury. Metope of Athena and Theseus (Delphi Museum)

3. Aegina, West Pediment. Head of Athena (Munich Glyptothek)

4. Aegina, East Pediment. Head of Athena (Munich Glyptothek)

5. Aegina, West Pediment. Oriental Archer (Munich Glyptothek)

6. Aegina, East Pediment. Herakles Archer (Munich Glyptothek)

7. Aegina, West Pediment. Greek Archer (Munich Glyptothek)

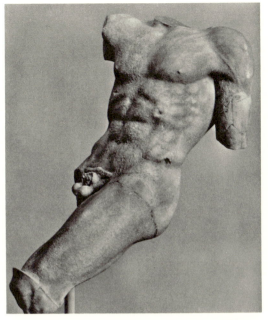

8. Aegina, East Pediment. Warrior Falling
Backward (Munich Glyptothek)

9. Gaul Falling Backward (Venice Archaeological Museum)

10. Aegina, East Pediment. Head of Moribund Warrior (Munich
Glyptothek)

11. Head of Dead Persian (Rome National Museum)

12. Aegina, East Pediment. "Companion I," detail
(Munich Glyptothek)

13. Olympia, Temple of Zeus, West Pediment. Detail of Figure B (Olympia Museum)

14. Olympia, Temple of Zeus, East Pediment. Kneeling Girl, detail of back (Olympia Museum)

15. Parthenon, East Pediment. Detail of Selene (Athens, Akropolis Museum)

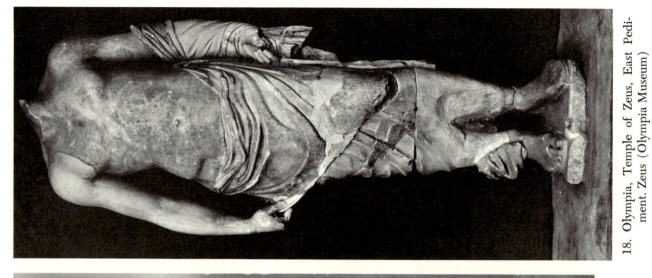

18. Olympia, Temple of Zeus, East Pediment. Zeus (Olympia Museum)

17. Ilissos Kouros (Athens National Museum)

16. Olympia, Temple of Zeus, East Pediment. Oinomaos (Olympia Museum)

21. "Zeus-Hero" from Pergamon (Istanbul Museum)

20. Dresden Zeus (Dresden, Albertinum)

19. Delphi, Siphnian Treasury, East Pediment. Zeus
(Delphi Museum)

22. Olympia, Temple of Zeus, East Pediment. Figure K (Sterope?) (Olympia Museum)

23. Olympia, Temple of Zeus, East Pediment. Figure F, Hippodameia? (Olympia Museum)

24. Peplos Kore (Athens, Acropolis Museum)

25. Kore 682 (Athens, Acropolis Museum)

26. Olympia, Temple of Zeus, West Pediment. Lunging Lapith (Olympia Museum)

27. Delphi, Temple of Apollo, Poros Pediment. Giant (Delphi Museum)

28. Borghese Warrior (Paris, Louvre)

29. Olympia, Temple of Zeus, West Pediment. Lapith Bitten by Centaur (Olympia Museum)

30. Olympia, Temple of Zeus. Metope of Amazon, Head of Herakles (Paris, Louvre)

31. Olympia, Temple of Zeus, East Pediment. Seer, detail. (Olympia Museum)

32. Selinus, Temple E. Metope of Herakles and Amazon (Palermo Museum)

33. Xanthos, Heroon G on the Acropolis (London, British Museum)

35. Selinus, Temple E. Metope of Hieros Gamos (Palermo Museum)

34. Xanthos, Heroon G on the Acropolis (London, British Museum)

36-37. Fleeing Maiden from Eleusis (Eleusis Museum)

38. Xanthos, Heroon H on the Acropolis. Sphinx Pediment (London, British Museum)

39. Angelitos' Athena, Acr. 140 (Athens, Acropolis Museum)

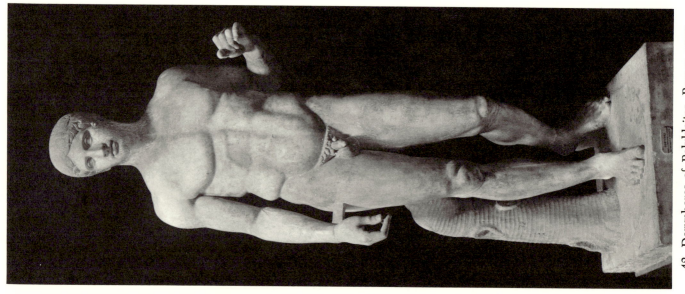

42. Doryphoros of Polykleitos, Roman copy (Naples, National Museum)

41. Kritian Boy (Athens, Acropolis Museum)

40. Aristodikos (Athens, National Museum)

43. Kritian Boy, detail of head (Athens, Acropolis Museum)

44. Kritian Boy, head, left profile (Athens, Acropolis Museum)

45. Kore 684, detail of head (Athens, Acropolis Museum)

46. Propylaia Kore, detail (Athens, Acropolis Museum)

47-48. Delphi Charioteer (Delphi Museum)

49-50. Attic Draped Youth (Athens, Acropolis Museum)

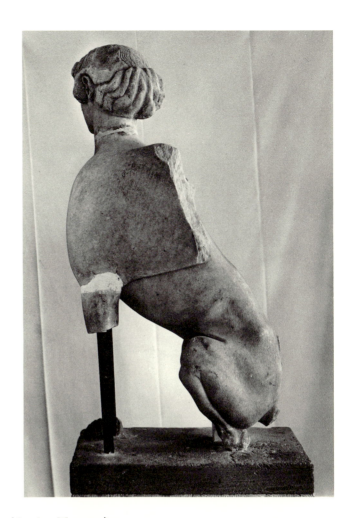

51-52. Aegina Sphinx (Aegina Museum)

53. Sphinx, Acropolis 632 (Athens, Acropolis Museum)

54. Lid of Lycian Sarcophagus with Sphinxes (Istanbul Museum)

57. Nike of Paionios (Olympia Museum)

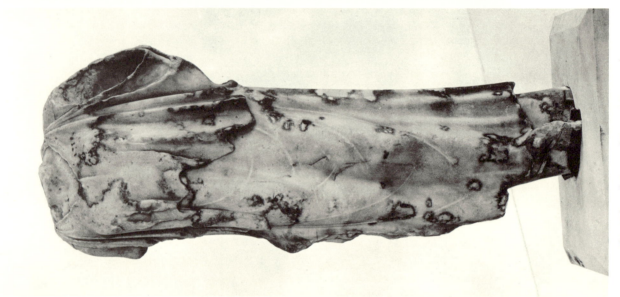

56. Nike of Paros (Paros Museum)

55. Nike from Delos (Athens, National Museum)

60. South Italian Bronze Peplophoros (Reggio Calabria Museum)

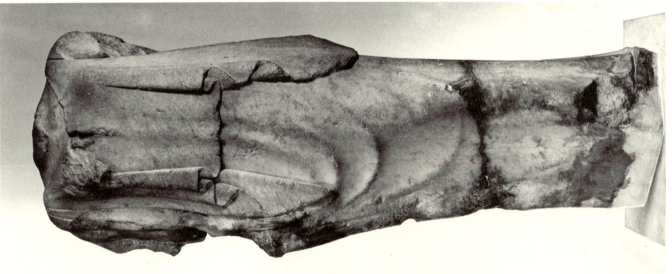

59. Peplophoros from Xanthos (London, British Museum)

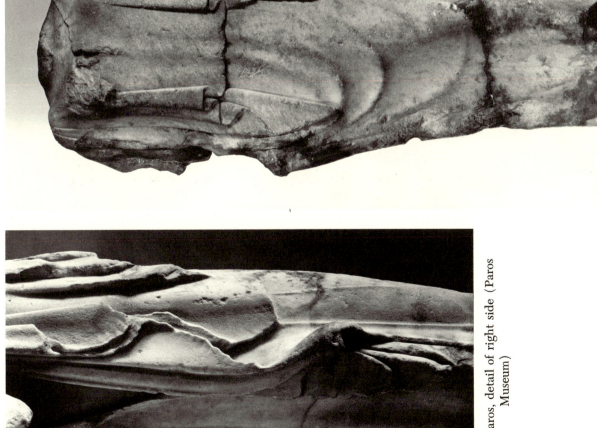

58. Nike of Paros, detail of right side (Paros Museum)

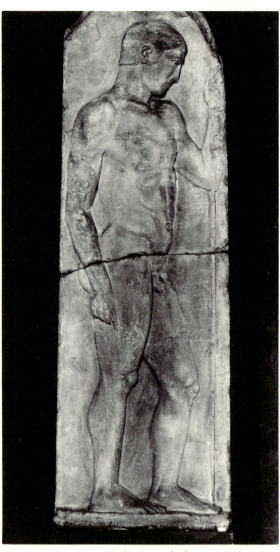

61. Nisyros Stele (Istanbul Museum)

62. Banquet Relief from Thasos, detail of attendant and dinos (Istanbul Museum)

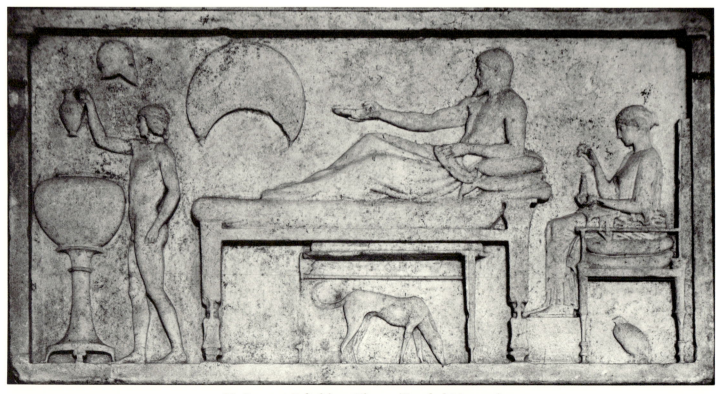

63. Banquet Relief from Thasos (Istanbul Museum)

64. Banquet Relief from Thasos, detail of seated woman
(Istanbul Museum)

65. Banquet Relief from Thasos, detail of reclining man (Istanbul Museum)

66. Stele of Girl with Doves, from Paros
(New York, Metropolitan Museum)

67. Giustiniani Stele (Berlin, Staatliche
Museen)

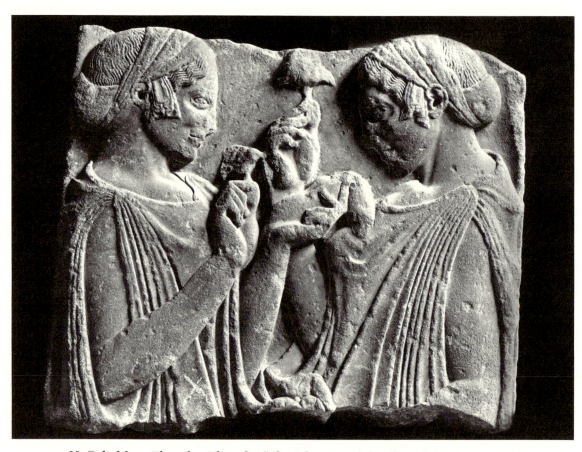

68. Relief from Pharsalos, Thessaly: "The Adoration of the Flower" (Paris, Louvre)

69. Stele of "Mourning Athena" (Athens, Acropolis Museum)

70. Stele from Sounion (Athens, National Museum)

71. Ludovisi "Throne" (Rome, National Museum)

72. Blond Boy (Athens, Acropolis Museum)

73. Olympia, Temple of Zeus, West Pediment. Apollo, detail (Olympia Museum)

74. Blond Boy, right profile (Athens, Acropolis Museum)

75. Corinth Head, right profile (Corinth Museum)

76-77. Volo Head (Volo Museum)

78-79. Capitoline Youth Head, left profile (Rome, Capitoline Museum)

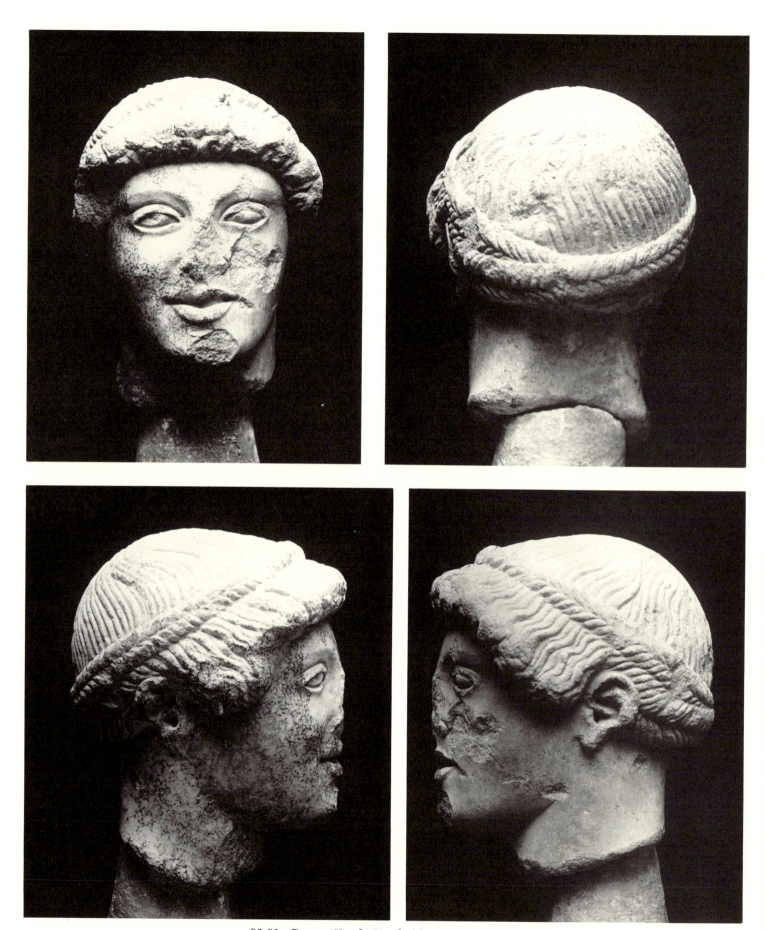

80-83. Cyrene Youth Head (Cyrene Museum)

84-87. Cyprus Youth Head (Nicosia Museum)

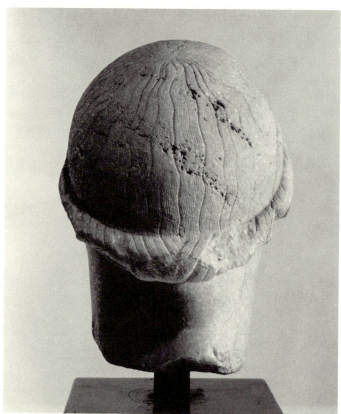

88-91. Cleveland Youth Head (Cleveland Museum)

92. Agrigento Kouros, detail of head (Agrigento Museum)

93. Selinus/Castelvetrano Bronze Youth, right profile (whereabouts unknown)

94-95. Omphalos Apollo (Athens, National Museum)

96. Apollo Choiseul-Gouffier
(London, British Museum)

97. Omphalos Apollo (Athens,
National Museum)

98. Bronze from Cape Artemision (Athens, National Museum)

99. Bronze from Cape Artemision, detail of head, right profile (Athens, National Museum)

100. Head, Acropolis Museum 2344 (Athens, Acropolis Museum)

101-2. Head, Acropolis Museum 2344 (Athens, Acropolis Museum)

103. Hestia Giustiniani (Rome, Conservatori Museum)

104. Penelope, head (Copenhagen, Ny Carlsberg Glyptothek)

105. Head of Aspasia/Sosandra Type (Crete, Herakleion
Museum)

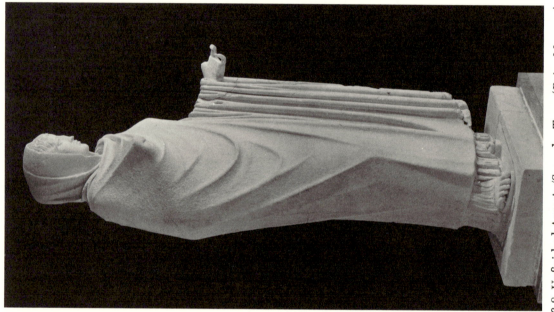

106-8. Unfinished Aspasia/Sosandra Type (Baiae Museum)

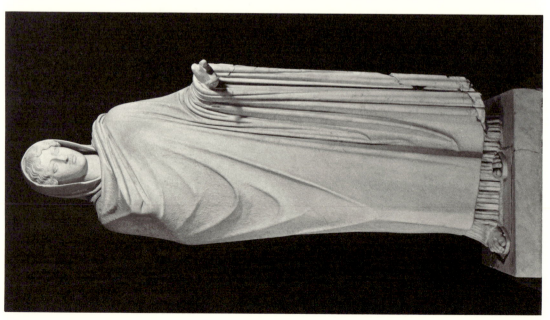

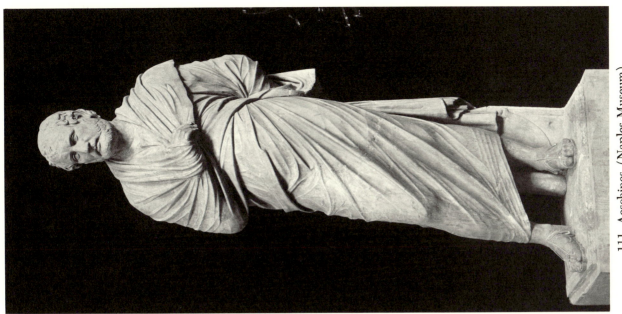

111. Aeschines (Naples Museum)

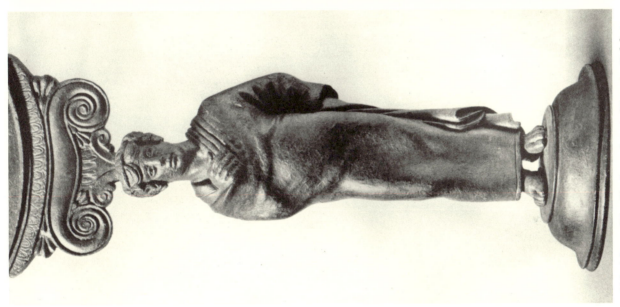

110. Mirror Handle from Locri (Reggio Calabria Museum)

109. The Baker Dancer (New York, Baker Private Collection)

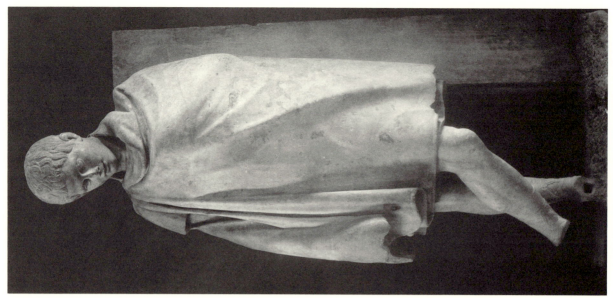

114. Boy from Tralles (Istanbul Museum)

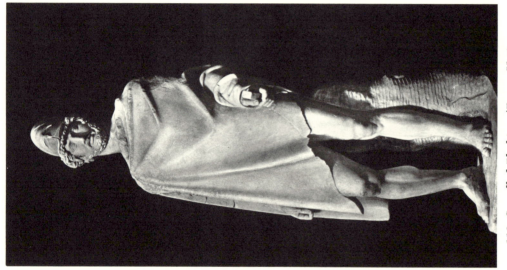

113. So-called Phokion (Rome, Vatican Museum)

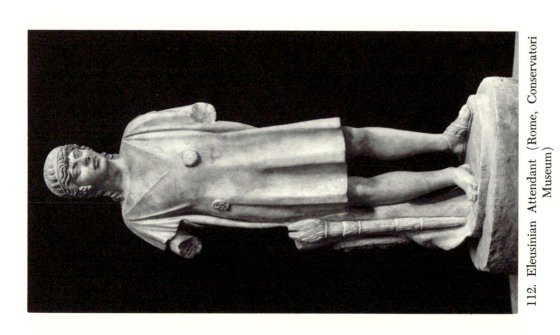

112. Eleusinian Attendant (Rome, Conservatori Museum)

117. Head of Aristogeiton? (A 5), right profile (Rome, Conservatori Museum)

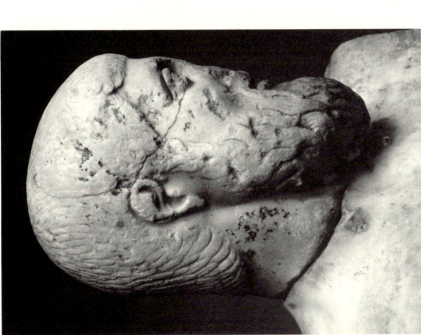

116. Head of Aristogeiton (A 4), right profile (Rome, Conservatori Museum)

115. Aristogeiton (Rome, Conservatori Museum) A 3/4.

119. Hip-Herm Ludovisi, Diskobolos (Rome, National Museum)

118. Bronze Statuette of a Diskophoros (New York,
Metropolitan Museum)

121. Head of Perseus (Rome, Conservatori Museum)

120. Head of Perseus (London, British Museum)

122. Myron's Diskobolos, reconstruction

123. Frankfurt Athena (Frankfurt Museum)

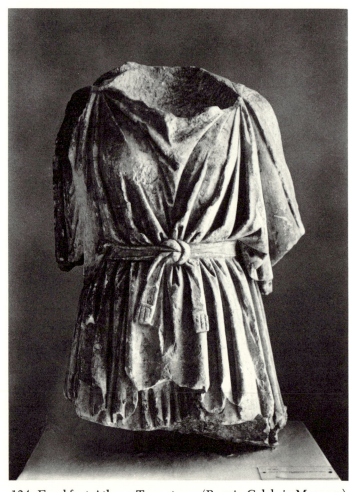

124. Frankfurt Athena Type, torso (Reggio Calabria Museum)

125. Seated Goddess from Tarentum (Berlin, Staatliche Museen)

126. So-called Leukothea Relief (Rome, Villa Albani)

127. Xanthos, Harpy Tomb, reliefs of West side (London, British Museum)

128. Xanthos, Harpy Tomb, reliefs of North side (London, British Museum)

129. Terracotta Pinax from Locri (Taranto Museum)

130. Terracotta Pinax from Locri (Taranto Museum)

131. Thessalian Grave Stele from Krannon (Volo Museum)

132. Thessalian Grave Stele from Larisa (Volo Museum)

133. Grave Stele from Sinope
(Kastamonu Museum)

134. Grave Stele from Sinope
(Kastamonu Museum)

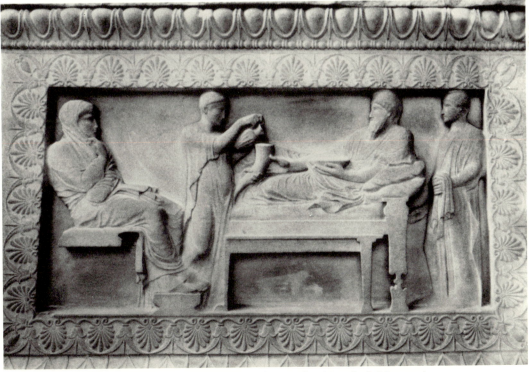

135. Satrap's Sarcophagus, short side (Istanbul Museum)

136. Phoenician Sarcophagus (Istanbul Museum)

137. Herm of Themistokles (Ostia Museum)

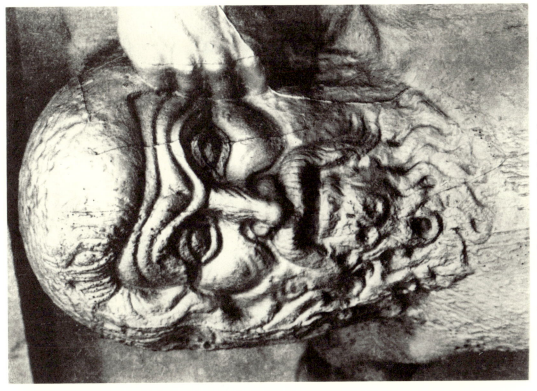

138. Parthenon South Metope 31; head of centaur (London, British Museum)

139. Penelope from Persepolis (Teheran Museum)

140. Penelope in the Vatican (Rome, Vatican Museum)

141. Parthenon, North Metope 32, detail (Athens, *in situ*)

142. Parthenon, East frieze: Poseidon, Apollo, Artemis (Athens, Acropolis Museum)

143. So-called Lanckoronski Relief (Richmond, Virginia Museum of Fine Arts)

144. Munich Plaque 185 (now destroyed), Poseidon

145. Munich Plaque 186 (now destroyed),
Herakles/Omphale

146. Munich Plaque 187 (now destroyed),
"Aspasia/Sosandra"

147. Munich Plaque 188 (now destroyed), Apollo

148. Munich Plaque 189 (now destroyed), Athena (?)

149. Apollo Pitti, detail of head (Florence, Palazzo Pitti)

150. Relief in Genf (Genf, Private Collection—once in Mittelschreiberhau)

151. Relief of Seated Man (Providence, Rhode Island School of Design Museum)

152. Seated Apollo Citharode (Rome, Vatican Museum)

153. The Three Graces; so-called Chiaramonti Relief (Rome, Vatican Museum): Fuchs' a

154. Relief-adaptation of the Three Graces (Rome, Private Collection): Fuchs' i

155. Fragment of Relief with Three Graces: central Charis (Athens, Acropolis Museum): Fuchs' g

156. Fleeing Maiden from Eleusis, detail of head (Eleusis Museum)

157. Ludovisi Akrolith (Rome, National Museum)

158. Akrolithic Head of Apollo from Cirò (Reggio Calabria Museum)

159. Athena from Pergamon, attributed to Myron (Berlin, Pergamon Museum)

160. Athena from Pergamon, left side (Berlin, Pergamon Museum)

161. Herakles Statuette, left side (Boston, Museum of Fine Arts)

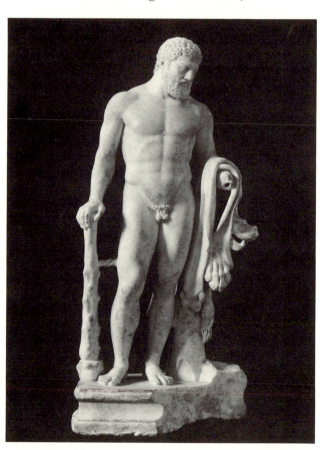

162. Herakles Statuette, front (Boston, Museum of Fine Arts)

164. Bronze Spinario, detail of head (Rome, Conservatori Museum)

163. Eros Soranzo (Leningrad, Hermitage Museum)

165. Esquiline Venus, detail of head (Rome, Conservatori Museum)

166. Esquiline Venus (Rome, Conservatori Museum)

167. So-called Müller's Peplophoros (Rome, Capitoline Museum)

168. So-called Ludovisi Peplophoros, Candia Type (Rome, National Museum)

169. Athena from Leptis Magna (Istanbul Museum)

170. Three Bronze Dancers from Herculaneum (Naples Museum)

171. Two Bronze Dancers from Herculaneum and small Praying Girl from same context
(Naples Museum)

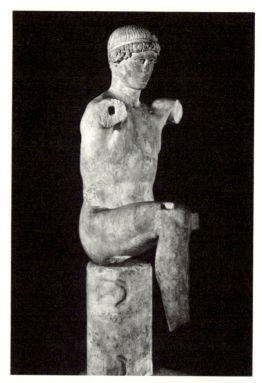

172. So-called Conservatori Charioteer
(Theseus?) left view (Rome, Conservatori
Museum)

173. So-called Conservatori Charioteer
(Theseus?) right view (Rome, Conservatori
Museum)

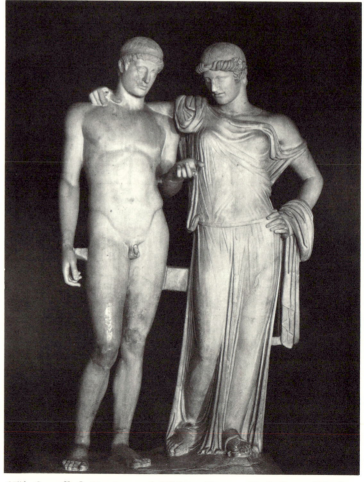

174. Stephanos' Athlete (Rome,
Villa Albani)

175. So-called Orestes and Elektra Group, Pasitelean (Naples
Museum)

176. Kassel Apollo, right profile (Kassel Museum)

177. Eirene and Ploutos (Munich Glyptothek

178. Bronze Head of Youth from Acropolis (Athens, National Museum)

179. Head of Woman, Electra Type (Munich, Hirth Collection)

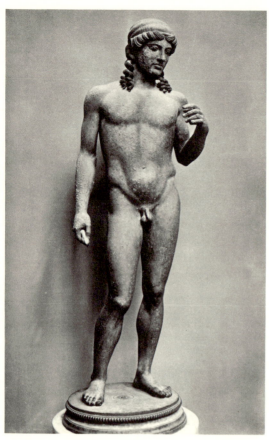

180. Bronze Apollo, Mantua Type (Naples Museum)

181. Ephebe from Via dell'Abbondanza, Lychnouchos (Naples Museum)

182. Ephebe from Via dell'Abbondanza, detail of head, back (Naples Museum)

183-84. Ephebe from Via dell'Abbondanza (Naples Museum)

185-86. Basalt Head, "Orpheus" (Munich Glyptothek)

187. Head of Emperor Hadrian, right profile
(Ostia Museum)

188. Antinoos Mondragone (Paris, Louvre)

189. Antinoos, Mondragone Type (Berlin, von Stauss
Collection)